Dagie's Story

Part 1: Germany

Dagie's Story - Book 1: Germany
By Dagmar Weiss Snodgrass

Copyright 2019

Photographs are the property of Dagmar Weiss Snodgrass or are used by permission from the Halvorsen family collection.

Editing and proofreading by Dragon Publishing & Editing
Cover Design by A Writer for Life
Published by Dragon Publishing & Editing

Books written by Dagmar Weiss Snodgrass

Papa and I and with Zara Tustra
Candy Bomber

Coming soon …

Dagie's Story, Part Two: America

This book is dedicated to my family. The ones that God has taken away from the Weiss and Monk families, and to the family that is here to love and to support my efforts as a writer. My husband Dale, my daughters Linda and Barbara and their husbands Preston and Ted. And not to forget the many grand and great grandchildren that are the love of my life. There are too many to mention them all by name. I want to leave this writing for them and the general public. For all that read this to know that when one believes in God and turns their life over to Him, all things are possible. He turned my life around and I walked through shadows. He now helps me to walk and soak up the sunshine...

Dagie's Story

Part 1: Germany

By:

Dagmar Weiss Snodgrass

Berlin, Germany prior to WWII

Brandenburg Gate, 1930

Chapter One

Many years before I was born, right after World War I, my homeland Germany went through many changes. Changes that left a dark mark on my country and the world. When the world thought or spoke of Germany, it would leave them with a very bad taste in their mouth. Time going by couldn't change anything for the German people, because what was done was done. No matter what we tried to do, it couldn't be undone. Most of all is the fact that all of the German people themselves didn't want to forget any of it. Why did they not want to get out from under any of it you might ask? They kept the flame of remembering these sad times alive, so other world nations would be warned. Warned not to fall into the same trap they had fallen into. Thinking all was well, when it was not. My country fell into evil-doing hands and when it was recognized, the evil had grown so powerful it couldn't be undone. The so-called brown shirts took over and fear of them took over my homeland.

On the fourth of February, 1934, I was born as the youngest of three children in the Franz and Elisabeth Weiss family. My brothers Edgar and Erwin were thirteen and twelve years older than I. Dad was thirty-seven and Mom was thirty-six when I came along. Dad was a police officer and had to deal with much during this bad and sad time for all of Germany.

History marched on and our family saw evil taking the place of goodness all around us. The brown shirts came and they removed good friends from us. All because they believed differently from what we did. They were smart, talented, prominent people and were called German born Jews. German families lost loved ones that went and spoke

1

up against the brownshirts and the country's leader. A man by the name of Adolf Hitler.

Hundreds, no thousands, no millions of good people under Hitler's regime lost their lives in concentration camps. Camps like Auschwitz, Dachau, Buchenwald and many other such places. In this awful of times I grew up and my hometown was the capital city of Germany, Berlin. At first, I was too small to understand the danger that we lived in. It was a day by day all around us. I had parents and brothers that took very good care of me. I remember that I loved music and when I heard it coming to me from the streets, Mom would open the apartment windows, hold me in her arms and let me see what was going on outside. Young boys and girls came marching down the street playing on drums and other instruments. The boys wore brown shirts and pants, the girls wore brown shirts and skirts, all of them marching and also singing.

As I got older, my parents told me these boys and girls belonged to Adolf Hitler's youth groups. At the age of ten they had to join these groups. It was a must, an order given from the higher up, for all ten-year-olds to belong. If the parents had any objections, it could result in grave consequences for the entire family. Their sons or daughters could be taken from them and grow up in a children's home. There might have been visitation rights given to the parents. But in any case, their child could be influenced by Adolf Hitler's doctrine.

In plainer words, they would be brainwashed. The poor parents wouldn't recognize their child any more. By allowing them to participate they kept some control over their child. And maybe, in their home life, were able to repair some of the damage caused by the group teachings. This is, if they raised an understanding and listening child.

I was too young to understand any of this. When I looked out the window being held by my Mom, I enjoyed the music and singing of the marching band. I enjoyed to see the flags waving in the wind from every window on National holidays. It was very pretty and this is what I liked about it. I had not any idea that all of this was a display of power, and that my homeland, in the years to come, had reason to be afraid of it. I was a child and had the protection of my family.

Dagmar Weiss

As I got older, I understood more. By the age of six, I was taught what I could say and what not to say. Also, what to do and what not to do. I learned like my family to be a keeper of secrets. It was a hard lesson to learn for a six-year-old, but I learned fast. My parents and my brothers taught me well and by the time I went to school, I was a very good trained secret keeper.

My brothers, being older, had their time in Hitler's youth group behind them. My parents acted smart and let them go to work for the farmers. One year of hard work in a farm community, it softened their indoctrination somewhat. When they returned home, Mom and Dad took over to undo the harm that was done to them.

When the family took me to national events, I didn't know that my father, from higher up, had orders to be there. And it was this way for the multitude of people standing next to us. What I saw and liked was the glitter and fanfare around us. My father carried me sitting on his shoulders so I could see so much better. My hands clutched his curly hair so I would not fall. I felt secure this way. I only turned loose when I clapped my hands together.

Franz Weiss – 35 yrs old

I was delighted to see the soldiers in their fancy uniforms and doing the goose-step. The band played beautiful march music and followed behind the leader. I was small and didn't know what was to come our way. I didn't know how much my family would have to suffer. I didn't know how much my country would have to suffer. At the age of four, five, six I acted like a child. I saw and heard no evil. But sad to have to write this, it was there. It was all around us. The bare eye couldn't see it but a heavy hand was laying on Germany. I would get to feel it, when at the age of six Mom enrolled me in first grade.

Chapter Two

In this time my family made changes. In 1940, my parents went through a divorce. My older brothers understood the how come and why. I, however, did not. I had a difficult time to understand that the love of my parents for one another changed from what it was before to a friendship kind of love. I think I believed it could change their love for us three children. If it happened to them, it could happen for the three of us. Their love for us was very important to me. It took a lot of talking from my parents with me, and a lot of tears shed by me, before I understood that their love for us three children was a forever kind of love. That nothing could change this.

I understood when Dad moved away, he would stop by to visit us often. When the time came and Dad stood with a suitcase in his hand in front of me and Mom, I realized how big a change it was for our entire family. He took Mom's hand and said goodbye. But unlike my mom, I was able to kiss him like I always did. I gave him more than one kiss and then I had to let him go. When the door closed, Mom and I sat in the kitchen and cried. I had his promise to console me. He said he would come back soon.

Little did I know how hard all of this was for Mom. A new chapter in her life was beginning. A new chapter for all of the Weiss family, and the hardest was yet to come. As Dad left us, so would my brothers. Edgar and Erwin didn't want to be drafted into Hitler's military. They went in as volunteers and were promptly taken for service as SS soldiers. Hitler made war starting in 1940, my first school year. Mom and I were now alone, missing the men in our family.

Elisabeth Sauer Weiss age 22

The days seemed long, the apartment was large and lonely for the two of us. Mom found a solution to the problem. She rented a spare room we had to a nice young lady. Her coming and going made us feel less alone. Soon she and Mom became the best of friends. And for me she was a new member of our family. Dad came to visit often and it kept a smile on Mom's and my face.

The mailman brought the court-ordered money for the household and my brothers' mail to us. Both the checks and letters came every month on time to the mailbox. If we didn't have mail from my brothers serving time in Finland, Mom looked very worried. She had this look on her face that made me feel sad. The smile on her face was gone till a letter was in her hand from my brothers. When Dad came and read it, all three of us had reason to smile.

Mom learned to live her life after almost twenty years of marriage as a single woman having motherly duties. She did all of this with still having love for the man that left her and a heart filled with love for her three children, Edgar, Erwin and Dagmar.

When my Dad left the police force because of his own political views, he had her support. Dad told us in strict confidence that "Hitler made the police into killer of women and children." He wouldn't and he couldn't be part of this. To his and our surprise, after he faked a nervous breakdown, they retired him from the police force. Being a smart individual, after a time he found work in the radio industries. Like working for the A.E.G. and for Lawrence or Telefunken. What we didn't know was the target he had on his back from the time he left the police, till they decided to close in on him. But we found out later and all of us had a terrible time dealing with it.

Chapter Three

Dad couldn't be with me at my first day of school. It was Mom that held my hand, in the other I had a bag of candy from Dad. It was a tradition for children to have a gift of candy to take to school on the first day. I believe mine was the largest and the most colorful because Dad wanted to make it up to me for not being there. Being six and a little smart I understood why he had to miss out on the things like this. I forgave him. With a smile looking at my candy bag, I forgave him.

I was excited not to be called a little girl anymore. With being a schoolgirl, I was a big girl now. I wanted to show Mom just how big and how grown up I was by asking to share in our household responsibilities. The minute we got home, I would ask her to let me be her helper.

We came to the school and assembled in the yard around the flagpole. Over the loudspeaker the national anthem was played. The flag was raised up, as the music played and we sang and greeted the German flag. It seemed like a long song and a lot to do for me. My arm got tired and I dropped it to my side. In a second, I heard someone behind me say to raise my arm and to continue with this greeting. I was not to drop my arm till the ceremony was over. I felt my arm being pushed by someone and not in a gentle way. It was a hard push and it scared me. Mom standing behind me did nothing to stop it. I didn't dare to turn around to see who was doing this. I stood there knowing I must do as I was told. The person that did this left a lasting impression for me to remember to hold my arm straight up when I heard the national anthem played.

I thought when Mom and I went home, I could ask her about this. She would explain things for me. And if she couldn't, Dad could when he made his next visit. I didn't know that my schoolyard experience was only a very small incident, and many major ones would follow. How could I know, how could I understand, when I was only six years old?

After we left the schoolyard, I met my teacher. She was a tiny, friendly young lady and I liked her right away. Since my classroom was located on the second floor, she instructed me in how to greet the teachers in the hall and on the staircase up to my class. I was to give the German greeting I learned in the schoolyard this morning or it was allowed for me to curtsy. She said it was up to me what I liked and wanted to do. I said I like to curtsy. This was the way my parents had taught me to do. With this said, she smiled at me. When I looked at Mom, she had the same pleased smile on her face as my teacher.

I was a happy girl on the way home. I forgot the rough treatment I received during the playing of the national anthem. I wanted to concentrate on opening and eating the candy from Dad. I wanted to share with Mom and lay aside the candy for Dad that was his favorite kind. Dad liked the caramels and Mom, she preferred the sugar candy. I was the one easy to please because I liked all kinds. To look at the size of this nice decorated bag, there was enough in it to last me all week. Or maybe even longer.

Making it up the two flights of stairs, Mom opened the door to our apartment. I made it to the kitchen, emptying the bag of candy on the table. I made three neat piles, one for Mom, one for me and the last pile was for Dad. It was a surprise for us when in the afternoon the doorbell rang and when we opened there stood Dad. He came by from work to see how I liked the first day at school. I don't know which one of us was happier to see him, Mom or I? Mom gave me all the time I needed to tell him about the day. I told him what scared me and what I liked. I told him how much I liked the teacher I was going to have. When I had nothing more to tell him, my parents said they would have their grown-up talk in the living room. I was to play with my dolls, eat the candy and stay in the kitchen.

It took a long time for their grown-up talk. When they came back to me, it was time for Dad to say goodbye. If it was dark outside, Dad said good night. I didn't like for him to say either one to us. I wanted to get out of bed and say good morning to both of my parents. But this was not happening any more. It was Mom and I and I and Mom, with Dad coming to visit.

The first week, Mom walked me to school. She stood behind me and made sure I held my arm and hand up till the national anthem was over. She walked me to the door of the class and she turned me over to the teacher. She came and picked me up and at the beginning of the new week, I would walk alone because I was a big girl now.

Proud to be big and my parents could trust me, I was put in charge by Mom in helping her dust the furniture. I had duties that only big girls could do and when Dad came to visit, Mom would tell him what a good helper I was. It made Dad smile, Mom too and my smile was the bigger than theirs. Both of them made feel good inside and very important.

Came Monday coming down the stairs from our apartment, I had to move over to the side. Men walked by me carrying heavy bags on their shoulders that looked like they were filled with sand. I wondered about this and wanted to ask Mom about it when I got home.

Since I started school, my circle of friends has grown. Before, I had only three other friends. Two girls, Ruth and Eva, and one boy by the name of Lothar. We got along well and now had only the weekend to play together. In class I had twenty or twenty-five other kids to learn and to have fun and play with at recess. The teacher was always with us, guiding and giving us instructions.

It was a time of war and Germany had air raids by day and by night. If it happened when I was at school, all classes went to the shelter in the basement of the school. We followed the teacher one behind the other, standing against the wall or sitting next to each other on the floor. When the siren sounded the all clear signal, we didn't resume classes, we went home. Most parents came looking for their children and so did my Mom.

I was fortunate my home was only two blocks away and if I ran all the way, I reached it in five minutes easy. Today I was in a hurry to get home. I leaned on the doorbell impatient for her to open and let me in. I loved my teacher and today playing all kinds of games at recess, she kept me next to her the whole time. I was excited about it as it made me feel special. She also said that my mom dressed me pretty. Mom needed to hear all this from me. I always had to change my outfit when I got home. I wore my school clothing more than just one day.

As we sat eating the evening meal, Mom told me about her day. She said the men I met on the stairs that morning did carry sandbags up to the attic and emptied them there. When I asked why, she explained it was to extinguish small bombs that the enemy planes could drop through the roof and set the house on fire. She said the neighbors elected the air raid warden. It was Mrs. Maier who took the job. Not any of the men wanted this responsibility. Mom then showed me a gasmask that was issued to us should there be such an attack. Mom's fit her, mine was too big for me.

Looking at each other wearing this, we looked like monsters. I thought this funny, but it was not. When the air raids got harder and harder, we had nothing to laugh about. Mom said the basement that was the laundry facility for all that lived in this house, had to be turned into an air raid shelter. Everyone took a chair down to have a seat, for as long as the air raid lasted.

I counted our chairs and not one was missing. Mom said she was not afraid, we would stay, unlike the others, in our apartment. We would have to see how it goes. When we used the attic for drying the clean clothes, it paid to be extra careful not to get sand from these piles in every corner on the clean wash. We had so much to learn at the beginning of this war. Doing the laundry to have clean clothes to wear would be the least of our worries. Mom told me when the sirens sounded to think it was a thunderstorm to cover my head and stay in bed.

I knew hiding under the cover that this storm was not made by mother nature. It was a man-made storm. It brought death and destruction to all in its way. I hid under my warm blanket, waiting for it to be over. I was scared the whole time. I didn't not dare to tell Mom about my fears, she always had so much on her mind. She was worried about my brothers. It was up to me to be her big and brave girl. But for Dad, I didn't need to be any of this. When he came visiting, he came to be with his little girl. And this is what I was and will always be … his Dagie.

I knew Dad would tell my why, when I looked out the window, soldiers in trucks would come and take friends and neighbors away. They treated them rough and their behavior frightened me. The book and toy stores I liked, we could not enter any more. They had yellow stars on doors and windows. Mom said we were not allowed to shop in them anymore. I didn't understand any of it but I was sure my Dad would explain it. And when he did, maybe I didn't have to be afraid anymore. No, I was wrong, because it got worse.

Chapter Four

Coming home from school, climbing up the stairs to the second floor, I saw yellow stars on the doors of our neighbors. When I first saw a star on someone's coat or jacket, I asked if I could have one for my coat. I thought they were pretty. Then I saw them decorating store windows and we were forbidden to enter. Or I saw many stores with broken windows because someone had thrown a rock through the glass. This changed my mind of wanting to wear the star. Small as I was, I realized there was a threat behind this star. A threat maybe my dad could explain to me. All I knew at this point was the fact I felt fear. Fear of what was going on around me. Mom said when Dad made his next visit, both of them wanted to have a long, long talk with me.

Dad came that evening and talk we did. It was not the kind of talk I wanted to have. Just Dad and I alone. It was a parents' with their little daughter talk and their daughter needed to hear and understand every word they said and take it to heart. I knew how important this talk was going to be when I had to sit in my chair from my play table right in front of them.

Dad started by wanting to know if anyone at school or parents from my friends had asked me questions about our family. I said no, no one had done this. Dad said good and "Dagie, if anyone does, you must always say that you don't know and tell them to go and ask your mom and dad. Anything we talk about is not to be repeated to anyone." He then gave me the example by saying if someone said "Did your mom last night listen to the news on the radio or did Mom listen or not to Adolf Hitler's speech last night", my answer should be "I don't know" to them. What we talked about in our family was not for other people to know. And he said when Mom and Dad had grown up talk, like they often had, the radio would be turned on loud so the neighbors wouldn't hear them. I laughed when I heard this as there was a wall between our and the next-door neighbor apartment. I thought Mom and Dad were being funny to think someone could hear them talking.

Dad was not at all being funny when he took a water glass out of the kitchen cabinet and placed it against the wall. He then invited me to put my ear against the open end and listen. Oh, I was surprised as I heard the neighbors talking. Dad placed the finger over his lips and smiled when he said "What we just did can be done to us." He put the glass back into the cabinet and said, "We need to remember that every wall has ears. And that there are bad people living around us and they could do us harm. They pretend to be our friends when in reality they were not. They pretend to be good, when they were not. We couldn't trust anyone outside our family."

I asked what would they do to us, if someone said anything bad about us. Both told me that the police or soldiers could come and take me away from them. Maybe I would be given other parents, or I would grow up in a children's home. Many, many bad things could happen if someone wanted to harm us for some reason. Both of my parents said they would hurt if someone came to take me from them. They looked at me and wanted to know how I would feel if this happened. I answered I would cry and try to run away from the bad people. My parents said that there was not any running away. I would always be found. Mom said all the people that the soldiers put on the trucks, and I saw this from our living room window, they too would like to run away. It can't be done. Someone would be sent to

16

search for them and bring them back. I asked where do they put them when they are brought back? Dad did not smile when he said "Dagie, they go to prison." I knew that prison was a bad place and didn't want for anyone to have to go there. Dad wanted to know if I understood why I shouldn't talk with others about our family. I understood perfectly.

I didn't like the parent with daughter talk we were having and was getting ready to cry. It didn't do anything to take my fears away. I was more afraid at the moment than what I had been before. Dad wanted to find out from Mom how come we didn't use the air raid shelter as everyone did. Her answer was that it was not all this bad. When it got worse, we would join the others, but not till then. Dad just looked at Mom and said, "Ellie, it will get worse and I would feel better knowing you and Dagie are tucked away in the basement."

I had put my arms around his neck knowing time had come for him to say goodbye and be on his way. I gave Mom away by telling him I was to think of guns shooting at planes dropping bombs on houses as being a bad, bad thunderstorm. I was to be good and wait for the storm to end. Dad warned again how dangerous it was staying in the apartment instead of going down to the shelter with the neighbors. To me he said to remember what we had talked about. He walked out placing one of his fingers over his lips saying … "hush, we need to be good secret keepers."

Mom and I didn't know till sometime later that Dad kept a big secret of his own from us. He did not go home to be alone. He had found a second love that was special and the young lady's name was Adelheid. In time to come, she would be my brothers' and my stepmother. I can write here that for our mother, we would always be her first love. For her it was Dad, Edgar, Erwin and Dagmar. She never looked to find a replacement for she had lost. She could have, but Dad for her was the one and only love. We three children knew that the love for her family ran deep. In the following years it proved itself how loyal and true she was to her family and friends.

Mom went back to the kitchen. I waited till I couldn't her Dad's footsteps anymore. He was only gone for a few minutes but I missed him already. I had to wait till I saw him again. I hoped it wouldn't be a long wait. I then followed Mom to the kitchen. She was waiting for me. She looked at me and said she had to do something to me she didn't like to do. She didn't like it because I had done not anything wrong to deserve it. She would have to give me a spanking. She had the carpet beater in her hand, used to beat the dust out of carpets and throw rugs. This was also the tool that was used on me when I was a bad girl. Before I knew what or why it was happening, Mom laid me over her knee and gave me this so undeserved spanking.

When it was all over, I cried my eyes out. But Mom had a grip on both of my arms saying I needed to always remember this and if I did anything that I was forbidden to say or do, the next spanking would hurt me more, much more. And the carpet beater would be left by the kitchen door. Easy for Mom to reach and ready to use on me. We had a spare room next to the kitchen and things from my big brothers and all of my toys were kept in it. I went there to hold my favorite toy from Dad in my arms while all the tears flowed. It was Mr. Brown Bear that soothed my hurt feelings. When I stopped crying and listened, in the next room I heard my Mom cry. Having to give me this spanking so I would be a good secret keeper, hurt her so much more than it hurt me. My bottom was sore and I would remember this underserved of all punishment.

I tried to understand why she had to do this to me. But it was somehow confusing to me. Mom spanked me hard enough for me not to forget this. And the old carpet beater left by the kitchen door, would be my constant ugly reminder. Would my mom be able to forget about it? No, she wouldn't and couldn't. What she did was done for the love she had for all of her family. But trying to teach a six-year-old about the dangerous times we lived in, she had to find a way to make me understand. This was the only way that left a lasting impression on me and believe me that it did. She wanted to keep us together and safe from all harm. This is why she had to hurt me. To teach me to understand that families in Berlin, not just in Berlin but all over Germany, lived in dangerous times.

This night when the sirens sounded, again we stayed in bed. In mom's opinion, the storm brewing in the clouds over Berlin was light. For as long as it stayed this way, we slept in our bed. I always took Mr. Brown Bear to sleep with me. When I was scared, we were scared together.

Chapter Five

I loved going to school. I and the other kids liked the teacher, Miss Blumenberg, more and more. From Friday through Sunday, I played with my three companions, Lothar, Ruth and Eva. We fought over whose boyfriend he was, either Ruth's, Eva's or mine. We liked him and he seemed to like being with his three girlfriends. Was there the air raid signal given, Ruth, Eva and our boyfriend, Lothar, had a play table set up in the shelter. They continued their playing while I laid in my bed, holding Mr. Brown Bear. I was thinking of them sitting in the basement playing. I was holding my breath each time I heard a loud noise and wishing that I was in the basement playing with them.

Getting out of bed in the morning was never a problem. I loved getting ready for school. Mom saw to it that I washed and dressed nice and clean. Breakfast was a slice of brown bread with margarine and jam if we had any. If we didn't, Mom topped the spread with a tablespoon of sugar. It sweetened up my morning. To drink I had a cup of milk only if we happen to have any. If we didn't, I drank some of Mom's bad tasting coffee. Or much better for me, some water from the kitchen faucet.

Everything we bought was bought with ration stamps. From the things we wore and food we ate, all was bought with ration cards. Mom was always a week ahead in when she went shopping. Often the owner of the store refused to sell to us. We ran out of the first week meat coupons and we needed to use the ones from the second week. This is when the begging started between Mom and the owner of the store. When the store owner got his way and we walked away empty handed, Mom blamed Adolf

Hitler for it. She would say the man with the little beard under the nose is starving Germany to death.

I knew with what she said, she meant every word of it. It was one of the secrets I needed to keep. Come to think of it, Mom and I shared many secrets like this one between us. She said our meal tonight was soup cooked with lard. Since we couldn't buy meat, it would have to do this time. Next week we had the coupons to purchase the meat to cook stew. She told me to be sure to drink the small bottle of milk at recess. This would help and be good for me. I promised to do this and happily to school I went.

Today the day would be different from any other ... For me and everyone in class the day changed. The morning went by as usual, when I curtsied my way past the teachers to class. Recess was fun, the teacher always played with us. And she always thought of new games we could play. When the bell rang to call us back to class, sometimes we asked to play a little longer. We wanted to play some more and our teacher understood why. Being first graders, we were still playful and she knew we needed extra time to get used to being in school.

So, it was today, when she gave us the extra time to play. Getting back to class we just sat down, when the doors opened and two men in uniform entered. We stood up to give the Adolf Hitler greeting but Miss Blumenberg behind the large desk motioned with her hands to remain seated. We did and watched how these two men took our teacher by both of her arms out from behind the desk and they walked her to the classroom door. Again, all the class stood up and as we were taught, wanted to give the national greeting. But our teacher again turned, freed both of her arms from these two men and motioned us to remain in the seats. The door closed behind them and a few minutes later, another teacher came and took over the class.

I didn't know what to think, we all were surprised by this. I knew when soldiers came, this was always bad. I wanted to get home in a hurry today tell what happened to Mom. I ran home all the way, burst through the door when Mom opened to tell her this news. She just looked at me and said, "Dagie, let's hope she is back tomorrow. Tonight, when you say your prayers, say one for your teacher."

Before we ate the soup Mom had cooked for the evening meal, I still had time to play with the many dolls I had. I lined them up against the wall by the kitchen door right next to my reminder, the carpet beater. I liked to play school, all the dolls were the students and I was the teacher. However, it was not any fun this time. I wondered about Miss Blumenberg and if she would be back in class tomorrow.

The only men in uniform I liked were my two brothers. And of course, my Dad when he still wore the police uniform. All the others I really was not sure about. When I saw what they did, all they did for me was to scare me.

When it was time to go to bed, I held Mr. Brown Bear and we both prayed. We prayed for Mom, Dad, my brothers and Miss Blumenberg. I said please dear God, do not let the sirens go off loud this night. We do not need another storm over Berlin because all this scares me very, very much. I do not remember if a storm coming our way from England to Germany was brewing in the clouds over Berlin during the night. If the sirens sounded, it would have woken me up.

In the morning I rushed around to get to school. I wanted to be among the first to say hello to our teacher.

Mom knew why I was in such a hurry and she helped me to get ready. Again saying, at recess to drink the bottle of milk and she added to be careful. I knew from the carpet beater that was standing behind the door it meant to keep watch over what I said.

Rushing up the stairs to get to class, I was expecting to see Miss Blumenberg sitting behind the desk. But she was not there. I thought maybe she is late today. When the door opened and we stood up to greet, another teacher came in. One of the kids some time later asked if she would be back tomorrow. But the answer from the substitute teacher was she didn't know. I knew better than to ask questions even though I wanted to ask.

I would rush home to Mom and tell her of my fears. I didn't think she would be back. And I was right. Day one, two, three, four and five went by, then came the weekend. Came Monday we had a new homeroom teacher. I now knew she would never come back to teach or to play with us again. Telling Mom about it, she said there are many people like Miss Blumenberg we wanted to pray for. I shouldn't forget to include her in my bedtime prayers. Well, I promised myself never to forget and when Mr. Brown Bear and I curled up together, we prayed for Mom, Dad, my brothers and the teacher all of us kids liked to much. I also prayed that the man-made storms coming from England to Germany would not be so hard on us.

Chapter Six

In the following days a lot happened. The happiest times we shared as a family were the times my brothers came home from Finland. They were home for a week or two from fighting a war. Dad joined us to have time with his sons and all their friends stopped by for a visit.

My brothers came, each having a care package under their arms. It was large and filled with food items. On the inside Mom found a short, typed message saying with the compliments of Adolf Hitler for his troops. We were glad to get the extra food. We didn't have enough for the two of us and now we had two more to cook for. Extra food was needed and it was of help when my brothers were home. Mom said when Edgar and Erwin were with us, we didn't have to go hungry. But when they left and the food was all gone, hunger struck us again. We would go to bed with tummies growling. And Mom would tease, saying our tummies wanted to have a friendly talk with one another. In the morning after eating the slice of bread, it would be their happy time and their fussing would end.

Going to school she reminded me to drink the bottle of milk at recess. Or to eat whatever they gave us, that was good and something extra. We got such a surprise at times. But it didn't happen often. Sometimes we got a cookie, other times it was a red apple. When I told her we had something extra at school, she smiled. She said every little bit helps. The cookie was always too small to take home. Only the apple was big enough to share. When I came home with something for her, again she said, every little bit helps and every bite we shared helped both of us. To hear this made me feel good.

Every day we waited for the mail. When it came, Mom shared her letters with Dad when he came to visit. He did the same for Mom. Day by day the newspaper was read. It let us know who lived and who died. Who died in the front lines of the war or here at home in the everyday air raids. Mom had family and friends that lost what they held dear.

Mom had to give me the sad news we lost uncle Werner Zimmerman and uncle Heinz Koppe. Aunt Lene and Aunt Friedchen lost their husbands and my cousins their dad. I was so very sad for them. My mom saw I had a hard time dealing with this. She said that all we could do to help was to pray. When I went to bed, I did the praying and my prayers got longer all the time. For a little girl, I had so much on my mind. And when I prayed, I also remembered the teacher I had liked to much.

One day my brother Erwin came home again. He had the care package with food under his arm with Hitler's message inside. But he came home on a sad mission. He brought the few belongings of his best friend, who was killed in action, back to his friend's parents. His friend was killed fighting next to my brother in a man to man knife fight. Erwin wanted for us to go with him, when he spoke to his friend's parents.

One afternoon after I came back from school, the three of us made this sad visit. Tears were shed when we got there and when we left. When I looked at my brother, he had tears in his eyes. The tears didn't stream down his face. I saw that his blue eyes had tears in them when he had to say farewell to his friend's family. They invited us back. Mom promised we would come and visit. Erwin said he would write a letter now and then. And when we came to visit, we could tell them how he was doing. Tell them how the war was progressing or not in Finland. He promised his friend's parents he would try and take good care of himself. And with this said, they hugged Erwin and the tears flowed again.

I was the one looking forward to visiting. They had a dog named Hänsel like the Hänsel out of Hänsel and Gretel in Brother Grimm's fairy tale book. I had fallen head over heels in love with him. And I think he did with me. I asked Mom if I could save the soup bone for my four-legged friend from now on. All this could only happen if we had a soup bone to cook with. Mom laughed and said, "You know I use the bone twice over to get all the good I can out of it. But after that, sure, you can give it to Hänsel."

At each visit Hänsel would greet us at the door. He had a good nose and started sniffing at the bag I was bringing him. Should my hands be empty, I thought he was disappointed. Soon he forgot about it and played with me till we went home.

Mom and her new friend shared many talks. I knew they were serious talks. I often wondered about this, but never said anything to her about this. Dad showed me that walls could have ears. Didn't these walls have ears like ours? Or were these different walls from ours? I really didn't understand but I worried about it. Could we be in trouble? I thought all these things but didn't dare to ask about any of it. I knew I was a child to be seen when we went visiting. I was to be seen but not heard. Yet, I heard a lot. And what I heard concerned me greatly.

At night I added all of this to my prayers and gave it to God. I was sure he understood all this so much better than I ever could. All the prayers I said were prayers to help us.

Chapter Seven

I was now a second grader. I like my teacher but not as much as the first one. My brothers came to be with us as often as the ongoing war would let them. The care packages they brought now had a goose or duck attached. Mom hung them with a long cord around the neck to the outside on the kitchen window. Till on the next day she would clean and cook them. This was meat we didn't buy with a ration card. It was given, with the compliments of Adolf Hitler, to my brothers Edgar and Erwin Weiss.

When Mom cooked such a dinner, Dad was always a guest. But only Dad. The lady that now held his heart, with all of us knowing it, she was not allowed to come with him. Dad had introduced us, but to us she was not yet family and maybe she would never be. We loved Mom, and somehow, we must have hoped that Dad would find his way back to his first love. Meaning Mom and us.

The fanfare of Germany being successful in winning the war continued to be broadcasted in films and on the radio. Erwin was the one saying not to believe all we heard, read and saw, or saw in films. He called it Hitler's propaganda, trying to make the German people believe something that was not the truth. In all that my family talked about when they sat together, I prayed for the walls not to have ears. Or no one to be home next door and listening. I became with every day, more and more, the best secret keeper in Berlin, Germany.

After my brothers left to go back to the front lines, we changed our minds about not going to the air raid shelter. So did the neighbors living across from us. When we came running out to the stairwell to rush down to the basement, so did they. The Mr. carried his wife and she was bleeding. We found out when the house shook and the glass in the windows came flying out, she was hit by it. She was going to have a baby and the husband and neighbors tried their best to help to calm her, bandage her, till more help would arrive. No one wanted for her to be so afraid that she could lose the baby.

This night was the night Mom placed two chairs in the basement. One large one for her and my little one next to hers. Berlin - Marienfelde was bombed on this awful night. Many died and Mom said many more of us would die if this war didn't end soon. Going to school I saw the houses burned to the ground in the neighborhood. I knew people laid buried under the rock and wood. I needed to tell Dad about it. I was afraid that Mom and I could be next under such a rock pile. And Dad living elsewhere wouldn't know about what had happened to us.

When Dad came by, I told him we now had a place in the shelter with all the others. He was glad about it and told it to Mom. About my fear of being buried under the rubble of a house he had this to say. After one of those heavy bombing attacks he would come looking for us. And if the house should have fallen on us? He said, "I promise you to dig you out with my bare hands." Then he asked if I believed what he said. Oh yes, I believed him. I cannot count on my fingers and toes how often Dad stood in the open doorway after a bombing attack. Ready to hug us and always ready to be of help.

There was a large paint factory, now building airplanes behind the house. This is what the planes coming over from England wanted to destroy. We living around it, we were in the way of it. War was war, we all knew it and we all thought it was plain awful. Awful was what we saw when things are on fire.

I always, in my imagination, found something pretty and interesting in the sparks flying. I thought of them as being fireflies, sparkling and dainty. I had the imagination of a child and used it often to keep the harsh reality away and maybe make me feel less afraid. When I said something to Mom about these sparks, she was not happy with me. It was Dad saying for her to let me be a dreamer for as long as possible. He would say to Mom, "Let her dream. One day like us, she will have to grow up to face the real world." After what he said, Mom took it easy on me. I knew, like Dad, that she was in my corner.

Coming home to her from school, I always had a tale to tell. Like today, when teaching history, part of the map was covered with blanket. I saw Germany and Italy displayed, all other was not for us to be seen or asked about. The teacher said that Italy was a friend but the rest of the world didn't like us. And if we couldn't see them as being friends, they were to be called enemies to all of Germany. I asked Mom why no one liked us. She couldn't explain it to me. She said ask Dad, he will tell you!

Nights spent sitting in the air raid shelter with gasmask on the knees and shovels and axes in the corners, showed us how very much the world disliked us. Mom wrapped her arms around me, covered my head and all of me with my favorite blanket and said, "Dad will be here when the storm is over. He will make both of us feel better."

Coming out from the shelter, the sound dropping bombs made was over. The sparks that I made into fireflies were flying and catching on fire what was not already burning. The house behind us was hit. People cried when they saw what was happening. I looked to the open doorway and outlined with all the fireflies dancing around, there stood Dad. Ready to hug and ready to pitch in and help.

They formed a bucket brigade to get the water to the burning house. I heard Mom and Dad shouting to move the water buckets from hand to hand faster. I tried to help, so did my friends Ruth, Eva and Lothar. But we four were still too small. Our hands were too tiny to lift the heavy buckets. We sat together on the cold ground and watched how our parents worked to help their neighbors.

One of the neighbor ladies that had the apartment on the third floor wanted the baby carriage brought down from the burning building. When Dad heard her cries, he dashed into the flames. Mom protested but he did not seem to hear her. She called after him not to be foolish. After a while, that seemed like an eternity to us, he came out from the burning house. He was coughing hard. Mom cupped her hands and gave him water to drink from the bucket. It did the trick and he stopped coughing. The rescue mission for the much-needed baby carriage was accomplished.

Dad had burned spots on his arms, hands and face. The suit he wore was ruined but he did not care. The neighbor had the carriage for the baby to sleep and to go for rides in. And this with the help from my brave Dad. I cried when I saw how hurt he was.

His name was mentioned in a letter someone mailed to a government official. We never found out who did this for him. But he received a letter for his bravery in difficult times. And if you can believe it, he got a new suit he didn't have to pay for out of his own pocket. And this with the compliments from Adolf Hitler. The wounds he had soon healed. I was proud. He is and always will be my hero.

The house in the back of ours burned down from the top to the second floor. These neighbors had to find a new place to live. The first-floor neighbors stayed, hoping not to be hit again. The days went by with non-stop bombing. It didn't look good for anyone living in the capital city of Germany. When the air raid siren sounded, bombs fell and Dad came to look for us. The lady that had captured his heart had to share him with us. Mom was sure she didn't like this, but then Mom said, "this woman knew that Dad had children and that Dad loved all three of his children." This, she said, would always bring him back to us.

Chapter Eight

Another day after school, Mom and I made a visit to a cemetery nearby. Mom bought a small bundle of flowers for one of the graves. We found the place after looking for a while and laid the flowers down. On the small marker was a name of a mother and her child. It was the neighbor and her baby that rested there. Mom said, "Look, Dagie, is it not sad? She really didn't get to use the baby carriage for very long. God had other plans for both of them. When Dad comes, we want to tell him about this."

We lost many people we cared about in so many different ways. Some died because it was war. Some were taken away because soldiers came or the Gestapo got them. And some, for our own good, didn't want to be our friends anymore. Mom and I visited with the families of friends to my brothers. And we were made to feel welcome by all of them. At one of these visits when we got ready to go, Mom's friend asked for us not to come back. Mom said, "Why? What is wrong, of course we wanted to come again." But Mom was told if we did, she wouldn't open the door anymore. Mom was hurt and didn't know what to make of this. She looked at her friend and said she did not understand any of this. Mrs. Kupps stroked my hair and said, "Your responsibility is to your daughter. You need to keep her safe and secure. For your and her sake, I cannot let you visit me anymore. If you come back, I will not open this door to you. And I am not doing it to be mean. I want to protect both of you."

Later we did understand what she was doing and why. She was not Jewish but her husband was. This made them and their son undesirable to Hitler. Her husband was deceased and her son was a soldier and placed to fight in the front lines. He was the first in my brothers' circle of friends to lose his life. Others followed in Paul's footsteps. We lost many in this way. Mom and I often went to a cemetery, bought a bundle of flowers to decorate a special friend's grave with them. I never heard my Mom pray out loud, but she stood there with her head bowed and held my hand in hers the whole time.

It was not an easy task for Mom to write letters to Edgar and Erwin, telling them they lost another wonderful friend. Sad for all of us, but more so for my brothers. These young men grew up together. All of them had dads that were or had been like ours a police officer. When they were old enough, they played football for Hertha BSC. They drank beer at their favorite hangout, The Ratske Restaurant. They talked about sports and, of course, about girls. They laughed and thought it funny if one of them managed to steal a pretty girl away from the other one. They laughed and joked around whenever they got together.

Their favorite swimming place was the river Spree, that was running right through the middle of Berlin. All of these young men, when asked, would claim when they were baptized as babies it was done with the water from the river Spree. It ran deep through their veins, forever they would be Berliner boys. So, when they got together and laughed and joked around, they knew when they went back to the front lines, they could also die together. Seeing each other was a celebration of life for all of them. Because the next time, one might be among the missing. When this happened at their next get together, they lifted a glass of beer up high. It was their last greeting and a goodbye to a dear friend. A friend they would never want to forget. Mom and I said goodbye in a different way. We always bought flowers at a shop or vendor and visited another lonely cemetery. We all had our own way to deal with grief. Mom always waited a while before she made a visit with the family. She knew when to stay away and when it was the right time to give a helping hand. Dad always said of Mom she was the woman that had a soft heart. It was so soft it was made out of butter. When he said this, I knew what he was saying. He paid her a huge compliment. He was saying our mom was nice and a very good person.

When he was gone, I thought about his words and wondered why he left such a good person? How could he give his heart to someone else, when she was so good? I must say I was very confused by all of this. When I had questions I wanted to have answers for, I always went to Dad. But this time I couldn't ask him. With this I was all alone. I had to figure it out on my own. And it might take me a long time to figure out what was so difficult for me to understand. It could be I would never find the answer for it but I would pray about this. Yes, my prayers every night became longer and longer all of the time.

If my brothers came home on what they called getting a much-deserved furlow, maybe a talk with them would do me good. They could help me to sort it out. Help me to understand the things I could not talk with my parents about. I wondered how long it would be before they would get such a much deserved and needed furlow. In the meantime, while we waited for their return, I went to school, Mom and I went through the everyday hunger pains together. Oh yes, our tummies liked at bedtime to talk with each other as Mom liked to call it. But they had to wait till morning to be fed breakfast. I must say it was hard to go to sleep when my tummy was talking. I was sure it kept my Mom awake too. Then morning would come and all would be better for the two of us.

We visited the air raid shelter with our neighbors when the sirens blew. Dad showed up after every awful air raid. He didn't forget how afraid I was of a house falling on me. I never forgot the promise he gave me, to dig me out from under with his bare hands, should this happen. By coming, he calmed my fears and maybe my mom's as well. Every night I prayed for this war to end. But it was not happening, no matter how much I prayed. It went on and on, from one day to the next.

When sitting in the air raid shelter, I hated the thin whistling sound the dropping bombs made. I hated the silence that always followed, when they dropped near us. When they were dropped right over us, the thin shriek sound was short and the silence after it was long. This is when we jumped off the chairs we sat on, and face down we laid on the floor. Going to bed after coming up from the shelter, my prayer was always the same. God, please bless Dad, Mom and my brothers in Finland. Bless the teacher I once had and others like her. And please let the bombs fall in other places, but not on us.

Day and night the bombs kept falling. Many people got hurt, many died. My prayer should have been for the bombs to stop falling, so no one would be hurt. So no one would have to die. I was small and I didn't know any better. What I did know was that prayer was important and God listened to little children's prayers. Oh, how we needed his help. In all this time the war continued and Berlin and other cities kept burning. Mom said for me to keep praying and this is what I did.

Chapter Nine

The time came when we were under an air raid and I waited for Dad to show up and he didn't come. We went through one on the other and he still didn't come. What was wrong? Because this was not like him. I worried, Mom worried; it didn't help for us to worry, he didn't come. The end of the month came around and Dad always brought the household and the child support money by, but Dad did not come. Mom looked at me when she said, "Dad would not do this." Something was wrong and we need to find out what it was.

The next day, Mom kept me out of school and we started the search for Dad. First, we went to his home. Praying the house was there when we got there. If it was not, we didn't have to go on with the search. The man Mom and I cared so much about was then buried under all the rubble of wood and stone. But when we turned the corner on Dad's street, we gave a big sigh of relief. The house was standing.

Dad lived on the first floor. We climbed up the stairs, hoping it was Dad opening the door to us. Mom rang the bell, we recognized by the light footsteps, they were not Dad's. When the door opened, Mom faced the young woman that took Dad away from us. She invited us inside and she was surprised to hear Dad was missing. She said she thought for some reason when Dad didn't get back to her, he was still with us. She said she knew he cared much and thought the reason for his staying away for this length of time was serious. Now she was concerned like my mom. Mom and she agreed to look for him. Mom would go to his place of work and hoped to find answers. In this both Mom and Aunt Adelheid, as I called her, would work together.

At home, Mom wrote a letter to my brothers. They needed to know about Dad. The next days, Mom kept me at home from school. We went to Dad's work place and all I could see was the shaking of people's heads to Mom wanting to find answers. This went on for many days. At night I heard her crying. She didn't know it, but I shed my own tears and prayed to find my dad. I hung on to my teddy Mr. Brown bear and we prayed and prayed. Sometimes I only prayed for Dad and not the others. He was important to me and I wanted for him to come back and hug me. I missed him.

However, right now, I really knew that I needed to be a big girl for Mom and for Dad. I needed to pray that every day Mom and I went looking for him, a miracle could happen. We wanted to find him and know he was well. When the air raid siren sounded as we walked, Mom and I took shelter in a hallway of a house. Sometimes when we were spotted walking, we were invited by strangers to join them in their shelter. Mom always told them our hope, our mission was to find Dad. When we left, to be on our way to another office building to ask more questions, we left friends behind that understood. They wished us well in the search to find Dad.

In the days that went by without a lead to what happened to him, I heard Mom cry after she went to bed. To me she said to keep up and pray for Dad. I holding my friend Mr. Brown Bear, we prayed non-stop. Non-stop between all the air raids we were having. When we came out of the shelter and saw the damage the war made, we remembered Dad. He always came to see us and if he had to do it, he had promised to rescue us from under the rubble of the house that had fallen on us. We depended on his help and rescue for us. We believed in him. Here we faced another bad storm and he was not there. He couldn't come. Our mind was asking, where are you? Don't you know how much we need you?

The trouble was we couldn't make phone calls to find Dad. This would have made everything faster if we had a phone. Private citizens like us didn't have phones. Mom did everything by letter writing and us going places to ask about Dad. One day we got help. In a government building we entered a large room. I was sitting not far away from Mom on a chair, watching with interest what was happening. The man behind a big desk opened a large folder and showed it to her. I noticed it had a lot of red marks among the dark writing. After a while, Mom thanked this man and we went home.

Walking down the stairs Mom squeezed my hand and said, "Dagie, we did it, we found Dad." "Where?" I asked. "Where is he? Can we go see him?" Mom said, "Yes, we will go see him tomorrow." Tonight, she wanted to write to my brothers, as we needed their help. I didn't let up, wanting to know what the man said to her. She gave in by saying "Dagie, Dad is a political prisoner of Adolf Hitler." He was held a prisoner in the KZ of Plotzensee in Berlin. All the red markings I saw among the dark words on paper spelled one word. And it meant "political". My dad was held prisoner by the man that had a beard under his big nose. The man whose voice I didn't like to hear on the radio. He was the one that took my dad away from us. I didn't like him. In my prayers I wanted to tell God about him. Maybe with me praying, God would do something to help and bring my dad home.

When we came home, as always when she was very upset over something, she turned the 8X10 picture we were to have hanging on the wall of Adolf Hitler around to face the wall. She nor I wanted to have to look at him. When we went to bed at night, I wondered why my dad was in prison. He was a good man. When Dad was a police officer, he had told me that prison was for the bad people. What was my dad doing there when he was not bad? Well, when we went there, I was sure we could explain that a big mistake was made. We would get him out and bring him home.

When tomorrow came, we hurried to leave. We had much to do and Mom and I wanted to get started on the rescue mission we had in mind for Dad. It was taking time till we reached Plotzensee. Part way we walked and the other part we rode in a trolley. The prison was a dark place. It had windows with bars on them. A big door to walk through with a guard walking with us as we walked from one court yard to the other.

Each time we went through the door, the guard would lock the door behind us. I thought what a bad place this was to be in and my Dad was here. Here in prison with many others. What did they do to deserve this? I knew my dad didn't deserve any of it. And maybe there were others here that didn't deserve this anymore than he did. We reached the building that the guard said Dad was in. Again, I sat on a bench and watched Mom talking with someone that looked like a soldier. He sat behind a desk talking for a very long time with Mom. Looking at their faces while they talked, neither one looked happy. I could tell it didn't go well.

Prisoners went by me with large containers that seemed to have soup in it. They looked like they wore pajamas. Striped pajamas. I couldn't imagine Dad wearing something as ugly as this. But we had come to take him home. He wouldn't have to wear this ugly outfit much longer, they would give his own clothes back to him. I sat, I watched and waited. When Mom came out, she took my hand and she said, they will not let us see Dad. I said, we do not get to take him home? Mom said no, not today. We will go home and see what we need to do next. Again, we followed the guard from the back of the prison to the front door.

With a sad heart we went home. I cried and Mom cried. For the moment this was all we could do. Something good for us came out of this bad day. We now could visit Dad if they let us see him. His address was changed from Zehdenicker Str number 7 to Berlin - Plotzensee - KZ. He was alive and knowing this, we now wanted to believe he would be released and come home.

I started back to school. The air raids came more and more often. Hungry was an everyday tummy ache for Mom and me. Money somehow was sent to Mom to pay the bills. Dad could not mail it from prison so somebody other than dad must be taking care of this. But who was it? Surely not the man with the beard under his nose. He was not a kind man and I was sure he wouldn't do this for Mom and me. I kept wondering about all of this. But I did not go and ask Mom about any of it. When letters from my brothers came, Mom was happy to know they were doing alright. We both smiled when the postman brought mail from them.

Then one day I woke up with a bad fever and came down with a bad case of measles. It was all we needed for me to be home and very sick. More school I was missing, to the point of I might not make it to the next grade. Having the measles meant I had to be kept away from others. If there was a bombing attack, we didn't go down to the shelter with the others. My friends played sitting at a small table down there. We did not want for them to get what I had. When the siren sounded, Mom and I stayed in the hallway between the living room and the kitchen. The doors to both rooms, Mom kept closed. If the windows splintered in the other rooms, the glass wouldn't hit us.

In the day time, the windows had blankets on them to keep the light away from me. When the doctor visited, he had Mom place scarves over the lampshades. He said direct light was harmful and with having measles it could go into my eyes. It can cause blindness. We did what the doctor ordered and from day to day I got better. I resumed normal school activities, and I wrote letters to my dad who was still in prison. Mom said this would cheer him up.

If I got too sad thinking of my dad and sat there crying, Mom gave me the book that had a photo of him inside of it. One of my favorite books was the Brothers Grimm story book. She said, "Look at your dad, he is smiling at you. Now he wants for you to give him a smile back." It always did the trick and Mom knew that it would. I wiped away the tears and smiled back at his photo. After all, I needed to be my parents' brave little girl. Every day Mom was always at my side, she never left me. I think if she was in contact with Aunt Adelheid, it had to be by mail. We never went to Dad's apartment again after we found out where he was. There was not any need for us to see Aunt Adelheid. I didn't like her any better than I did Adolf Hitler. This man was the very mean person that imprisoned him and she was the lady that took him away from us. I knew that I didn't like either one of them.

Chapter Ten

Then one day, coming home from school, my brother Erwin was there. Mom's letters reached him and he was given a furlow. He told us that Edgar was on his way home to us. We could expect him any day. Our family had a crisis, they came to help their Dad. Mom told Erwin they wouldn't allow us to see him when we went to visit at the prison. To this Erwin just said, "They will not do this to Edgar and me. This uniform I am wearing will open the prison doors. I promise you that we, when we go there, will see our Dad." Mom just replied she hoped they were right thinking this. And I was hoping the same. The day Erwin went to the prison I sat at my play-table looking at the brother Grimm's story book with Dad's photo in it. Praying in my heart Erwin would get to see him.

Erwin was the first to make the trip to the prison. Edgar was visitor number two. Erwin was right when he said the SS uniform would open the large prison doors that they kept closed to Mom and I. Edgar went there when I was in school. Mom stayed home and did not go with Erwin nor Edgar to the prison after he arrived home. They talked about it in the evening and I heard bits and pieces of their conversation. Sitting around the kitchen table with the radio standing on the shelf turned up loud, they talked and their faces looked serious. I could tell by looking at them that all didn't look good for our dad.

I wanted so much to ask what was going on, but I didn't dare. Because I was to be seen but never heard from. I wanted to know why was Dad put in prison? Did he say something and the walls where he lived had ears? Did he forget to turn the volume on the radio up when he shared secrets? I wanted to know but didn't dare to ask questions.

If I did, they would say I was too small to understand it all. Well, they may be right. However, I was not too small to worry or to be a good secret keeper for everyone. I questioned what I was. Was I a big girl or was I a small girl? I wished they would make up their minds what they wanted for me to be. I couldn't manage to be both big and small at the same time. Oh, grown-ups could be so confusing for someone like me.

In all of this family trouble, I was seen as needing to be a big girl. I guess they didn't think about how upsetting it was when they changed their minds and I had to be the small girl again. I was to be the little daughter and sister Dagie, that played with her dolls and Mr. Brown bear. I really loved the playtime when I got it between air raids and with bombs dropping down from the sky. But if they wanted for me to be the big girl, then I wanted to know all that was happening in our family. Then why will they not tell me about it? What was it that was done with our Dad? And why, why was this done to him?

With my brothers on furlow, all friends that were not in the military came by for a visit. The doorbell did not stop ringing. They made dates to meet in the evening at their favorite hangout "Ratske". Mom and I went with them. Mom drank a dark beer with the boys as she called them and I got a soft drink called Sprudel. Our stay at club Ratske was always short. I had school the next day. Erwin and Edgar stayed longer. They only rushed home at the sounding of the air raid sirens over Berlin. They wanted to be at our side during the air attack. Mom brought a couple of extra chairs down and my brothers carried them up to the apartment when it was over.

Standing in the kitchen, I heard my brothers say to Mom they'd rather face the enemy in the front lines face to face instead of sitting in a shelter like we did. In hand to hand combat they had a chance to defend themselves. We, however, were like sitting ducks waiting for death to happen. When I heard what they said I thought this is why Mom kept me sitting next to her. I was not allowed to sit with my friends at the play table. If a bomb would hit our house and make it cave in, and if we could not get out from under, Mom and I would die sitting together. Dad would find us sitting close when he came to dig us out with his bare hands.

I prayed, oh, God, don't let this happen to us. Dad is in Adolf Hitler's prison in Berlin - Plotzensee. He isn't able to come to help us right now. He was the one that needed God and our help. For this reason, my brothers came home. I needed to pray that God and my brothers could do it and spring Dad out of prison. Then another thought hit me. When the siren went off, did all the prisoners get down to the air raid shelter? Or did they stay locked up in their cell without any protection against the falling bombs? This was a scary thought I had and I was afraid for my Dad and all the prisoners in Berlin - Plotzensee. My head was full of questions I did not get any answers for. I was the obedient child that was seen but not heard from. My head and heart wanted to get answers. I wondered should I dare to ask?

I also wondered if Dad went hungry like we did. Erwin and Edgar brought again two care packages of food to us and with this we again ate better for a while. Coming from school, Mom surprised me with a cake. Before we ate the evening meal, I had playtime with friends. In the dangerous times we lived in, we still found time to act like kids. We played catch, hide and seek, drew pictures and so forth. We lived in a children's world. When the sirens sounded, it destroyed our world and brought us back to reality. The world of living in World War II took over. We all prayed for this war to end, no one knew when this would be.

Erwin and Edgar Weiss

Chapter Eleven

One day the doorbell rang, we opened and there stood Dad. We couldn't believe it was really Dad. But it was so, it was him. I hugged him so hard I almost knocked him over, so happy was I to see him. Mom wanted to know if he was a free man, but he shook his head saying no. Hitler let him come out from this awful place to marry the woman I called Aunt Adelheid. My brothers and I would have a stepmother.

We would never call this woman Mom, we had a Mom and we loved her. Adelheid was the intruder and not welcomed into the family by us three children. My brothers thought as I did, besides she was only a few years older than they were. For them she would be Adelheid, our Dad's new wife. Now here stood Dad with me, telling Mom he would marry her replacement. I knew that when he left Mom would cry. I understood Mom well. She would go to the living room, leaving me to play in the kitchen. She would shut the door and cry for a very long time. When this happened, I needed to be Mom's big girl and help her through this new heartache.

I stood next to my parents for this long talk. Dad said someone from his place of work had turned him over to Hitler's Gestapo. They arrested him and a court, without a lawyer present to defend him, sentenced him to serve six-month prison time in Berlin - Plotzensee. In court, false witnesses testified against him. He said the rest was history. From court he was taken straight to prison. No chance was given to get in touch with the family. He said he was grateful Mom started to look for him and did not give up till she found him. He also said that because of Erwin and Edgar being SS soldiers, Heinrich Himmler send a letter to the prison. This letter opened the doors to both of them when they came to visit. And it might be the reason they let him out to get married. After the week they gave him for his honeymoon, he needed to go back to serve the rest of the prison time.

All the time Dad was talking, he looked at Mom and seemed to have forgotten about me. The prison was a death camp, he said. On a daily basis many, many lost their lives. It was a living hell, as no one knew who could be next to die. He said it didn't matter if the sentence was not a death sentence, at random they executed prisoners.

While he was talking, he raised his arm, the suit sleeve fell back. I saw they starved my Dad, his face was my Dad but what was under the suit that covered him up, this was not the Dad I knew. He was a walking skeleton, just skin and bones. And this was not all of it. The front row of his upper teeth was missing. Who was so cruel to do this to him? Again we questioned why was this done to him, I just couldn't understand any of this. Dad said he had other things to tell my Mom but he would do this at some other time. All the time my parents had this conversation I thought of Dad showing me that the apartment walls had ears. He wanted for me to be careful in all I said. Maybe he forgot for one single moment, that the walls at his place of work also had ears? If this was it and my thoughts were right, my poor, poor Dad. We needed to get him out of this horrible place and soon, or all of us would not have a Dad. And I wanted to speak with Aunt Adelheid one more time if mom would take me there. I wanted to tell her to keep a carpet beater behind the kitchen door, like Mom did for me. It would remind Dad not to say anything, just like it reminded me. He needed like me to keep his mouth closed. This would help him and would keep him out of trouble.

Dad came back for a visit with mom when I was at school. They must have had the talk that was meant just to be between the two of them. This talk was not meant for me to be a part of. I asked Mom later if Dad told her how come all his teeth were missing. She said yes, he told her. She would tell me about it when I was older. I knew by what she said that again I was her little girl and not seen by her as her big girl. The big girl that I liked to be in order to be of some help. Over Berlin the air raids came regular night by night and day by day. I went to school and was in a hurry to get home to be with my brothers. Dad married Aunt Adelheid and took time away from her to be with us. One night he took Edgar and Erwin to meet with friends and have a beer at Ratske's. This time Mom and I didn't join them, we stayed home. They needed father with son time, before Dad had to return to the prison. Dad gave the prison a name. He called it hell on earth for everyone in it.

I was not in bed yet when they came home and had a story to tell. Mr. Ratske was picked up by the Gestapo. From what all three of them told us, he had too much to drink and went outside, saying and shouting words against Adolf Hitler, Germany's leader. All three tried to stop him and get him off the street. They told him to calm down and to stop shouting. Mr. Ratske was big and tall and nothing they said and did made an impression on him.

Soon they heard sirens of what they thought was a police car coming. All was lost, they had to make a run for it. My brothers wearing the SS uniform and Dad out from prison with a pass. It was a situation that spelled disaster for all of them. They had no choice but to abandon a friend of many years, in order to save themselves. Mom didn't let go, she wanted to know more. What would happen to Mr. Ratske? No one knew, but all knew this was not good.

I was standing there listening to every word, maybe this is why they didn't talk about it more than what they did. Again, I had my own thoughts about all this. I was half a child and half a grown up and understood more than they gave me credit for. Poor, poor Mr. Ratske, most likely they took him to prison, like they did my Dad. The same awful things that happened to my dad would now happen to him.

In the following days before returning to Finland, my brothers went by club Ratske. It was open to the public, but it was run by the staff, the owner had not returned. All of them worried about Mr. Ratske and when my brothers left, they made Mom promise to write the minute she heard anything about him.

With my brothers gone, Dad was the last to leave us. Two went back to fight in a war, the other went back to finish serving a prison sentence. And we, Mom and I, we served kind of a sentence, sitting next to each other in the air raid shelter, waiting for a bomb to drop on us. They hit all around us but up till now, we have been spared. The paint factory behind us took a direct hit. Some neighboring houses burned down, but amidst all the destruction our house was still standing.

On a day when Mom and I were out and about, we ran into Mrs. Ratske. Mom was glad to see her and asked about her husband. Sad was the news Mrs. Ratske gave Mom. She received a letter from some person in the government, letting her know that her husband passed away from a heart attack. Mom and she stood and talked for a while, no one believed from what I heard them say, that Mr. Ratske died from this. But this was another one of those secrets we wanted and needed to keep.

Coming home, Mom wrote the letters to my brothers telling them about the man that had been their friend. To me she said this "Dagie, we must pray not to get a letter like this about your Dad. These things happen every day to people we know and we could be next to get sad news like this." Again, I sat at my table by the kitchen window, Brother Grimm's story book in front of me, with Dad's photo inside of it. I looked and looked at it, pleading with God not to let my Daddy die.

The mail we got from my brothers said they both thought this was going to happen to Mr. Ratske when he was taken away. They were sad that they were not able to help him. The Ratske family had lots of friends and all mourned the loss of a dear friend. However, someone called the police to come and get him and this person was not a friend. Mom said this person was called an informer for the Third Reich, this person was a tattle-tale to the Gestapo. And since we knew all the walls had ears, we needed to be very careful. Most of all we would try to stay more to ourselves. We wanted to be careful with the old friends we had and not make any new ones. At this time in Germany, old friends or new friends all could turn out to be for one reason or the other a tattle-tale.

Chapter Twelve

In all the World War II troubles we celebrated holidays. Most of all, Adolf Hitler's birthday. Youth groups were marching, flags flying from every window, but not from ours. Our window looked like a dark hole in this apartment building. Mom said she liked it this way. It was a free day from school because it was the big man's birthday.

We heard the doorbell ringing and I followed Mom to the door. A man stood out there we didn't know telling us to hang out the flag. Mom said our flag was broken. I knew right there, Mom had told a lie. The flag was leaning against the wall in the spare room next to the kitchen. I kept my mouth closed, I knew the carpet beater stood behind the kitchen door waiting for me. I was not about to risk it by correcting my Mom. But I was wondering why it was alright for her to tell a lie, when she told me to lie is wrong. I thought what was right for a grown-up to do must not be right for little kids like me.

Mom closed the door saying we will get the flag fixed; it will wave in the wind by the next national holiday. Like she said, maybe it would fly in the wind by this time. Who knows, a lot can happen between now and then. I could tell that when Mom closed the door, that she was angry. She kept grumbling to herself as she went to the living room to turn Adolf Hitler's picture around facing the wall. Who in the world does he think he is, she kept saying, to dictate to us every step we take? Small as I was, I wondered about this myself.

My brothers were made to serve in the SS even though they didn't want this branch of service. Dad went to prison because someone told a lie about him. We children had to stand at attention in a strict way, in the school yard and sitting in class. Our teacher and friends (well my teacher) were taken from us, never to come back. Stores were broken into, windows were smashed, because the owners were Jewish. Churches were emptied of all that was pretty. Who in the world is this man, that had so much power to destroy all that is good? I wondered, wondered and wondered. I prayed, prayed and prayed.

When I asked Mom, she put her hand over her mouth to tell me it was another secret we needed to keep. And she said, "Dagie, only the Devil can do this. What we saw in Berlin was the Devil and his helpers working overtime hours. Often, we had to turn a blind eye to what was going on all around us. We had to do this for our own good."

When mail came from my brothers, Mom cried as she read the letters from the beginning to the end. Erwin wrote about the Salla battle and the many lives lost on both sides. He said he was decorated with the iron cross second class. And it was for saving and not for taking lives. This is what made him proud. Mom nodded when she read to me what he wrote and she said, to save a live deserves a medal. But to take a life brings great sadness to the one who takes it and for the families that mourn a loved one.

Erwin wrote, that two of his fighting buddies tried to talk the enemy into giving up, and they were killed. The enemy had a hiding place in a cave and didn't want to give up. Erwin wrote they were threatened to be killed by flamethrowers, if they did not come out of the cave. He said he just had to try to reach them and he got on top of a tank using a bullhorn, and surprise – whatever he said, made them give up. He said yes, they were prisoners now but God willing when this war ended, they could go home.

Mom looked at me and smiled when she said that my dad in World War I, at the same age as Erwin, was decorated with the same medal. Like father, like son must have come to mind when she read me a part of Erwin's letter. We had reason to be proud of both of them. They received the same medal, only many years apart. Dad in circa 1916 and Erwin in 1941-1942. The next letter written by Mom to Dad she would mention this good news. And if the newspapers had a write up about this, as they often did, we would mail the article with the letter to him. To Ewin however Mom would mail the newspaper article with a letter telling him how proud she was of him. But most of all she wanted to write for him to stop taking risks. She wanted for him to stay alive and come home to us when the war was over.

Sometimes the Newspaper wanted to report some good and not only all the bad news. We read a feel good as well as a feel bad section in the paper every single day. The good softened the blow of the all-time bad writings. Sure enough, Erwin's name was printed along with other names. The letter we wrote to Dad we didn't get to mail, instead we told him about it face to face.

Dad showed up at our door and we were the first he came to visit when the prison doors opened to set him free. Sitting with Mom at the kitchen table he said he was sure Erwin and Edgar's visits and the note or letter from Heinrich Himmler, who was the leader of the SS and head over the prisons in Germany, had something to do with him not being a dead man. He stated he was lucky to be alive. Then my parents told me to go and play for a while with my dolls. They needed to have a long grown-up talk and I was still too young to understand any of it. Again, I obeyed them and went from the kitchen into the living room and cuddled my teddy Mr. Brown Bear. Both of us grateful for God to have answered my many prayers, Dad was released and home with us. I was a very happy little girl for this was the day God had chosen for letting him come home to us. I did like I was told, I played with my toys, through the closed doors I heard my Mom cry. Somehow, I didn't worry about these kinds of tears, they must be very happy ones.

When the time came for Dad to go home, it was hard to let him leave. He told me when I kissed him that Aunt Adelheid was waiting to see him. I had almost forgotten in the excitement, that he didn't live with us anymore. He promised he would come back very soon. When the doors closed behind him, he was on his way to be with his new wife. That night I almost wished for the sirens to sound so that he came back like he had always done before, making sure we were alright.

Mom had me put the dolls and toys away when she said, "Your dad lived through some bad times in Adolf Hitler's prison. He is a very sick man, I needed to understand this about him. We needed to give his body and mind time to heal before he would be completely himself again. It would take a very long time for him to get better." I knew by looking at Dad that he needed food, to gain back some of the weight he had lost. Under the suit he wore, he was skin and bones. I said to Mom and he needed new teeth to be able to safely chew the food. Without good teeth he could choke on it, like I almost did when one time my mouth was too full.

I asked what happened to the teeth had had, why is he missing so many of his front teeth? Mom shook her head, I could see right now was not the time to ask all these questions. Maybe some other time is better. All she said was when I was older, both of them would want to have a talk with me. She said then I would understand the difficult time in their life.

I don't believe the sirens sounded that night to bring us down to the air raid shelter. But something else kept me awake. It was Mom's crying that didn't let me sleep. It was not easy to smile when around us we had nothing to smile about. But today Dad was released from the prison. The tears she had rolling down from her eyes should be happy ones. But maybe she was crying because he went home to Aunt Adelheid, when she wished he was still with us. I closed my eyes tight not to think about this. Because like Mom I wanted for him to still live with us like he used to do before the divorce happened. The days went by and now when someone leaned on the doorbell, we could tell if it was family or a stranger. We made up our own ring-a-ding since the incident with not having a flag hanging from our window. It was three long and two short rings and open sesame, Mom opened the door.

She always had a smile when she knew it was Dad standing there. He came more often and not only after a severe air raid hit Berlin. They had become true friends. Dad's prison experience formed a tight bond between them. The more trouble Dad had, the more he needed his comfort giver and best friend, Ellie Weiss. He told her about not finding work after being released from prison. He said the card deck was stacked against him, since he had been a political prisoner. Getting a police pension kept us all afloat for the time being. Money being this tight presented a problem in his second marriage. He worked on repairing radios and relied on his drawing skills to bring in the extra money that was needed.

Mom showed sympathy for all that concerned him. When he needed it, he came to her more and more to get it. And she always gave what was needed. If it was the listening ear, or the asked advice or the helping hand, Mom gave it to Dad. To me she said, "This is Edgar's, Erwin's and your Dad. I will always help him. It's the right thing to do." I believed that Dad knew how much he could count on her. He knew she had the love in her heart for the father of her three children. This love would never go away and she would never let him down. He could depend on her.

Chapter Thirteen

The war, it moved along and we were forced to move along with it. Families' special days we celebrated as best we could. Getting together whenever it was possible and taking a head count. We were always glad when we came up with the same number from the last time.

On birthday get togethers, I was the lucky one. I was born on Grandma's day and Grandma always had a cake. If it wasn't for Grandma, maybe there wouldn't have been a cake for me. She did her best to make her and my birthday extra special.

It was amazing to her entire family that she managed to bake two or three large cakes to feed the birthday visitors. Germany was on a starvation diet. She must have saved up for this and gone without for a long time to bake all of this for her family. When we left, she had a gift for me wrapped up in paper. It was a piece of birthday cake to eat on the way home. Mom smiled when she said this is what Grandparents do when they love their grandchildren. This made me feel good and it made me feel loved. I went to bed and prayed to God like I did every night, "Please bless all the people I love and take care of my Grandparents because they love me. And should the planes come tonight to drop bombs, make them drop them elsewhere but not on us. Amen" I don't remember having to get out of bed that night. God gave me and grandma a birthday present by not letting the sirens go off. With Mr. Brown Bear in my arms, I slept peaceful all night long. And for my Grandma my wish for her was to have sweet dreams. All of us loved our grandpa Hermann and grandma Emilie Sauer.

Came Christmas we hoped to have a peaceful night. Everybody celebrated Christmas and should take time out from dropping bombs. This was wishful thinking on my part. War does not give anyone a time out or a holiday to enjoy. From Germany, the Air Force (Luftwaffe) flew to England to destroy London and other major cities. From England, the Royal Air Force and the American Air Force came to do the same with us. In fighting a war there is not one bit of peace or rest to be found. No matter how hard one looked or wished for it.

The news in the movie houses proclaimed victory. Berlin and other cities showed not any sign of it. Berlin and other places laid in ashes and we lived in the middle of it. Schools had to slow down, I was home more and more.

When mom bought the newspaper, it printed there are foster parents living in villages and small towns not so touched by the war because there was not any industry there. They were willing to open their home to us children, coming from a, by war, torn up city. My parents talked about it and asked if I wanted to go. They thought it was good for me to leave them and to get out of Berlin. I was not at all sure about this and I said it to them. I couldn't believe that they wanted to send me away. When they told me I might have a foster brother or sister to play with, the whole plan sounded much nicer. After talking it over for a while I gave in and said yes, I was willing to go. But I didn't want to be way for long. I wanted to go only for a short time, just for a little while.

They arranged for me to leave on what they called Adolf Hitler's children's train. My few things were quickly put in a box because we didn't have a suitcase. Dad made a drawing of a funny looking dwarf on the side of the box. This was a good way for me to pick out my box from the many others. When the day came for me to leave, I wanted to change my mind. All of the sudden I was afraid to be away from Mom and Dad. I had second thoughts and asked to be taken home. My parents told me they loved me, but this was not the time for me and them to make changes. It was too late for this. On the end of the line someone was waiting for me to give me a home for a while. And I must not disappoint them by not coming.

The train I was taking was from the front to the back and from the back to the front really Adolf Hitler's children's train. It was going from Berlin to Obornik. There foster parents waited at the station to take us to our new home. For us kids, the threat of the falling bombs was over. For the parents we left in Berlin, the threat continued. With day and night air raids, we could lose them and be orphans. This was the threat that accompanied us to Obornik. All of us were too young to understand that loving parents removed us from danger, yet they stayed and faced it.

When the train started to move, I wanted to get out. I wanted to run back to Mom and Dad and beg them to please let me stay. But a soldier stood by the door and looking at him, I didn't dare to leave my seat. There was not one boy or girl in this compartment that I knew. I felt out of place and wanted to cry. The little girl in me wanted to cry, the big girl in me fought back the tears and looked out the window. The train started to move faster and faster and I liked seeing houses and trees going by so very fast. Soon we had left the city behind us and I was interested in what I saw.

The kids started talking, singing and laughing. We made so much noise that the soldier at the door laughed when he told us to stop it. He had to say it one more time, and then another time but this time he was not laughing. We all knew he meant it and we immediately calmed down.

I didn't like the men in uniform. I did not have any reason to like them. This soldier with us wore a grey uniform. I didn't know what kind it was. The mean soldiers wearing a brown uniform, they scared me the most. I remembered them because they came to my class and took our teacher away. They came after neighbors and friends of ours. They shouted at them, they pushed them around, then loaded them on trucks and drove them away. Maybe these men wearing the brown shirts took my Dad away. No, I did not like them because they were mean to good people. But this soldier in the compartment with us kids wore a grey uniform, maybe it meant he was only a little mean or not mean at all. I hoped he was one of the nice soldiers and would be friendly to us all.

I sat in my seat looking out the window and also watching the kids play games. I minded my own business and liked it this way. I thought of the lady that would be my foster mother. I hoped she liked me and I wanted to like her. I had a name tag hanging around my neck. My name was on it and hers. Mom had told me that like my Aunt Lene, she was a widow with two children close to my own age. Mom also said all of them looked forward to having me as a part of their family. All of them wanted to take good care of me.

When Dad and Mom said goodbye, I had to promise them I would be a good girl. They said they would write and Dad promised me to draw pictures and send them. I did promise to continue to be a family Weiss secret keeper and make them proud of me. I would do my school work and clean up all of my messes and I will say my prayers at night. Mr. Brown Bear, my teddy bear, was packed in the box with my clothes. I was not leaving him in Berlin. Being boxed away like he was, Mom and Dad didn't have to pay for a ticket for him to ride the train like I did.

It seemed like a long train ride from Berlin to the small town of Obornik. When we arrived at the destination the soldier opened the door and helped us down. I decided I could jump the few steps down on my own, I did not need his help. I looked around and thought my heart would stop. The men waiting for us all wore what I disliked so much. They wore brown uniforms. These men were the brownshirts and I did not trust them. I knew that I was in big trouble.

From the other compartments, soldiers brought their group of children to join ours. We kids formed a line to get to the inside of the waiting room. And one by one as we entered, we filled up this area. Foster parents stood outside and inside waiting for names to be called and go home with one child or more. All of us stood guarded by the soldiers that had been in the compartment with us. From what I could see, the waiting room on each side had two large doors for coming in and going out. So the foster parents with their child in tow were coming and leaving through these doors. It was a steady stream of come, come, come and go, go, go. It was wonderful to know so many people had come to help the children that got off Adolf Hitler's children's train.

Before it was my turn to walk through the doors and meet my foster Mom, I took one last look at the train that brought me with all the other children to Obornik. The locomotive was still billowing steam, or was it smoke? It was getting ready to pull out and say goodbye to us and Obornik. What would this train's next mission be? More children leaving the big city to find refuge from this war?

Or would it become a Red Cross train bringing wounded or fallen soldiers back from the front lines? If this train could talk, it had a story to tell.

My turn came and I stepped to the inside. I thought looking around someone please come and take me away from here. All around this room calling out names and asking more questions stood the men wearing brown shirts with a swastika armband. I looked at them and thought I should have made a run for the train when I thought it was leaving. Maybe with so many people standing around, no one would have noticed me trying to be an escape artist. But no, with the men in the grey uniforms, one of them would have seen me and brought me back. I was doing right by staying and not making any trouble for myself and others.

The roll call went from A to the letter Z. Since my name was Weiss and started with a W, I didn't think anything about being among the last. When my name was called and nobody was there to claim me, I got very scared. I stood with all the men in a brown uniform and no one was there to rescue me. I thought of Mom and that I didn't belong here. I needed to be home with her. I missed her and it was only this morning when I left her and Dad.

Some of the men in uniform left. Only a few of them stayed and now and then they glanced over to me. I knew I was a problem and they were talking about me. One of them came and looked at my name tag. He asked if I went by another name or was Dagmar what the family called me. I looked up at him and told him Mom and Dad called me Dagie.

With this said, he took my hand in his and told me that I was going home with him. He told me he had a daughter; her name was Betty. She was a year younger than

I and she would love to have someone like me around to play with. He did not let go of my hand and scared as I was, I left the train station with a man wearing this dreadful brown uniform.

I was surprised to see he had a car and a driver waiting for him. The car was black and had the German flag attached to the front. It was a sign that the man riding in it was important. Getting into the car I was glad when he had to let go of my hand. And I was glad to have it back and kept my hands folded in my lap. I was on my way to a new home and family.

Looking at the man sitting next to me, I noticed he kept smiling and I thought, he does not look mean. He told me that he would write to my parents that I was staying with him and his family. He didn't want for them to worry about me. I thought good but what would they think of me living in a home of a man wearing a brown uniform. Would they be scared for me?

Chapter Fourteen

When the car stopped, I saw a beautiful house with a garden and a fence around it. I had never lived in a house before and seeing this made me believe that my foster parents were not just important but they must also be rich. Inside I met my new Mom and sister Betty. Their family name was Halbleib and they told me I could call them Mr. or Mrs. Halbleib but would like it, if for as long as I was with them, to call them Mom and Dad. Like their daughter Betty did. I nodded yes, I would do this. I also learned we had Polish servants in the household that saw to everyone's needs.

They took off my coat and hat and one of the servants brought me a bowl of soup to eat. I ate it slowly, taking care not to blow on the soup because it was still hot. And I took care of not to slurp when eating, because this was showing I had good manners. My mom had taught me to be polite in every way possible. To slurp or blow on things was having bad manners. Not to do this was having good manners. I wanted to make my mom proud of me. And coming to the home of Mr. and Mrs. Halbleib gave me this opportunity, showing them how well she raised me. Spending time away from my parents, I wanted to be the good and nice little girl they brought me up to be. And now, living in the home of someone wearing a brown uniform, I needed to be extra careful and extra, extra polite.

By now it was dark outside and it was time for bed. Betty's room had two beds and one would be mine. My box must have been brought to the house and Mr. Brown Bear was sitting on my bed. I was glad to see him. For me to go to sleep without holding him was unthinkable. I liked my sister to be. She took my hand and smiled at me when we met. She was pretty, her hair was dark brown and the color of her hair matched her pretty brown eyes. Yes, I thought that we could be good sisters and good friends. Her bed stood at the right side of the room and mine was on the left. We had the window in the middle for looking out to the garden. I saw that Betty's Mom had a tummy and I knew this was called having a baby tummy. Betty said before we went to sleep, they were wishing for a baby boy. I wanted to include this in my prayer, when I prayed for Mom, Dad and my brothers. But my prayers would have to wait till the lights were off. This was between me and God, Betty and her Mom and Dad didn't need to know about it.

On the first day with my new family, I found out everything was different. Not done in the way my own family did things in Berlin. It was nice, and new for me but very, very different. Maids took care of everything including Betty and I. They helped in keeping us clean and well dressed for each day. They took care of cooking and cleaning. And when needed on weekends, took Betty and I out for walks. These so helpful people spoke a different language from us. When they worked next to each other they spoke their own language. I noticed when Mr. or Mrs. Halbleib or we kids entered the room they switched to our language. It was a polite thing to do as my new mom explained it to me.

My foster mother had to rest a lot. She stayed in bed often and we kids had visiting time with her. Time spent with her was always fun. She explained to Betty and me she had to be in bed so much, not to lose the baby tummy. My foster Dad, I only saw at the evening meal. After this he gave Betty and me playtime or talk time with him before going to bed. And after he got home, he changed clothing. Gone was the brown uniform. He wore a shirt and pants like my dad did. Gone for the time he spent with us was the uniform that I disliked. He was with us kids and was Betty's and my dad. I learned this is really what he wanted to be when he was at home. To be Betty's mom's husband and Betty's dad. This was of importance to him. And he was mine too if I wanted to call him dad. Every morning he was picked up by the driver, driving the big black car. I thought how wonderful this was, for him not to have to take a trolley, bus or underground train to work like most people in Berlin had to do. He, like his wife did during the day, made time for us sharing his evening hours. I learned that I could relax around him. He was nice, he was loving with us. I totally forgot that he wore a brown uniform when he left for work. I loved him and his wife. And of course, my new sister Betty.

The people working for this family liked their jobs. The time that I was a part of their family, I learned a valuable lesson. A book cannot be judged by looking at its cover. It had to be read to know what it is all about. And a man should not be judged by what kind of uniform he is wearing. But by his actions and the words that come out of his mouth. By this we can tell if a person is good or bad. This family was a good family. It was the right place for me and I fit in well with them.

I was a fortunate little girl when this family took me in. I learned when the days went by, that like my family in Berlin, they had to be secret keepers. Not from each other but from the outside world. I fit well into their family circle as I too was a good secret keeper.

I had not any trouble going to school. I made friends but I never brought a friend home with me from school. My playmate was my sister Betty. I really didn't need anyone else.

When letters came for me from Mom and Dad, my foster parents read them to me. But only the part that was meant for me. The other part was for them. Every time a letter was brought by the mailman, I was a happy girl. Dad kept his promise to make drawings and Mom wrote she loved and missed me. She told me when my brothers came home on furlough. And she told me about Grandma, Grandpa, as well as all my other relatives. So far, the forever dropping bombs have not taken any of them away.

I prayed my prayer every night after the lights were turned out. "Please, dear God, drop the bombs someplace else but not on the people I love. I do not want to be all alone in the world and have to live in a children's home." I thought about my friends Lothar, Ruth and Eva. They didn't leave on a children's train like I did. Mom didn't write anything about them. I knew of them that at the bombing raids they would sit in the basement and play games at their table. Mom didn't have to write me about them, because I knew them well. Did I miss them? Of course, I did. But right now, as I promised my parents, I needed to make the best of times here with my foster family.

There were other things I thought about and they puzzled me. There were things taking place in my foster parents' home that didn't make any sense to me. One minute I was told not to speak with the neighbor kids living next door to us because they were Polish and not German. We were told we must keep away from them. On the other hand, my foster mother packed baskets with food and medical supplies and carried them to the Polish neighbors after it got dark. Betty and I helped her. She said she needed us to help carry because she did not want to take a chance on losing the baby tummy.

We always went when it was very dark and went to many homes in one night. Everyone was glad to see us and it seemed like they knew when we were coming. At these private visits, it was perfectly fine to talk and play with the children. And Betty and I had a wonderful time with them. To me, it didn't seem right that at times it was alright to be friends and the next time it was not.

I never said anything about this to my foster parents but could not understand grown-up people. I kept my mouth shut but always had my eyes and ears open. Many visitors came to the house at all hours of the day. But also at night after we kids went to bed. My foster Dad belonged to the SA. These were the men wearing the brown uniform. Or they could be called the brownshirts. They were friends of his and visited us often.

Then visitors came very late at night. And for some reason when they came, Betty and I were placed in the attic room. Betty took her favorite doll and I Mr. Brown Bear to bed with me. We had strict orders from Mr. and Mrs. Halbleib, Betty's parents, never to come down stairs during the night. For this reason, a potty was placed in the far corner of the attic for our use. In another corner stood a bushel basket of apples should the munchies hit us.

I being older than Betty often wondered about the attic adventure we had. What was going on down stairs that we had to be banished to the attic? We minded well and waited till morning till one of the maids came to bring us back to the nice bedroom we had downstairs. But I was wondering about everything that went on in this household. I didn't think I could ask my foster parents about any of it. Somehow, my heart told me it was not for me to ask. But what I did instead, I put it before God after the lights were turned off. I prayed to him and he would know what to do with all this secrecy.

PS. Many years later I thought about what was going on in this household and the secret life my foster parents lived. I came to this conclusion. My foster father wearing the brown SA uniform the Nazis wore was a Nazi in the day time for the world to see. However, in the dark of the night when all good deeds were done by this family, he met with people from the Polish underground. All living and working in this house had to welcome the Brownshirts that were 100 percent Adolf Hitler friendly. But I come to believe looking back on it many years later, that under Hitler's big nose, God bless them all, the Halbleib household sheltered and welcomed the Polish underground.

My foster family went all out to celebrate the holidays. The spring with its pretty flowers, the lazy summer days sitting in the garden. The winter with the snow on trees, shrubs and on the road. We liked sitting cozy by a warm stove.

Then one day we heard a cry of a baby in the house. Betty had a baby brother. We heard him but we couldn't see him for a while. Mrs. Halbleib had to stay in bed and rest for a few more days before we could visit both of them. We were so excited when we could go and say hello to him. He was so cute and could cry very loud. But my prayer was answered, Betty and family had the little boy they wanted. I was happy for them and every day for an hour or so, we girls visited with him.

Christmas came and the mailman brought a parcel for me to the house. Mom and Dad always put something in for Betty and now they remembered Betty's little baby brother. For me getting mail or a parcel with goodies meant my family was alright. I could never forget that they were facing the constant danger of falling bombs. I, since living with the Halbleib family, did not have to be concerned about it anymore. A restful night was mine since I was with them.

The radio let us know which towns got hit the most. And if I was in the room during a news report and Berlin was mentioned, they turned the radio off so I couldn't hear the bad news. My foster parents and the staff did this because they knew I would worry about my mom and dad. They did not want for me to cry. But when I went to bed and the room was dark, I pulled the covers over my face and cried. Betty and my teddy Mr. Brown Bear heard me but I knew they would never tell. They were my friends and would keep my secret.

Chapter Fifteen

Then the mailman brought a letter from Berlin. In it, my mom asked for me to come back. She wrote that she missed me and wanted for me to come home. My foster parents left it up to me to stay with them or to go back to be with Mom and face the day and night air raids. I said thank you for taking care of me but I wanted to go and be with my mom. The Halbleib family was very good to me and I would miss them. Most of all I would miss Betty and her baby brother. But it was time for me to go back to be with my own mom. To see my dad and play with my friends Lothar, Ruth and Eva.

When our minds were made up to let me go home, it didn't take long and my box was packed with Mr. Brown Bear inside and it was on its way to Berlin. The Halbleib family took me to the Obornik train station and alone, I was on the train to Berlin. I was told not to leave the train till it got to Berlin. There, Mom and Dad waited for me. I loved the family I was leaving but it was time to be back with my own.

Alone I sat in the train compartment moving at a good speed toward Berlin. On one of the stops on the way, a soldier opened the door and he and many children joined me. I scooted to sit next to the window to make room. The language they spoke I noticed was not mine. I started my journey sitting alone but now this train was again a children's train with a soldier as a guard.

Driving along and coming to another stop the soldier got up and said in a loud voice, "Everyone out!" Then he repeated it one more time and said to hurry up and he meant for everyone to leave this train. I was thinking since he was a soldier and in charge, his command was also meant for me. I got up and he didn't stop me and I followed the children out of the station.

The soldiers turned us over to Catholic sisters and they took over for them. I didn't know what to do and not anyone asked me a question. I was with them and was now a part of them. We were taken to a dark brick building and up to the second floor we went. The sisters divided us into small groups, giving each of us a pillow and a blanket. We understood it was for the bed we needed to make up without help from the sisters. We had a surprise when we were told for each of us to pick a bench alongside the wall and this would be our bed. The sisters turned on the lights and they had to stay turned on because the glass in the windows was painted over with black paint.

I had made a mistake by leaving the train when they did. I knew my foster parents thought I had reached Berlin and was safe being with my Mom and Dad. They had not any idea this was not the case. When the sisters came none of them spoke to us. They brought us a cup of oatmeal to eat and something to drink that looked like juice.

None of the children that I was with came to me wanting to be friends. But they understood my language. They understood the soldier that ordered for us to leave the train and now the sisters giving us instruction in case of an air raid. We were to remain sitting or lying on the bench. The pillow was to be held in the front, to protect the face. We needed to face the wall and not the windows. Glass could splinter and hit us if it got bad. When the siren gave the all clear, it was alright to not face the wall anymore.

I kept thinking of the time Mom and I stayed in the apartment instead of being with the neighbors in the air raid shelter. Now I needed to pretend like I did then, we were having a bad thunder and lightning storm and it will pass.

We must wait till the storm blew over and then we will be alright. Maybe in the morning, my parents will look for me and find me. I was very scared, alone and wanted to go home.

When the sisters came around to take care of us, I wanted to look for the one that gave us a smile. She was the one I would dare to talk with. They came giving each of us a wet washcloth for wiping hands and face but they did not give smiles. They must have taken us to the bathroom when we needed to go, funny it is that I do not remember this. What I remember very well is waiting to be found by Mom and Dad and to be rescued from this dark and dreary place.

I got up to walk and to look around. I wanted to make friends while I was there, but not anyone seemed to be interested to become my friend. I found some books and looked at them to pass the time. I saw stacks of games on a table but I was not invited to play by this group of kids. I started to amuse myself by scratching off the black paint on one of the windows, making me a peek-a-boo hole to look out of. This made some of the kids laugh. It broke the ice and I didn't feel so alone any more. I smiled at them and finely they smiled back.

When a woman I had not seen before came into the room she saw the scratched hole in the glass. She didn't say anything but when she came back, she handed me a washcloth. My dirty finger told her I did this. Germany was under a black-out order. This meant that all windows needed to be covered not to let the light shine to the outside. And here I made me a peekaboo hole. I wondered after I wiped my hands with the washcloth, if I would be punished for it.

I was lucky that nothing happened to me but I thought it would when the same woman came back, took my hand and walked me to an office to be questioned by another lady. I answered and heard the woman in front of me say "this is the child." Then I was taken back to join all the other children. On this evening I had the best time with all of them. Most of them did speak German, only a few among them didn't. We played by singing and dancing and acting like long-time friends. I loved it and could have kept this up all night. I had such fun but then a woman came and blew a whistle to stop us from singing and dancing.

When the time came for lights out and to sleep on the bench, I was taken out of the room. I was given a room with a bed in it. Over the bed it had a cross hanging on the wall. The room was simple, a bed, chair and one table. The only thing pretty in it was the cross on the wall.

For the first time before going to bed I removed my outer clothing. Then I prayed. I knew that I was going home. Mom and Dad had searched and found me. If there was an air raid that night, I didn't know it. I slept in a warm bed instead of on a cold hard bench. Soon I would be with my parents. The box with Mr. Brown Bear in it got to them a long time before me. I must say, the whole time I was in this place, I missed holding my cuddly friend.

The opening of the door woke me up. The lady that took me to the office yesterday looked in on me. I got dressed knowing this was the day I went home. I do not think I ate breakfast before leaving. I remember wanting to see the children and saying goodbye to all of them. We had such fun playing together the night before. I walked by every door on the way out. The rooms were dark and empty. Where did all the children go? They must have left before I did.

The same woman that was responsible for me since yesterday took me to the train depot. There she placed me in the care of a soldier that was going to Berlin. He promised he would turn me over to my parents when we reached Berlin.

Most of the trip there he slept and I looked out the window. People came, sat next to him and me and left, it never woke him up. He was very tired from fighting in this war. Looking at him I felt sorry for him. But he too like me had family waiting for him that would be glad to see him. We were both lucky to go home. I thought how glad I could be that I was small and a girl. I was too young to be told by Adolf Hitler to sign up and fight in a war.

Soon the picture on the outside of my window changed. Not anymore fields with small houses. I saw burned buildings, one right next to the other. It meant we made it to Berlin. The train pulled in, my soldier friend woke up and said "we are home." Yes, this was Berlin and we were at home here.

Chapter Sixteen

With the soldier following behind me, I was jumping down the steps from the train, I saw them. There they stood, my mom and dad. They thanked this young man for taking care of me and he was on his way to see his family. Oh, I had so much I wanted to tell my parents I didn't know if it would take hours or a month to tell it all. But I would try to fill them in on all the time I was away from them.

Meeting my playmates Lothar, Ruth, Eva and the young lady renting the other room from Mom was nice. My playmates asked right away if I could come down and play with them. Mom said yes, I could in a little while. And of course, we would again spend a lot of time sitting in the air raid shelter with the other neighbors. This was a time none of us liked. Mom, again, keeping me tucked away next to her, covering me up from head to toe with a blanket. Dad always came to see if the house was still standing and we were still alive. Not one time it entered my mind how difficult it must be for him to reach us. Buildings burning and traffic interrupted by the holes in the streets must have made it hard for him. Fire engines and all the other emergency vehicles going every which way. Not once did I think of all this, but now I know that I should have. Dad was a promise keeper and as promised he came looking for us. Leaving Aunt Adelheid alone to make sure his first family was still among the living. Praise God for such a dad as mine.

When he came visiting, we talked about my foster parents and my mix-in with the children's group. All of us agreed I was very lucky to have had such good foster parents. More so, Mom and Dad were in agreement that it was good they found me before all the children left. If they hadn't, I would have been on the way with them to an unknown destination. They told me since they spoke a different language and had a guard with them, it was their belief the sisters turned them back over to a guard. They told me they may be on their way to a work camp or some other camp. (Now, after WWII, we knew this could be not just a work camp. Maybe, it was a concentration camp.)

Mom and Dad said that I was the lucky one, to have come home to them. The friends I had for such a little while, they believed didn't have a mom and dad waiting for them at the end of their journey like I did. I thought I will keep these fun kids in my prayers. My prayer list had become so long, that many nights I and Mr. Brown Bear prayed us both to sleep. I talked with Mom about this and she said not to worry, the Father in Heaven understood everything.

Mom wrote letters back and forth to Mr. and Mrs. Halbleib. I believe they wrote to Mom to get both of us out of Berlin. To find another place of refuge from the forever falling bombs. They must have written at the moment there was nothing open for rent in Obornik, or we would have moved us close to them. However, they knew of a place that was still taking refugees from the big cities and making room for them. This place was Rietschutz, not too far from Warsaw.

They wanted for us to find out about it and give it a try. This happened to be correct and it was odd, or a God given to us, that one of Mom's sisters with her two sons, Horst and Rolfi, was already living there. She helped in finding us a room. Mom looked for renters to take over our apartment and rented it out furnished. We could not pay for two places, here and there. She found two nice ladies that wanted to take over our place right away and they made friends with the renter that was already there.

Mom started packing and this time, we had more to take, not just one small box. Before we left Berlin, my brothers made it home on furlough. We had a bit of family togetherness. In times like this, it was needed. Fun and laughter were shared, as we all lived each day "one day at a time". When my brothers left and went back to the front lines, having to live in their own kind of hell we hugged them goodbye. Then we too said goodbye to Dad, leaving him behind in the danger zone.

Mom and I got on the train that was taking us to Schwiebus. My tears flowed, waving goodbye to my Dad. He looked so small and not tall at all looking down at him from the train window. He smiled and waved at us walking next to the train as it left the station. A three to four-hour train ride brought us to Schwiebus. This was the city not far away from Rietschutz. Aunt Lene and the boys stood at the station saying hello. I now had two cousins to keep me company. Horst was one year younger than I and his brother Rolfi was about three years old. He was a cute little boy with blue eyes and very curly blond hair. Aunt Lene loved both of them so very much. She always said, "they are all I have from Uncle Werner to remind me of him." Her husband was among the many killed in this war. She seemed to be happy that we came to be with her. She needed someone to talk and share things with. My mom was her older sister and the two got along well. Looking at my Aunt I thought she was pretty. But I thought she was not as pretty as my mom. No one was as pretty as my mom.

Coming into the little village of Rietschutz our new home was one room under the roof of a guest house. It was comfortable and we would like living there. The landlady's name was Mrs. Magen and she took a liking to us and we to her, the minute we met. She told Mom if she ever got bored staying upstairs, to come down and lend her a hand in the restaurant she was running for this farm community. Mom agreed to do this and I was assured to get all the free lemonade after school I wanted. What a sweet deal this was for me. I smiled big knowing I could have this treat anytime I asked for it. Maybe my cousins Horst and Rolfi could have some too, if we asked for it. Mom looked at me smiling as if she knew what I was thinking. She was good at it, she could always read my mind just by looking at my face. She told me when I wondered about it all moms could do what she did. Moms knew their children very well.

Rietschutz did not have a school. We children had to get up early to get to the next village and go to class there. The teacher taught all eight grades and I had a good time being with so many kids of all ages. Instructions were given to us, on what to do on the way home should we hear or see planes in the sky. It was for us to hide under trees, shrubs or lay down on the ground in the middle of a wheat field. Many times, we had to look for cover and we always found it. If it was in a field, we picked flowers to take home for our mothers after the planes were gone. By as many flowers we brought home, it told how often we had to hide away. It was a daily happening for us to hide in the field. Mom run out of vases to keep all the flowers I brought home. It was scary and we all knew that the day would come when we had to stay home from school.

The war was coming our way from the direction of Warsaw. Mom said it would wind up being in our front yard and she was right. The day came when the doors of the school had to be closed. Horst and I didn't mind. We got to play together more often. It was clear to us that our moms, friends and neighbors had much to be concerned about.

When the first troops came, they came to open a Russian war prisoners camp on the outskirts of Rietschutz. It was not under the black-out law like us villagers. The camp was lit up like a Christmas tree. And planes – enemy planes – would not drop bombs down on their own. All of this was explained to us in one of the many meetings held by the Mayor. Children were not allowed at these meetings. But mom always told me what was going on. The meetings were held down stairs at Mrs. Magen's restaurant. Their loud voices carried all the way to the upstairs. And if I sat in the stairwell, I heard every word they spoke loud and clear. It was not very comfortable sitting on the steps listening. So, I stopped trying to eavesdrop. I waited for Mom to come and tell me all about it. When she liked something that was said, or when she didn't.

When the prison camp was set up, we all went out and stood looking at the barbed wire fencing stretching all around it. We saw the Russian soldiers standing behind the fence. Most of them smiled and waved at us kids. To be friendly, we always waved back. They were talented people and made straw purses and baskets. They made all sorts of pretty things. Then every morning they went through the same ritual standing by the fence, hoping someone would want what they had made that night. Hoping to get food for their pretty work. They worked for the farmers and must have gotten the straw to make things from them. They threw the finished item over the barbwire, showing with their hands they wanted food for their fancy work. When I stood there, I got such a pretty purse for Mom and she sent me back with a loaf of dark bread for the Russian that made it. But when I came back with the loaf in my hands, he was

not at the fence anymore. I gave it to a German soldier that
came out to me. Telling him he should give it to the nice
young man that gave me the purse for mom. I didn't realize
that with hundreds of prisoners there, the German soldier
didn't know which one to give it to.

We still slept through the night but the radio told us
about the war getting closer and closer. There was not any
getting away from it. We knew what was going to happen
but the animals did not. Every morning the rooster crowed
happily, sitting on top of the fence post, waking us up.
Walking around the village, the geese and duck families
waddled to the slow flowing water of the small creek going
through the middle of Rietschutz. They had not any idea
that things were going to change around them. And this
was happening at a fast pace.

Troops were coming and cutting down trees and
shrubs. Trenches destroyed the pretty fields and the farmers
harvest. But before all this happened, we had sad news
from Dad. We lost the apartment we had in Berlin. We lost
friends, neighbors in a day air raid. My dad wrote the
whole street was destroyed – it became a no-man's land.
Berlin was hit and hit hard by day and by night.

Mom and I had lost our home. Mom cried as she
worked hard for what little we had. But things can be
bought. Lost lives cannot be replaced, this is what both of
us mourned. The people we had lost and would never see
again. She bowed her head when she said, 'May God help
us.'

Mom went to help Mrs. Magen in the restaurant.
She wiped tables, floors and washed the glassware. I
watched and drank a glass or two of lemonade while she
worked. We wrote letters to Edgar, Erwin and Dad and we

were happy when we heard from them. From Edgar, we heard less and less and I saw Mom worry more and more.

The radio news was a lot of propaganda about how Germany was still winning victories over the enemy. We all knew all of this was not true. From one day to the next we knew what we heard and read was nothing but lies. The Mayor of Rietschutz called one meeting after the other. Mom and Aunt Lene came back from them, shaking their heads and other times their fists.

Then one morning, Mom and I heard steps on the stairs and when we opened the door, there stood my brother Erwin. Arms in slings, under the pants he had wrappings around his legs. He was smiling, and so glad to see us. A wounded soldier had come home. Home to get some loving, tender care a field hospital couldn't give him. But his mom would and could.

We had a doctor in this farm community, he would be our helper. Between Mom, Aunt Lene and him, Erwin would recover from the many wounds in his arms and legs. He told us the field hospitals were full, that is why they let him come to us. And with the war zone coming closer and closer, we were in easy reach.

Everyone that met my brother liked him. The young man in the SS uniform stole the hearts of many. Most of all, the hearts of the young girls. The farmers stopped by, bringing eggs, vegetables and fruit to eat. This was not done till Erwin showed up. We were grateful as it helped Erwin and us. Fresh milk I picked up every day at an appointed time, after the milking was done. Mom said we were being spoiled and getting used to all the spoiling that has come our way.

Since my brother was a wounded warrior and could use some spoiling, we gave our bed to him. Mom and I slept on a pile of thick blankets on the floor. Besides being wounded, Erwin suffered from shell shock. I called it bad, bad nightmares. His body made the bed shake when he had a nightmare like this. Mom woke him up saying "Son, you are at home. Nothing bad is going to happen." He never told us about his nightmares but we knew, he had the hand to hand combat fights. This was his nightmare, the nightmare he didn't want to share with anyone.

Every day, Erwin made it his mission to stand in the path of the Russian war prisoners, coming under guard down the main street from the farmers' fields. In his wounded arms he held paper bags with fruit, bread, tomatoes, and whatever else he could put in. I needed to help him as when he was done giving this away, his arms and legs hurt.

The first few times he did this, he tore the bags open and let it all roll out onto the cobblestone street. But it almost caused a stampede as all the prisoners pushed and shoved to get some of it. It was frustrating for the guards. Since my brother's SS uniform outranked them, Erwin said smiling, they had to put up with him. And the guards didn't report him to the Camp Commander. It was clear to us, they also had a good heart and showed it by keeping order with the war prisoners. But every single day for as long as Erwin was with us, they let my big brother be the prisoners' helper.

Coming back to the room, Erwin said to Mom that he believed soon the shoe would be on the other foot. He knew and had accepted that he and Edgar and all the others fighting this war would soon become war prisoners. The war was lost and they would have to face up to it and get ready to pay the price. It was hard for us to hear that if my brothers made it through the war, they would have to be prisoners. And for how long would they have to face prison time. And who would take them prisoner. It could be the Russians or maybe it was done by the Americans? Erwin said he would try to find the American lines if he could. He wanted to have nothing to do with the Russians if he could help it

I sat and heard my brother give instructions to our mom, what she needed to do when the end came. Then after he was done, Mom said, "Erwin, please do not go back to your Company. Stay with us and wait for the war to end." If the end is as close as you say it is, why can't you stay here with us? To this he shook his head no and said that someone would come and find him and it would cost him his life. He would be shot as a deserter. No, he said he is not running or hiding away from his duties. What he continued to say to Mom and me was sad to hear and very scary.

The time came and he had to leave. It was at night when we took him to the train depot in Schwiebus. The train was going in the direction of Warsaw. He said goodbye and told Mom not to worry. He would do his best to stay alive and one day come home to us. He said "when you write or see Dad, tell him that I love him." He gave Mom the bush knife he had on the inside shaft of his boot and said, "I do not think I will have to use it anymore. You keep it for me till I come back." When the train rolled into the station and stopped, he slowly climbed up the steps and found a window seat. The train pulled out with Mom and I running next to it. We wanted to see him for as long as possible and remember him in this way. He smiled seeing us run next to the train but it was a sad smile, Then, we had to stop running, the train was gone and with it went my brother Erwin

Somehow, we made it back to Rietschutz, but I don't remember how. We took over the bed that Erwin occupied for a while, wishing he was still sleeping in it. We didn't mind at all sleeping on the floor while he was with us. Now we wondered where he was. Did he get to his company? Was he fighting? Was he able to sleep? We were sure if he was able to sleep, it was not in a bed like he had with us. It was more likely sitting in a trench or laying on the cold ground to catch a wink here and there. In this he was not alone, many with him lived the same nightmare.

From Dad, we received mail. From Edgar, we heard nothing at all. It was getting cold, as winter was coming. Looking out the window before it got dark, we saw pretty sunsets. In the dark of night, when the sky showed a gloomy red, it told us a different story. We knew fighting was taking place in the distance. Sometimes we could hear a rumbling like thunder. These rumblings and lightning streaks in the sky were not made by nature. They were man-made. Awful to see and knowing many were killed by all of this.

Mom and I went to see Aunt Lene and her boys every afternoon. When we got there, she told us the news that soldiers were combing the nearby woods, looking for a deserter. We all hoped that he would not be found. I knew if Mom and Aunt Lene saw him, somehow, they would try to hide him. Mom said, "with this war about over, why would anyone want to kill this young man. He was like most of the German troops, only a scared, hurt by the war, young man." Maybe like my brother Erwin, he could suffer from shellshock. We never heard if the patrol found him, but it was our prayer that he got away. Far, far away.

Chapter Seventeen

Every day, sometimes in the morning other times in the afternoon, Mom and I dressed warm and made the short walk over to visit Aunt Lene. My cousins and I liked playing with the neighbor's dog. The dog was friendly but was trained to be a watchdog. He knew us kids and it was fun to go and play with him like we did. I think he was waiting for us to come to play with him. He was a St. Bernard, had a large head and strong body. The farmer promised if there was a heavy snowfall this winter that Brutus (this was his name) would pull our sleds.

For the weekend, if there were a couple of extra eggs that the farmers gave us Mom and her sister did some baking. A yeast cake in the shape of a loaf of bread was baked and tasted yummy on Sunday.

Every night we looked out of our window to see if the redness of the sky moved any closer to us. So far, it has not. And it also meant that our soldiers were not giving one inch of ground to the so-called enemy. We living in Rietschutz wished for a white flag to wave and call this war over and done with. We watched and watched the sky every night. Then we saw that the red glow at night stretched closer and closer. A sure sign that our troops lost ground and the noises we heard in the distance became louder and more plain for the ear to hear.

We had refugees going by or turning in to stay a while in Rietschutz. They came in wagons pulled by oxen teams and horses. The highway leading by the village and going on to Schwiebus looked like it was on the move. It was on the move, with people from villages and towns in the war zones. Old and young were moving inland, toward the capital city of Germany, my birthplace and hometown of Berlin.

Soon, we too would go back, but since Mom and I had lost our home, Aunt Lene offered to share her apartment with us. She laughed a little when she said, "if hers was still standing by the time we returned. A lot could happen, when a town and its people are under fire day and night." She was right in thinking she wouldn't be informed by anyone if her apartment house was still standing or not. Her in-laws died and her sisters and one brother had to watch over their own. In these times no one had the time or the energy anymore to be their brother's or sister's keeper. We would have to wait and see, when we reached Berlin, if with Aunt Lene we still had a roof over our heads. Mom always said to me to keep my hands folded and pray about it. And of course, this is what I did.

In the meantime, the village of Rietschutz tried to help all the refugees that filled the village square with their wagons. Farmers opened up their houses. In our house, the restaurant offered shelter and warmth. I walked from wagon to wagon and saw the elderly wrapped up in blankets. Each face I saw told a story. Each set of eyes showed a sadness. They left homes behind them that had been in their families for many generations.

The parents, grandparents in their wagons were sick and dying. They had to leave them in cemeteries along the way or bury them along the side of the road. They would mark the grave with something that belonged to this person. When the war ended, they hoped to go back and maybe, just maybe, bring home what belonged to them.

My mom said to me that the fear they had was etched in their face. Their faces looked lined and weather beaten. Their eyes had lost their shine. Their brows were furrowed and their mouth forgot what it was like to smile. When we looked at them, we hurt for them. Truth is, when they looked at us, they knew we would be next. All of it was only a matter of time. We, too, would be among the many fleeing from the war.

They did not stay long. The next day they moved down the highway to the small town of Schwiebus. If they moved on by train, they needed to sell wagons, horses and oxen teams. Or leave them with the farmers on the outskirts of Schwiebus. Not giving up all hope. they wanted to return one day and pick up what was theirs.

For a day or more, all in Rietschutz relaxed. Then the highway again showed movement. Red Cross cars, other cars, tanks, guns of all kinds came to take up the space the refugees had left open. Our soldiers, tired from fighting but having to go on, all of them marched into the village.

The officers found a place with the farmers. Our foot soldiers pitched tents next to the war prisoner camp. It was close to the Christmas holidays and it was to be Peace and Good will toward all men. But this is not found in times of war.

Mom looked at me when she said, "Dagie, the war has moved into our front and back yard. Let's hope it will end soon. All of us are tired and can't take much more of it." Tomorrow she will go and ask among the troops about Erwin. We both knew that if he had been among these soldiers, he would have already found us. Because he didn't come to us, we thought my brother was among the many missing. When she went to ask questions, she would also search and ask about Edgar. For a long time, we didn't have a letter from him. All this was a heartache for Mom and for me.

The last meaningful news we had from him came out of Finland, but the SS was always on the move. Erwin said the SS was sent to the most troubled areas. Edgar could be in Poland or fighting in France. This would be alright with us, because it meant he was still alive. With this positive thought, we looked forward to Christmas. Most of the time, we didn't put a Christmas tree up anymore. Our room was too small for a tree. Just branches in a vase, some tinsel and bulbs were our holiday decoration. A letter or card under this from Edgar would be a wonderful gift for Mom and me. News from someone having seen my brother Erwin would complete us having a good Christmas.

When Mom had conversations with our land-lady, she told us everyone in Rietschutz was baking cakes to bring to the tent town next to the war prison camp. Our troops are to celebrate this holiday. We all had the same thought, that it may be the last one they get to celebrate like this. The farmer that had a big house on the hill was giving free of charge milk and eggs for the baking to everyone. On a nice but cold day, Mom sent me with the milk can in hand up the hill to get some. If I was lucky, I would also get some eggs. I went up the hill with Mom's reminder not to ask for eggs. If they had any to give away, they would, like they have done before, give me a few. All I had to say was "Thank you" and bring them home.

The farm hands brought the milk into the kitchen straight from the barn. There was a line of people in front of me, so it took a while for me to get back to Mom. She always waited for me and was looking out the window till she saw me coming. With the milk container filled to the top, I came down the hill, waving with my free hand to Mom. Since I could wave, she saw that I didn't get any eggs for the baking. She had to find another way to manage to make a cake. But we had others as neighbors, the family living on the hill where not the only ones. Someone will give her the eggs she needed to put together a Christmas cake for the troops. I believed that my mom would find a way to participate in being a giver in these troubled times.

Now I was down the hill walking on the straight path with home in sight, I heard an unusual sound behind me in the sky. It was a fast-moving plane lowering itself down in a hurry. Then I saw and heard the bullets hit the ground behind and in front of me. I knew this was the plane of the enemy and I had become its target. It was only seconds or minutes that I was in such danger. All I thought about was not to spill any of the milk. I saw that my mother's face was not looking out from the window any more. The plane, as fast as it had come, it was gone.

I now moved fast. I was either running or very fast walking. Careful not to spill any of the precious milk we needed for baking. I made it to the front door, up the stairs and opened the door to our small room. Mom was kneeling on the floor below the windowsill, she had her face covered with both hands. She peeked through her fingers at me when she heard me say, "Look, I didn't spill a drop." I walked over to her and she kind of wrapped her arms around my middle and gave me a welcome home squeeze. Then she got up from the floor, took the milk from me, for the baking of the cakes. For a long time we didn't speak, but I noticed she glanced over to me now and then. I wondered what she was thinking about when she looked at me like she did. Oh, how I loved my mom.

Later, she and Mrs. Magen went outside to look at the path. The bullets had torn up the road but there was a spot undisturbed, it was my safe spot. I was standing or walking in this safe spot and the bullets didn't touch me. I must have had God's hand on my shoulder or he sent an angel to protect me. If he hadn't done this, I would not be here today.

It was a combined effort from Mrs. Magen, Mom and Aunt Lene baking cakes for the soldiers. The best part of it was when cousin Horst, little Rolfi and I got to lick the bowls and the spoons. The baker did not ask for money for the baking, it was done without charge. Did the war prisoners get to celebrate this holiday? This is something we didn't know. We must have been so concerned with our own troops, we forgot it was their Christmas as much as ours. A sad thought it is that there was the smell of baked cake in the air. Some got to eat and others did not. Some got to celebrate Christmas and others did not. As Mom would always say, tummies talked with each other when they were empty. They growled and growled till they were filled. When Mom's and my tummy spoke to each other the next day it got a slice of bread to eat and it stopped growling for a while. We thought the Russian war prisoners were not as lucky in this. Their tummy just kept on grumbling. Their hands kept on making purses and baskets out of straw. And they stood by the fence in cold weather throwing their work over the barbed wire begging to give them food for it. Mom and I were very much aware how sad it was for them. Sad for them and sad for us.

In the meantime, we children learned a few poems. Mrs. Magen had us recite them for the soldiers in the restaurant. It made them happy. When we finished, they clapped their hands and told us we did well. We all tried to be cheerful but this is hard in times of war. Then our house had electricity problems. The house was dark, the electric lines needed fixing. A prisoner under guard came to take care of it. He stood on a ladder outside the house by our window. I opened the widow and he smiled at me. I smiled back at him, he was not my enemy and I was not his. I was a little girl to him and to me he was a friendly young man that helped us fix the trouble we had. Later I told mom I liked him. She did too. She invited him and the guard into our room and fed both of them before they went back to the prison camp.

Mom sat and cried a little bit after they left us. She said the young Russian so much in his looks reminded her of Erwin. She wondered about Erwin and how he would celebrate Christmas. Was he still free, alive or not? Or had he been taken prisoner by now? Everything was possible. Food was something we did not have enough of but I understood why Mom felt compelled to feed the guard and this look-a-like of my brother.

Every day Mom went to help in the restaurant for a couple of hours and while she was gone, I read a lot. Mom wanted for me to keep up my reading skills. Since we did not go to school any longer, Mom gave me school work to do. Aunt Lene did the same with my cousin, Horst. When Mom came upstairs, I saw she was upset. She said there was a sign in the village square forbidding us to leave. We had to ask permission from the mayor if we wanted to get out.

She said this man did not have the right to make us stay when it was time for us to leave and to go back to where we came from. For us, this was to go back to Berlin. We saw him days before taking his family out of Rietschutz, to what he thought was a safer place for them. Mom said sure, he did come back after he took his own out of here but at the moment, this meant nothing to her. We had not any idea that only an hour later, we would leave, too. Mom went back down after she calmed down some. After all, upset or not Mrs. Magen could still use her help.

When she came upstairs again from doing what she was doing, she said, "Dagie, grab your coat. We are getting Aunt Lene and the boys. We are going to Berlin." I couldn't believe it but it was true. Mom took a suitcase and placed some clothing and paperwork inside, closed it and we were ready to go. Outside stood a Red Cross car with the driver waiting for us. Mrs. Magen followed us and, with tears, said goodbye. She and Mom had become such good friends in all our time there.

It was a late hour when we stopped at Aunt Lene's place and she hurried to pack a suitcase. We didn't give her much time to think about it. Out she came with my cousins and the nice soldier made room in the car for them. This man was from Berlin. Sitting in the restaurant, he recognized Mom spoke with a Berlin accent. They started a conversation between them and it was his advice we needed to leave now. He would take the responsibility for all of us. He told Mom to ignore the sign in the square. It was high time for us to get out of Rietschutz. We drove past the sign and by the light of the moon, without the headlights turned on, he drove down the highway. Schwiebus had a railroad. The only request he had for doing us this favor was to go to see his family. Mom promised she would do this. He wanted for them to know he was alive. He said to tell them how much he loved them. He wanted for them to know he thought of them all of the time. Over and over he said, "Please, tell them how much I love them."

We said "Thank you" and he got in the car and drove away, leaving us with the memory of the help he gave us. What would happen to him? What would happen to all the people we left behind? Mom said the writing was on the wall. Our guys would become prisoners and be guarded by the Russians that had been their prisoners all this time. The one-time prisoners would be free men and be thinking about going home to their families. The rest of us had hard times to face. Hard times the aftermath of war would bring to Germany.

We walked to the train station waiting room and we blended in with all the other refugees. Mom went to buy tickets for the train going to Berlin. Aunt Lene stayed with us and Horst and I sat on the suitcases. Every space in this room was taken. People standing and sitting along the wall. Sitting on boxes or suitcases like we did. Some had been there more than just a few hours. They had been waiting for days. Their faces looked tired. Some of the older women cried. Everyone sitting in this waiting room had reason to shed tears. They lost homes, loved ones in this war. What we all had in common was the loss of hope. We didn't dare to hope but we wanted to get it back. Get it back to bring again peace and order to the life we lived. We yearned for it and we prayed for it to happen. I never heard my Mom pray out loud. But my heart told me Mom and Aunt Lene prayed in their grown-up way to him. And I prayed in my children's way to be heard by him. Did my cousin Horst pray? I was not sure about this, because I never asked him if he did.

Soldiers sat there with such lost looks in their eyes. Some with bandages on their arms or around the head. Seeing this made us hurt for them. What could we do for them? There was nothing we could do to help them. We looked at them and wished that they still had a family waiting for them. That they still had a family to go home to be with. Now we were in this group, running away from danger. Only we all knew that the danger would follow us. With the end of World War II in sight, it would catch us. We waited for Mom's return with the tickets. The train on track one went part way, stopping in Zuelschau as its end destination. On track two, the train left an hour later but its end destination was Berlin. This was the train we wanted. Everyone in the waiting area was waiting on this train and it would be full to the overflowing.

When Mom returned, she had bought five tickets taking us to Zuelschau. Aunt Lene couldn't believe Mom had done this and she told her to return them and buy the other for us but Mom refused. She said she had her own reasons for doing what she did. Aunt Lene could do it her way but Mom and I would be on the train standing on track one. Fussing at Mom, Aunt Lene and the boys followed us to the departure gate one. The soldier standing guard hardly gave us a glance we walked past him but my mom looked at him. Before climbing up the steps to the train compartment, she again looked back at him.

Chapter Eighteen

The train looked dark and cold and it was. It had missing doors, broken or no windows at all. It looked like the train had been under attack but this was the train to take us closer to home. People were already on the train but the majority were waiting to get on the train to Berlin.

It looked like the people in our compartment had prepared for the cold weather. They had warm blankets and gave us one for cousin Rolfi. The little guy was cold and very tired. Leaving Rietschutz in such a hurry, we didn't have time to be prepared. But here we sat with people that showed compassion and they shared what they had with us, that had nothing.

The train pulled out of the station and now Aunt Lene wanted to know why Mom bought the tickets going only part way. Mom said the soldier guarding the gate told her to take this train. She said he overheard her asking for tickets to Berlin for five people. He just said, "If you have children, take this train and do not wait on the other." Mom said to her sister, "You might think that I am crazy but while he gave me the advice, he reminded me in looks and voice of my son Erwin. I took it as a sign, as the God voice talking to me. I had to listen and do what I needed to do. So, here we are, on the way to Zuelschau. When we get there, we wait on the other train and we pay the balance we owe for the tickets to get us to Berlin."

Mom said she was convinced we did right by taking this train. She was convinced she did right to listened to the inner voice. The voice she called the God voice speaking with her. The soldier standing at the gate made up her mind, that she needed to take his advice. Aunt Lene shook her head but it was too late for her to change her mind and go back to Schwiebus. Maybe she could have without any trouble at all. Our train was moving down the track at a snail's pace and all with us started to wonder why. Mom went to the non-existing doors to see what the hold-up was. She said people worked on the tracks. She saw them with lamps and maybe flashlights being very busy.

Now and then we made stops and let other passengers get on or off. Not many left, most of them got on the train. We had wounded soldiers with us. A woman having a Red Cross kit started to help them. One of them had a bad head wound. We thought he needed to be in a hospital and not be sitting with us on the train. To see him this hurt, it broke our hearts in pieces. These fighting men had a look in their eyes that made us want to cry. They had seen and had much to do in this war. They lost the will to go on. The look in their eyes said they felt all alone, what hope they had was totally gone. They looked like if they were on the road of no return. And if they returned it was called a miracle took place.

We felt looking at them, we needed to hug them back to life. To us they looked like the walking dead. Mom and Aunt Lene did this. They helped change bandages, thanks to the woman that had the Red Cross kit. And they gave out hugs to the wounded warriors on this train. I watched all of this and gave my hugs to cousin Rolfi. He started to cry wanting his Mommy to hold him he needed to be cuddled.

All of the sudden the train that moved slow was picking up speed. What trouble we had must have been taken care of. It was full speed ahead and the train was now making up for lost time. It was odd that the train to Berlin following one hour behind had not caught up to us. We moved so slow, with only now giving it more speed. Riding at night with no air raid siren sounding was a blessing. All on this train sat in the same boat, so to speak, feeling uncertain about the future.

When the train made it to Zuelschau, we said goodbye to everyone, wishing them the best and they wished us the same. We said thanks for the warm blanket for Rolfi and the slices of bread for Horst and me. We were last to leave the compartment, but before we could, the train started tugging and pulling. We sat down in our seat. We thought a conductor would come to help us when the train stopped to rest for the night. Then we needed to let the conductor know we were still on the train. He then could help us to get back the small stretch of track to the Zuelschau station. There we could wait for the train to Berlin and continue our journey to get home. This is if we all still had a home. It meant the house needed to still be standing and not be burned to the ground to give us a much-needed home. So odd in the time of no hope, over, and over again we grabbed onto a thread of hope. This for us to do must be a God thing.

The big surprise was ours. The train did not rest in Zuelschau but went down the track to Berlin. Mom looked at her sister when she said the soldier at the gate in Schwiebus gave her good advice. He must have been a God-send to all on this train. Aunt Lene nodded yes, now she was glad she came with us instead of waiting, like she was inclined to do, for the train leaving one hour behind this one. Mom thought about this as we were riding toward Berlin. She said, with us moving so slow because of whatever was done on the tracks, the other should have caught up to us. But it didn't. What happened? It had the most people on it.

The ride from Schwiebus to Berlin was under normal circumstances a three or four-hour trip at the most. With all the trouble on the track between Schwiebus to Zuelschau, and then to Berlin, it took the train all night till noon to get there. This train was not expected by anyone. The ticket booth was empty, with no one there to check or take the tickets from us. The odd part of it all was the fact only we five got off the train. Everyone else got off in Zuelschau thinking like we did at first, the train wouldn't go any further. Odd it was that nobody stood at the station in Berlin to get on the train. With no one in sight we couldn't pay the extra money we owed. We had only paid to get to Zuelschau and we owed to the railroad the money from there to Berlin. I heard my mom say to her sister Lene, "tomorrow I will go to make things right." Now Lene, let's go and see if the house is still standing or not. If it is, we need to find a store to buy some food. The cupboards at your apartment must be bare.

Leaving the station, we hoped Aunt Lene didn't lose her home. We walked through the streets with nothing but ruins of what used to be houses around us. Then we saw it, among all the devastation, her house was still there. We had a roof over our heads, if it wasn't taken from us with the next air raid.

Climbing up a flight of stairs, Aunt Lene opened the door to the apartment. Inside her place all was alright and we could relax. Putting the suitcases in the living room till they had time to unpack them, they went out again and left us alone. I was given instruction what to do in case the siren went off and we were under attack. The air raid shelter was in the house right in front of ours. We needed to get across a small courtyard to reach the shelter. If the siren sounded it meant for us to hurry. This could be hard for us with a toddler like my cousin Rolfi. I thought about it and my mind was made up to carry him with the help of his big brother Horst. Since I was put in charge over us kids while Mom and her sister looked for a grocery store, I told Horst what I expected of him in case of an emergency. He understood that both of us had to handle little Rolfi. While waiting for our mothers to return we looked through the kitchen cabinets. Not even a crumb of bread was laying there. We had nothing at all in the apartment. What we had was dust to clean off the furniture, because it stood empty for such a long time. Horst and I kept our fingers crossed that our Moms would find a store with a friendly storekeeper. That he would take the ration card stamps we had and sell us food to eat. And they did find a store and someone behind the counter that had compassion for us. They came home with something to fill the tummy.

Time to go to bed we shook the dust off the feather beds and pillows. Aunt Lene had a balcony and we stood out there and shook till we thought it was clean enough to sleep under. Mom and I shared a double bed. Aunt Lene and Rolfi had the other bed. Both beds stood together and they took up the middle of the room. The beds were large enough that Horst could have slept there too. But he was a bigger boy and needed to have a sleeping space of his own. Horst slept on the sofa in the living room. Lene said we would meet the neighbors when the siren sounded. And we did meet all of them on the first night home. They told Mom and Lene it was mandatory to sign us kids up to go to school. However, it was not possible to go to class, because of the constant air raids. The neighbors said, they spend most of their time sitting in the shelter as one air raid was followed by another. Our mothers listened and said, even though it was mandatory that they wouldn't even try to sign us up for school. We kids did without learning for a while in Rietschutz and we would do this till the war was over. Besides, we only needed to let our family know that we were here. To do this was important to us. All of them would be glad to have us back. My dad most of all.

Chapter Nineteen

Mom had her heart set to keep the promise she gave to the soldier that drove us to Schwiebus in the Red Cross car. The first day home, Mom and I went looking for his family. Rolfi was not feeling well so Mom and I went there without them. The soldier's family lived in the neighborhood that used to be ours. The neighborhood around the Andreas Paltz, all the houses around their house were either leveled or burned out buildings. After seeing this soldier's family, Mom wanted to go and see where we used to live. In all the rubble would we even recognize where our house used to be? We would have to go and find out. It was easy to find the house this family lived in. We climbed up the stairs and rang the doorbell.

A tiny lady opened the door and there were children playing in another room. We told her we brought greetings from her husband. With tears in her eyes, she let us in. She had her mother living with her. All of them wanted to know how the husband, father or son was doing. What did he look like and how was he feeling? They were so eager to hear all about him. But Mom could only tell them bits and pieces because she didn't have time to get to know him well. She told his wife and mother what she could about him. What she knew of him was that he helped us to get back to Berlin. He had a kind heart and Mom said we truly hoped, he would at the end of the war come home to them. We hoped this for many of our fighting men including my brothers.

While Mom was telling them over and over how he helped us to get out of Rietschutz, all this time I played with the children. There was not much Mom could say, except to tell them of his love for them. This was what he wanted for them to know and to remember of him. To remember it, just in case he would not make it home. He also wanted for them to know he would try his best to stay alive and make it back home, whenever this may be. All our soldiers knew they would face war prison time when all this ended. No one could promise their families when they would see them again. Only God knew what the future held for them. When we left, we left a grateful family. We felt good having made this visit. We kept the promise to a young man we left in harm's way in the small village of Rietschutz.

Before we made it back to Aunt Lene, since we were in the neighborhood, we stood in front of the rubble and ashes that used to be the apartment house we lived in. Erwin had seen it when he came on furlow before he found out Rietschutz was our home. He thought we were under all the rubble and ashes. Dad told him we visited Berlin, but Mom's warning God voice took us out of Berlin just in time. Back we went to Rietschutz before the bombs fell and burned down the house.

How glad my brother must have been to know he did not stand in front of our grave. We were alive, living in Rietschutz when the air mines took out house after house, all in one day. My school was also not there anymore. I stood and thought of the class I was a part of and the blond teacher I had that was taken away from us. She was someone that I couldn't forget. Looking down the street we remembered the places that used to be there and all of it was gone. The Resi movie house were my brothers earned money by ushering people to their seats. The Rose Theater, Dad took me there to see my first stage performance of Hansel and Gretel. The Ratske Club or Restaurant my brothers favorite place to meet with friends. All of it was gone. Nothing but rubble and ashes was left for us to look at. Mom took my hand and said let's go, this has been a long day. We turned to find the trolley station and taking trolley 77 we rode home. Home was now in Berlin Charlottenburg with Aunt Lene and the boys

When we made it back, Rolfi was feeling much better but Mom and I were tired. I do not remember if we went to the shelter that night but I believe we must have. There was also a time in the middle of the night after the raid was over, when we had to leave and go to a designated area because an air mine didn't explode. The mine crew, as we called them, came to do something about this. When it was done, we were told all was clear and we could return home.

In all this mess, we kids played while our moms had all the concerns and heartache a war brings. Mom and Aunt Lene talked about having to get in touch with relatives and for us, this was Dad before all others. Then grandparents, aunts, uncles and cousins. It would be devastating if we learned the family headcount had gotten smaller. Up till now, we were doing alright. With the falling bombs, however, this could change from one day to the other. Again, when the siren sounded, we got out of the shelter and one more time we made it through the night.

Mom wanted for me to stay with Aunt Lene and the boys when she went to pay for the rest of the fare from Zuelschau to Berlin. I did not like it that I had to stay. So, the time she was gone, I watched the kitchen clock, waiting for her return. When I heard the key Aunt Lene gave her open the front door, I was happy. She made it back and was safe and sound at home with us. She came to the kitchen table and laid all the money she had on top of it. Not one Mark or one pfennig was missing.

She told us to sit down, she had a story to tell us. We did and she told us the man at the ticket sale counter wouldn't take the money. She explained to him why we owed this and he told her to take the money, go home and count her blessings. The train standing on track two in Schwiebus never made it to Berlin. It had the most passengers. It never got to destination Berlin. He did not tell her what happened. All he said was for her to go home and to count her blessings. To be grateful that there was an angel standing guard in Schwiebus at gate one. This angel wore a helmet, had a swastika armband, and a gun in his hand. If he had wings, they must have been hidden under the uniform he wore. But this angel, with what he told Mom to do, saved our lives. The train leaving from track two never reached Berlin.

Mom said yes, this soldier reminded her of Erwin and it made her want to listen to what he said. She said God knew what he was doing when he stationed Erwin's look alike at gate number one.

She told this story to all the relatives and everyone agreed that we had been watched over by someone or something very special. Mom was also of the belief we should not ask why we were saved when so many others were lost. There was not an answer for this question. She said one day we would find out, but not while we were here on earth.

The days went by one on the other and one was always scarier than the other. To make it even more sad, Mom and Aunt Lene let old hurts and memories get to them. Soon it became clear to the two of them we needed to move away. We went to see Grandpa and Grandma Sauer, Mom's parents. Maybe they could help and, fortunate for us, they could. They had a key to Aunt Friedchen's house.

It was located in Berlin - Schlachtensee and stood empty for the moment. It was a small community of homes and people that worked for the railroad lived there.

Friedchen, another sister of Mom's, had moved her family away from the falling bombs and was still gone. Grandpa and Grandma thought she wouldn't mind if we lived there until she returned. These homes were small and had a garden around them. Uncle Heinz with help from Grandpa Sauer built this house. Uncle Heinz was killed in this war but Aunt Friedchen would return to the home from where she was as soon as she could. It was the home she shared with her husband and he built it for her with his own hands. It was built with much love for them and the three children they had. Hannelore, Mathias, (he was nick-named Matzel) and the youngest was Dieter. We knew should Aunt Friedchen with her children come back, we needed to search for a home for us all over again. But till this happened, this little house belonged to us. It was lent to us to live in for a while.

What little Mom and I had, we packed and, with suitcase in hand, we moved into the cottage in Berlin - Schlachtensee. It was evening when we arrived. It did not go unnoticed by the neighbor right next to us. Opening the garden gate, it squeaked and the neighbors must have heard it. They came over and introduced themselves to us. Their name was Mr. and Mrs. Leder. They had two daughters, Marianne and Hildegard. Right away they invited us, because of the air raids, to share their air raid shelter with them. We accepted their offer because we really had no place to go to. Mr. and Mrs. Leder smiled and said get settled and we will see you soon. We didn't have much to get settled with, our few clothes this was all we brought with us. We needed to use all of Aunt Friedchen's things while we lived in her house.

Checking the house, there were only two rooms we could use. The kitchen and the room next to it would serve as the bedroom. The last room was filled with junk. Old broken chairs and along the wall stood a torn-up mattress. Not any running water, electricity or indoor bathroom. We had a pump in the garden, the oil lamp for light and the outhouse for any other needs we had. Mom said we would be fine and live here till her sister and family returned.

We were grateful to have found a place that we could call home for a while. We were more grateful to Mr. and Mrs. Leder for giving us shelter from the falling bombs. The first night, while Mom hung our clothes up, Mr. Leder came with a wire cutter and made an opening in the fence. This way we had easy access to their dugout, leading from the outside to under their house. And when the Leders smiled and said we will see you soon, they knew it was only a matter of when the sirens went off announce we needed to run for shelter. Sure enough, we had to use it the first night there. Mom smiled when it was over and we went back to our place. She said nothing brings people closer than to sit and share dropping bombs and uncertain times together. The Leder family in this short time became our friends.

When the sirens sounded, stepping outside and looking up to the night sky, we saw something like Christmas trees above us. We had never seen this before. Mr. Leder explained it was a stakeout, where the bombs are dropped. Poor us, the pretty Christmas trees could be seen all around. This was to close for comfort. Mom hugged me, I hugged her, and with the Leder family, we sat together hoping and praying for the best. What I didn't use anymore was the blanket wrapped around me. All I wanted was for Mom to hold my hand. And she held it till the all clear siren sounded, then she felt she could let go of it.

The people living around us filled Mom in on all the news we had been missing in the time we lived in Rietschutz. The stories they told were not pretty. They were sad with sad endings. After what she heard, it was her opinion we cannot give up being hopeful. We have to live with the thought that, when the war is over, the Weiss family story will have a happy ending. With keeping this in mind, we made it from one day to the other. Taking it one day at a time and give it all to God was the motto we lived by.

Chapter Twenty

We had tall trees behind the little houses that could be danger spots for us. Anything or anyone could hide there. We found out about this when all men had to bear arms. Only women and children were left behind. Snipers took over the woods and one day, one of them took a shot at me. I was on a bench, sitting outside Mrs. Leder's house and held the only meal for the day in my hands. A bowl of soup that I spilled when the bullet went by my face. I dropped the bowl and jumped for the hole in the ground that was the door to the bomb shelter.

I called out for no one to leave the house, someone was shooting at me. Mom called out wanting to know if I was alright. I told her that I was fine. When they all joined me, they saw I was scared but also angry. I spilled my meal for the day on the ground and, unless someone shared, I went hungry. Mom felt sorry for me and she gave me some of her soup. It was a spoonful for her and one for me till the small bowl was empty.

We knew that the enemy was all around us and it was only a matter of time when they stood face to face with us. The women formed groups and stayed together. Mom had a hiding place and it was under the roof of our house. To get to it, we had to go around the back, over the roof of the outhouse and climb through a small door under the roof of the main house. There was a wood pile stacked up by the outhouse that made our climb up to the roof easy.

Mom hid, besides us five, four more people. Two women and two girls around my age. They lived behind us. We all thought there was safety in numbers. Once a day, everyone went to their own house to clean up or to get something we needed. We did this carefully and never stayed apart for too long.

It was morning when Mom and I sat by the kitchen window. We heard a rattling sound and saw a tank moving through the garden across from us. It took down the fence, part of the house, shrubs and trees. We thought it would come at us but it didn't. It turned on the dirt road and it made its way to the woods. When it made the turn, we saw it was not a German tank. It was Russian and had the hammer and sickle on the side of it.

Mom jumped into action. She went to the room with all the junk furniture and tore the mattress apart more. In it she hid Erwin's bush knife and photos he wanted her to keep for him. She knew if the Russians entered our house and found this, we as the family of an SS soldier would be in serious trouble. When Mom and I saw that the tank was gone, we ran to the neighbor's house, praying she was not in it when the tank hit it. We held our breath when Mom went inside to check it out. She made me wait outside and came out saying the house, thank God, was not occupied by the neighbor lady at the moment.

Well, it was not all empty, the parrot was at home and he was one angry bird. When the tank hit the house, he flew out of the bird cage and landed in the one tree the tank left standing. It was not far away from the house. Upset or angry was not the word for this talking bird. He was livid, this is the word to describe him and his actions. He was running up and down on the long tree branch, saying one bad, bad word on the other. My mom stood there wanting to put her hands over my ears so I would not hear all the ugly words this bird knew how to say.

Then Mom looked at me and I at her and we started to laugh. Here, the Russian tank had just rolled into the woods. We had faced a danger that was still lurking around us. But we were standing under a tree and laughing at a crazy, upset, angry bird. No matter how sweet we talked with him, he bad mouthed us and we couldn't talk him down from up there. We didn't stand a chance to sweet talk him to come down to us, he was one upset parrot.

We needed to run down the road and hope the owner was down there together with the other women and children. She needed to calm him down and get him out of the tree. Mom went to look for her while I stayed with Peter. This was the name of our cussing friend. Mom found his owner like she thought, living down the road with other neighbors. She came and cried when she saw what the tank had done to her home. But she believed, when the men came back to their families, it was fixable. The bird cage was smashed to pieces and Peter needed a new cage.

Standing together looking at the damage the Russian tank had done, we agreed a new cage was needed for our feathered friend and the badly damaged corner of the house needed fixing. We, too, needed a new place when Mom's sister Friedchen came back to what was hers, we then needed to find a home of our own. A place that no one could take away from us or throw us out from. This, for Mom and me, would be necessary.

With the tank moving through this area, we knew the war was over. The bombing raids were over. World War II was done and over with. We still needed to hide away in the hiding places. Gunfire was still heard, coming to our ears from far away and at night from close by. We saw only the Russian tank. Where were all the others? We hid away, we waited and we wondered about everything and anything!

Mom, Mrs. Leder and the other two ladies took turns in going out to look for food. We had emptied the cupboards. Now we were getting one slice of bread a day and this in the evening. We were starving. There was a weed growing along the side of the road. Mom picked it and it was cooked like spinach. Add a spoon of lard to the water, salt to season it and we had spinach soup. We ate it and pretended to like it. But to be honest it tasted terrible. But it was better than nothing and nothing we would have, if we didn't eat the awful tasting spinach soup.

The day hours were not so bad as we could see what or who stood in front of us. It was the night that spoke in many different voices and sounds. We still heard gunshots at night and the sound of these shots came from close by. One night someone entered our house and what he called sounded like Madka, Madka. We didn't know if Madka was a name of a person or something else. What we knew about him was he wanted to hurt. This man in our house was a bad man coming in to harm us. This we knew of him. Mom placed her hand over my mouth and the other moms did the same. The soldier went through our house and he kept calling for Madka. Later Mrs. Leder, my Mom and the other Moms talked about this word Madka and all had the same opinion this man was looking for a woman or more than just one woman. When we kids asked why, our Mom's told us he was looking for a girlfriend. They said he was up to no good trying to find a girlfriend for him in the middle of the night. Again, they said someone from higher up was protecting us. We were fortunate that this man, this soldier didn't find a girlfriend.

With seeing no one was there he then left and went next door to Mrs. Leder's home. He, thank God, didn't find us. But we learned a few days later, that when we heard gunshots, it was a signal from one Russian to the other on how many soldiers should visit the house down the road from us. Ten shots meant ten ladies lived there. The children saw what happened to their moms. And from what was told to Mom and Mrs. Leder, some of this happened to them. The girls were my and Hildegard and Marianne's age – eleven, twelve and a bit older.

It is very sad what a war and the time after has in store for people. It was living a nightmare. We that had a refuge in the attic under the roof of Aunt Friedchen's house did not go through this. We heard the shots fired in the dark of night and prayed for the ones living this nightmare. Mom and the other three moms placed their hands over our ears and held us close. Mom had more than one favorite saying and she often used them on me. She said let's close our eyes and hold them shut tight. When we open them, everything will be better and look better to us. I must say it did not look any better to me, open, shut or otherwise. It all looked bad to me. But then what did I know, I was only a ten going on eleven-year-old girl. I longed for a world that was pretty and safe to live in. Our world was torn up and unsafe, not fit for us to live in. But mom reminded me to be grateful for what we had. Our hiding place and the friends to share it with.

In the attic we would live for many days and it protected us from harm. We children did not leave this place. Mom and the other moms took turns in leaving and providing for our needs. Washcloth to keep us washed, potty that needed to be emptied in the outhouse every day. When we starved for a few days and our moms couldn't stand to see us children go through this, our moms stole from a neighbor to feed us.

The neighbor was one of the women down the road from us, living a nightmare every night. Her house was left empty and Mom knew this woman had stored food in the cellar of her house. Mom and Mrs. Leder broke in and took a part for us. They knew she would not share if they asked her. They made a promise never to tell what they had done. When this neighbor found out, she believed the Russians had raided her cellar. She was angry that the Russian soldiers came and stole her chickens. Behind her house she had a chicken coop and in the bright daylight light the Russians came and took all of her chickens. We saw them do it, looking down through small openings in the roof of the attic where we hid. It was Mrs. Leder that told her what we saw the Russians do. Now with Mom and Mrs. Leder doing the same, it was easy to put the blame on the Russians. Yes, they did steal her chickens but they were not guilty of the other. I think our moms felt ashamed about what they had done to a neighbor. Severe circumstances called for harsh actions. We wanted to survive all of us did. When we children said we were hungry, our mothers did for us what they had to do. After this we all kept quiet and I believe it was never mentioned again. Not between us girls and not between our mothers.

Chapter Twenty-One

One day rumor had it the Russians would come into every house. This is when we left the attic and went into the woods. No one found us and at night we returned to the hiding place. If patrolling soldiers by chance found us sitting in the woods, they would not have taken it easy on us. If soldiers combed the woods, they might have taken us for civilian trouble makers. Partisans like these civilians were called. Since it was only a short time after the war, such trouble makers could still be found and they were dealt with in a hard way. It didn't matter that we were women and children and had not a man with us. Just to hide away like we did, gave the impression we were up to no good. I hate to think of what could have happened if we had been caught. No one would have believed we hid away because we were afraid. Well someone bigger than us must have been watching over us on this particular day, because we got away with it. We were fortunate not to be seen by anyone when we left for the woods or when we came back from there. Sleeping in the attic every night, we all had the same thoughts. When was it alright to leave this place and start to live like normal people? When would the day come that we could leave this hiding spot for good?

Mom went to the outhouse one morning then got stopped by a neighbor. No not the one we stole from, it was another neighbor. She returned with wonderful news to share. And it was welcome news, that spread like wildfire once it got started. A Russian Officer would come and visit this small railroad community. With him, he was to bring law and order. This was something we had not had in a long, long time. The rumor of his coming gave us hope. This was also something we had not dared to have in a long, long time How often did we try to have hope and then in one awful happening it was snatched away from us. We living in the attic waited, everyone in this railroad village waited for the Russian Officer to come.

Then when we had almost given up on him, it happened. All nine of us heard noise coming to our ears from the street. The street was a sandy road leading by every little house down to the main road of this small community. There was something going on outside. We opened the attic door and climbed down from the wood shed and outhouse roof to the ground. Around us, women and children ran to the main road and we ran with them. As fast as the legs would carry us, we ran and ran.

Then we saw him. He was on horseback slowly riding down one road and then another. He turned and looked at the following he had. Only women and children followed him, the husbands that were taken from them had not returned yet. I think this officer riding the horse knew what he meant to us. He represented safety from more harm coming to women and children. We walked behind this man riding the horse and I thought he looked like a prince or maybe a king. He never stopped, but turned his head around many times to see how far we would follow behind him. We followed all the way down to the main street that went passed our village. There we stopped as he continued his ride. We cheered, some women clapped their hands together, this is when he turned around and waved at us. We talked and laughed when we went back to our homes. For the rest of the day, we dared to stay down stairs in our home. Mom and I talked about how nice it was to be out in the open and walk behind the horse and its rider. I was really excited about what happened.

We and our friends decided not to act foolish. We wanted to be careful a while longer and slept a couple more nights in the attic before we dared to climb down and stay in the house. After the officer on horseback made his visit, not any shots and other noises of the night were heard. I don't know who told us this, but he had a title, he was a Russian Commissar. The soldiers had to pay attention to him or they were in trouble. Where was he when all the cries echoed into the night? There was no answer for this. He was with us now and was our help, this was all that mattered to us. We started to sleep in our beds and it felt good not to have to lay on a hard floor like we had for many days and nights in the attic.

Once we returned to our homes, the missing men too returned to their families. Not all came back. Some died when they were forced to fight. When the waiting wives realized the husband would not return, they mourned their loss. It was the friends they had in the other wives that helped them to grieve and let the tears flow. The neighbor that had the talking bird and the damaged house remained alone. Her house was patched up by many helping hands. After a while, we saw a little smile return to her face and she moved on as best she could. But she had to do it alone. Peter her parrot was her faithful companion. And yes, he had a new cage for a home.

Mom had not any idea if my dad was alright or not. One day we heard the noise the garden gate made when it was opened. It still had the loud squeaking sound and needed oiling. Down the path came the man Mom and I loved. Dad searched for us and he found us. What a reunion we had! So happy it made us to know we made it through the war. Now, if we heard something about my two brothers, our happiness would be complete. We had to be patient and wait, for us it was to pray without stopping and hope that one day we get good news.

What all German people wanted was to make a lasting peace. We wanted nothing more than to live in peace and harmony with the world around us. We wanted to rebuild our country, towns and villages. A new Germany could rise from the ashes of yesterday. It would take hard work from all of us to rebuild our country. And not just to rebuild our country, but earn the friendship back from the nations we had hurt

Dad stayed with us for a few hours. Then he asked if he could take me with him when he left. He would bring me back in a few days. The minute he asked, I was ready to go. I forgot it left Mom alone in this still unsafe time. She allowed it and when it was time to go, I left Mom behind and walked next to Dad down the road and away from Mom. Was she worried about letting me go, knowing we walked all the way and the streets had jeeps and tanks patrolling the city? She knew I was with Dad and, should the need arise, he would protect me. Both of my parents would give their life for me, should I be in danger. She knew Dad was my protector and this is why she let me go with him. She also knew that I wanted to spend more time with him than just the few hours we had today. Mom was unselfish to my being selfish. Not one minute I thought that she was all alone at night without me at her side. Not one minute did I think she could be afraid without me. Today I think why was this that I didn't think of it? Maybe because I always thought of her as being a leader. The person that was always in charge. My Mom was courageous and had proved this to me over and over. Maybe this is why I dared to go with Dad and leave her alone. Yes, this must have been my thinking as an eleven-year-old girl.

I felt my father's love when he took me by the hand when we walked past the Russian patrol cars on the way to downtown Berlin. This walk took us by long lines of people standing with buckets by street pumps. The people of Berlin needed clean water for drinking and for cooking. The water was polluted and when taken home, needed to be boiled before using it. Too many dead were buried in mass graves or waiting in places tucked away from our eyes till they could be buried. Berlin was a big graveyard in 1945.

Dad and I walked through the main streets going through the Brandenburg gate and wanting to reach his apartment without getting into any kind of trouble.

With all that was going on, it was clear that we lived in a dead town. We the people had suffered enough and our heart, our mind, our spirit was broken because of World War II. The war left emotional scars on young and old. When the smoke cleared, Germany would want to rebuild. It would want to make amends and start with a clean slate. While Dad and I walked along side by side looking at all this, we talked about it. We talked about how long, how many years this would take to rebuild Berlin. Dad said it would not look like it used to look when this happened. It would have what he called a face lift. Old and new might blend and Berlin would have a new heart beat. It would march to a different drummer so to speak. We both knew that only time would tell if my dad was right with this assumption.

It was nice for Dad and me to imagine what the new Berlin would look like. It passed away the time and by evening, Dad and I reached his home. I met my stepmother and was polite when I greeted her. She was friendly and I behaved like Mom had taught and, before I left, told me to do. When Dad married this woman, my brothers and I never saw her as being family to us. She was Dad's wife and for this we owed to show her respect. He loved her but we three didn't. We loved Mom and we knew she was the glue that held our family together.

Visiting with Dad, we walked the streets of Berlin every day. We looked for food. The town was in ruins and all the stores were abandoned. Free for everyone to enter and take what was still there to take. Dad and I were interested in anything that smelled and tasted like food. We went into many stores and came out with nothing. Bare handed and feeling discouraged because being hungry was an awful feeling. One would think that by now we should be used to it, but no we were not. We searched and searched to find what would help us to live. And this was food. The stores abandoned by the owner had things left anyone could take. But things were not what kept us alive, only food would do this. The search for Dad and I went on till we found some. Inside both of us must have said prayers to find what we so much needed and looked for.

Then we came to the buildings that had been occupied by the one-time German government. It was the Reich Chancellery. A large building it was, with long hallways and many rooms. Entering one room after the other, Dad kept me away from one. He kept me standing behind him and he never stepped into the room. He pushed the door shut and said this place was a coffin for many. I understood what he was telling me.

When something like this happened between me and Dad, I felt so much sadness inside of me that did not turn loose. I felt for the people that were family to those left inside this room. The German people's heart was broken into pieces because of this five-year long war. We needed to rebuild our country and maybe we needed to grow a new heart. A heart that dared to have hope, believe in a future and dared to dream.

Yes, Germany needed to put away the nightmares of yesterday and believe that a new day was dawning for all of us. From what we saw around us, burned buildings, torn up streets, bomb craters and sometimes a man or woman hung on a street light, this day was not here yet. But surely it was coming when the four powers held a meeting. A meeting like Dad said would have to happen. They needed to decide what to do with us. If their upcoming and needed talk would   bring the best for us was yet to be seen. The future for a war-torn Germany was in the hands of a man called Stalin, Truman and Churchill. These men or more would, like Dad said, hold our country in their hands.

When Dad and I walked through the Chancellery, in one of the rooms we found a closed bucket. This we would take with us and open it when we got home. Dad found reels of film that interested him and he tucked these away under his coat. He looked funny walking with both arms crossed over his chest. He was protecting the hidden treasure under his coat. I was the one pulling the heavy bucket along, that was much too heavy for me. I wondered what was in it that made it so heavy. Besides this, I wondered how we would manage to get all of this home. I saw Dad was not giving up the reels of film he thought were a much-needed treasure find for him. But like I heard him and Mom say often, where there is a will, there would be a way.

I couldn't help laughing seeing him like this, but this was my dad. He and I always found something to laugh or smile about. I loved being with him. With him busy like this, it was my job to tote the bucket around. It was heavy, heavy but I tugged and pulled. I was not about to let go of it. I hoped when we opened it, we found something good to eat in it. It never occurred to us to leave it standing somewhere while we looked around and come back for it when we were done. Dad and I were the only people in this place; no one was there to take this away from us. So why didn't we leave it in one place, while we were looking around for more? I think war time taught us all, including me, to hang on to what was in our hands or someone would come and take it away from us. Being in an empty building or not, I was not going to lose this bucket I toted around with me. Dad and I were of the same mind to hang onto it for dear life.

On the way leaving the Chancellery, we ran into danger. Dad had opened the large door, only to close it again. He told me not to make a sound and stay behind him. I understood there was danger for us on the outside. Dad then opened the door slowly to look outside. He closed it again and told me a man ran into the ruins across from us. A Russian patrol was after him. We heard gunshots and after that was an explosion. It sounded much like a grenade blowing up. We knew this must have been aimed at the poor man looking for refuge in the ruins of the house across from us.

We waited a long time, before we dared to open the door and leave. Dad did not check on the man, we knew he must be dead. It was fortunate the Russian patrol did not enter the Reich Chancellery. Or we might have been killed, like the poor man across the street from us. Not any person was safe in Berlin. It was an open city. If someone went missing, it went unnoticed. Family missed them but could not do anything about it.

Here Dad and I walked along. He was hanging on to the reels of film, I was dragging the bucket over the sidewalk, making scratching sounds. Dad looked around and found a wide flat board. We centered the bucket on it and placed the bundle of film reels on it. Dad picking it up on one end and me on the other it made it easy this way to get it home.

Dad, eager to see what was on the film he found, turned the light on in the kitchen and held the film up under the light bulb. We saw we had Hitler's propaganda films. Dad said this was a good find and one day would earn some money. Should one of these days the family need extra money, then he wanted to sell them. But for now, they needed to be hidden till some time later.

After Dad discovering what was on the film it was my turn to find out what was in the bucket. Dad opened the lid and we looked at some green round things packed in water. I had never seen or tasted anything like this before. When I asked what this was, Dad said they were olives. This food, tasted like pickles and we could eat them. Dad's wife, Adelheid gave each of us a bowl full. And if we wanted, we could ask for more.

After we ate a second bowl, we felt kind of sick. I think we looked like what we ate, green in the face. Keeping it down or not, tomorrow we would have it again for breakfast. It was all we had and some potato peelings Adelheid had saved to cook at potato soup.

Dad mentioned to his wife Adelheid that he needed to take me back to Mom. We knew she had Mrs. Leder and the other ladies as friends and they looked in on her while I was gone. But come evening and it got dark, being alone could be scary. Even for a strong woman like my mom, it was now my Dad that thought it could be kind of scary for her. When I was with her, we went to bed together and I cuddled up sleeping behind her. She was protection, love and comfort for me. Maybe my being there did the same for her. To protect her, I was too young and too small. Comfort I could give her. When she cried, I cried. When someone made her angry, I became angry and wanted to stand up for her. When she hurt, I hurt. This is the way it was. I had love and respect for my mom. The days I was away from her, I knew I was missed by her. Yes, it was time for dad to take me back to her.

When I opened the gate to the garden the rusty gate announced our return, a welcome home was waiting for me. One of us would stay and this was me. One of us would go again and this was Dad. He had another wife and his place was with her. All we had was the promise, and we knew he would keep it, to visit often. Mom and I could depend on this.

When we left, I said thank you to Aunt Adelheid. This is what I called her when I spoke with her. I guess she didn't expect for me to call her anything else but this. And my Dad never asked for me to change it. I don't know what I would have done if he had asked me to do this, so I was very glad he never put me on the spot by asking this of me She was nice, smiled at me, and invited me to come back whenever I wanted. Then Dad and I ventured out, to face the unsafe walk all the way back to Mom in Berlin - Schlachtensee. This was where I as at home and where I belonged. We saw on the way back what we had seen before. Long lines of people getting a clean water supply. Their faces had a story to tell and so did ours. We didn't look alike but yet we were so much alike on the inside and on the outside our sad faces showed it.

We again passed the patrol cars and they paid us no attention and thank God they left us alone. We passed people climbing over mountains of rubble to dig and still find in it, something that belonged to them. We passed people begging for food and couldn't help them because we had none to give to them. We all had the same foundation under our feet. All of us wanted to grab onto having a family and a home, be survivors and have a better life than what we have had. We passed by groups trading items for whatever food they could get. This must have been the beginning of the black-market all over Berlin.

Undisturbed, we walked through the Brandenburg gate. Dad kept my mind busy by telling me about his family in Kaiserslautern. He was from the Rheinland and proud of it. He did not leave his birthplace till he entered World War I. Coming home from it, he stayed in Berlin and he became Edgar, Erwin and my dad. I loved it when he told me about his family. Most of them I had not met because they passed away before I was born. By Dad telling me about them, he gave all of them back to me. And by doing it the way he did, I met and thought I knew each and every wonderful one of them. Dad had a way of telling me things, that brought everything a life and was not told in just black and white but in blooming color.

The walks and talks we shared were meaningful to both of us. He was my dad and my teacher and I was his daughter and student. Talking like we did we made it, without trouble of any kind, home to Mom. Like I thought, she was waiting for us. The tears in her eyes when she saw me, told me of how glad she was to have me back. She said to Dad we were running out wood to keep us warm. And without any further to do, Dad grabbed a small saw and we made it into the woods to cut down a few small trees. We made it home with them. Outside, Dad and I cut them into small pieces big enough for the kitchen stove. I don't remember if we ate anything before Dad left, but we must have. I do not remember what it was Mom gave us, but something did fill Dad and my tummy. The question was if there was still enough of it for Mom after we ate. Or did she give her share to my dad?

Chapter Twenty-Two

The month after the war taught much to Mom and me. You either believed in God or it was possible to lose your belief and become a doubting Thomas. For us, it only strengthened what we already believed in. In this turbulent time, we ran out of firewood, most of all coal. Dad came to help and he and I went to the woods to cut down small trees. We needed to keep warm. All people living around us were in the same predicament we found ourselves in. Whether it was with firewood or whatever we had, one neighbor helped the other.

Since some of the men had returned, they helped the women whose husbands were still unaccounted for. All was talked about as if this railroad community was but one large family. No one took from anyone what didn't belong to them. All was openly asked for and shared. The secret that Mom and the other three neighbor ladies shared to keep us kids and them alive, needed to forever be buried and forgotten. I believe no one talked about it again for as long as they lived.

Mom must have been a miracle worker to come up with food for us every day. And by no means did this mean we ate three times a day. I remember we ate a cup of sugar a day. Why we had so much sugar and nothing else, I have not any idea about this. Aunt Friedchen, Mom's sister must have left it in the kitchen cabinet, because I do not remember us going out to buy any of it. And it was such a large amount something like five pounds or more. Even by using one or more ration cards it was hard to account for how Aunt Friedchen got all the sugar! But we had it, and it was for us to use as we saw fit. We ate it spooning down one cup at a time. After eating so many cups of it, it tasted horrible to us. BRRRRRRR almost too sweet and we wanted to throw up after eating it.

As it would happen, a day came when I couldn't get up from my bed. I could not walk on my own. The sun was shining, Mom wrapped me up in a warm blanket and carried me over to where we had three large fruit trees. The trees gave me shade from the bright sunlight. There I laid most of the day on a makeshift bed. Two lawn chairs my mom had pushed together to make me comfortable. Laying out there all alone, I had grown up thoughts the whole time. I prayed to God that I didn't have to leave Mom all alone in this world. Dad had Adelheid. Mom had only me. Edgar and Erwin? Who knows where they were? No, I did not want to leave our mom alone in this world. I asked God for his help while I laid out there and he gave it. Came late afternoon when Mom came to bring me into the house, I was still there when she carried me back indoors. We went to sleep like always, me sleeping behind her and cuddling up to her. The next morning, I felt better. I gained back some strength and I knew God had answered my prayers. Mom and I would continue together.

Dad came again and Mom told him about me. He had some news to share from Mom's parents about the one brother and the four sisters she had. All were ok and holding each other up, doing what they could to keep going. This is the news Dad brought to us. We knew we were blessed not to have lost more of the family in this war than what we had. Two brothers-in-law for mom, two wonderful uncles for me we lost. I thought please, God, let Edgar and Erwin be ok and come home. I could not bear the thought of never seeing them again. Mom, Dad and I prayed non-stop for their safe return.

On another visit, Dad wanted to know what Mom had done with Erwin's photo and the bush knife when the Russians came in. She said with a grin this was hid away in the mattress in the back room, but only for a short while. Since this was not a good enough hiding spot, she transferred it to the outhouse. In a secure container she said it was placed in the outhouse 'where the sun didn't shine'. She said when Erwin came home and she was sure he and Edgar would make it, photos of his service years would be there. All this was waiting for him, including us. We all laughed at the hiding place she selected. We were pretty sure no one would want to search in such a smelly place for valuables.

At still another time, Dad brought his radio to us and buried it in the bomb crater we had in the front garden. It was left for us as a last remembrance of World War II. It took away most of the garden by making an enormous hole in the ground. We sat next door in the Leder's air raid shelter untouched, only scared from the explosion of the blast. In this deep hole, Dad threw his prize possession, the radio, and covered it up with sand. He said that the Russians asked for all Berliners to turn over their radios. Dad bringing his to us by putting it in the bomb crater was his answer to them.

Again, a month or so later, he came back and tried to find it but it was useless. I helped him dig and dig for hours. It was never found again. However, my Dad could build his own radio and this he did. There was no end to the talents he had. Building, drawing, writing, math, this he was very good at. And story inventing and telling. He was wonderful in all of this.

He was a born teacher as I heard many that knew him say of him. The best part about it, one never knew when one was being taught. Every place I went with him became a classroom. Indoors, outdoors, a walk in the woods or around the block. He was the teacher and I was the forever learning student. To learn from him was fun. I was not the only student he had. Mom joined us often. I could tell it amused Dad when she did. They were not marriage partners any longer. But it was clear to me and everyone that knew them, they were solid in the friendship they had for each other. Every day we talked with one or the other of our neighbors. I liked playing with their kids for a while, to give their mothers and my mom time to have grown up talks.

Chapter Twenty-Three

Mom and I woke up one morning by hearing people shouting and a lot of movement was going on outside. We jumped out of bed, without putting a washcloth to face and hands, we followed the neighbors to the main street. When we reached the end of the dirt road and came to the paved main street, there they were. Jeeps, tanks, war machinery with a white star on the side. Not any red hammer and sickle was seen. A gleaming white star took its place. The Americans took the place that the Russians held in our part of town. With them they brought someone that had been missing in Germany for a long time. God came to visit and we all hoped that he would stay.

Amazing how we felt when we saw the white star and soldiers' hands reaching out in friendship. I still did not trust all of this. It was the weeks, months that laid behind me that would not let me forget the noises in the night we heard. The gunshots and people calling out to help them. No one at the time in the middle of the night could go and help. I was a girl like many others, that was a victim of this time. It would take a long time for me to be able to take a step forward. A lot of help from the man I believed in, the one that heard my prayers and answered them was needed for me. Oh, my goodness it was needed for all of Germany not just for me, or for just us alone.

The Americans, the English, the French were in the capital city of Germany. The Russians had moved overnight to midtown Berlin. Poor Dad, they were still with him in what would later be called East Berlin, the Russian sector.

Mom and I with many, stood in the middle of the main street looking with utter amazement at what was going on around us. And we were surprised by how many Germans could speak the language and talk with the American soldiers. All this was hidden away while Hitler was the dictator. I saw soldiers talking with a young boy and handing him something white to eat. Later I learned it was the American white bread and it tasted delicious. Not any of it was offered to me and Mom. I understood, there was not enough to go around to feed all of us. We stood a long time watching the crowd that gathered around us and all of us stared at the American troops. Unlike the Russians, they were friendly, showing us they didn't want to hurt anyone.

After we had seen enough, later sitting by the oil lamp that night, we both knew it was alright to sleep in our own beds. Not any scary sounds we would hear in the night. I cuddled up behind Mom and looked forward to what the next day would bring. Every day brought something that surprised us. Families dared to walk the streets more freely and they came visiting and told their stories of survival.

A coal truck (Lastwagen in German) brought heating materials. Dad was visiting when it came. He helped me carry by the bucket full what was given to us home. Sad it was that two buckets full of coal didn't last very long. Maybe one or two days we had it warm, then it was cold again. But Mom said, we must be grateful for having a little something, because it was better than having nothing at all. Of course, she was right, besides the two buckets full of coal were giveaways, we didn't have to pay for them. When we went walking around, we saw that the Americans set up a place for their troops to eat. They took what empty stores they could find and placed chairs and tables in them to turn them into a dining room for their men. Outside they had large containers, and what they didn't eat was thrown away. That's what the containers were there for, to hold the leftovers they didn't want anymore. Mom paid attention to what time they ate. Around five or six I was stationed across the street and watched. When it was safe for me to scoot over, I grabbed some of the leftover to bring home. I was always holding my fingers crossed that no one would catch and stop me. Whatever I grabbed in a few minutes time to put in a box mom gave me, became our evening meal. There was also a bakery store close by that we kept our eyes on. When a loaf was too brown or burned, it was a no sale for the baker and it was trashed. I stood waiting and when the baker was gone, climbed the chain link fence to bring home what was still yum, yum to eat. This helped us to survive.

All German people sat in the same boat. A shock wave hit us when the survivors from Hitler's concentration camps returned. Hearing what happened to them made us cringe. I think my homeland was one large bleeding heart. Camps opened to take care and house the Holocaust survivors. Workers were needed to work in these camps. My mom went to work at first for the American officers. There were three or four she washed and ironed for. This was the time when I first experienced the taste of a peanut butter sandwich.

Visiting Mom at her fine place of work, the cook saw me when he looked out of the upstairs kitchen window. The work room for doing washing and ironing was in the basement of a big house. The officers had taken this house as their headquarters. I was sitting by the window in the basement waiting for mom to finish her work and I was seen by the cook. Promptly, and unexpected by me and mom, he sent someone to the basement with a tray of sandwiches. The young woman that brought the tray down to me said, it was for me. There was enough there to share with mom and the other two ladies that worked with her. I didn't know what I ate, but I liked it. I thought it was funny that it made my tongue stick to the roof of my mouth. The four of us ate peanut butter sandwiches and none of us went home hungry because of the kindness the cook showed me. Water we drank to unstick our tongues. When this job came to an end because the house went back to its original owners and the officers were relocated, mom and the other two ladies found other employment. The three friends set out to find a working place for all three of them. They wanted to stay and work together as a team. They managed to find the same place of employment.

Mom's second job was for the returned Jewish families. She kept the hallways, bathrooms cleaned for them. They were waiting to leave Germany, go to the U.S.A., England, any place that would take them and give them a home. Mom again made friends with many of the ones she worked for. And many stories she heard from them that turned her heart upside down. Some she told me, others were so heartbreaking that she sat and cried and cried. These stories she wouldn't share with me, she kept them to herself. She told them to Dad when he visited, then both of them looked sad.

I was left on my own and learned to be responsible for the household. I had chores to do with Mom working such long, hard hours. Her work was demanding in the scrubbing and cleaning of long drafty hallways. She came home and said she was bone tired. But when the next day came, she was up and at it again. She worked after the regular hours for the Jewish families that paid with clothing, or stiff black-market prices for having a cleaning lady to work for them.

The families that came back from the death camps, somehow came into money. It must be that either the US government, Britain, France or maybe also Russia was reaching out to them. Money could by no means make up for their suffering and the loss of human life they have endured. We saw by what and how it was done, that the four nations were helping in whatever way they could. Money paid was never the answer for the card life had dealt them. But for the moment, it was of whatever help it could be.

The black market was taking off in Berlin and all over Germany. If you had something to sell or you had the money for something needed, the black market was the place to do business. It flourished all over Germany.

In this time, the schools opened and we kids returned to learning. My next-door neighbor, Hildegard Leder, and I were in the same class. We did not walk to school together because I had work to do before leaving. She was lucky to have none. Sometimes I envied her all the free time she had. But she was the youngest in her family. Her parents were together and not divorced like mine. Hildegard had Marianne, the older sister, and she did most of the housework. When Hildegard came home, the only work she had waiting for her was to finish homework for school the next day. Maybe she had some work to help with in the garden. When she did and I was out doing the same we talked back and forth. Yes, now and then I envied the freedom my friend had. After thinking about it, I felt bad and said to myself 'shame on me.' I was Mom's helper and the trust she placed in me should make me be proud. Mom and I did team work and each of us had to pull our own load. Mom, as the provider, had the heaviest load to pull. This is why when she went to bed, she was always bone tired. She often used the word exhausted. She said she was so exhausted that the minute her head hit the pillow, she was asleep.

Chapter Twenty-Four

The days came and went. Dad came and went. Nothing came to us from my brothers. We waited and waited to hear. A sign of life we waited for, but nothing came.

For me, the days went by so much nicer. I was a school girl and loved learning and being around kids my age. Dad came to help with firewood for the two rooms we kept warm. He kept Mom's spirits up and made me smile. He was a helper with the homework I brought home. We had two years to catch up on. This is the time I missed because of the war. I started in third grade when the war was over and at eleven years old, I should, by all rights, have been be a fifth grader.

The school year was divided up in six months. Six months with the teacher trying to cram one year of learning into this six-month period. I needed help with homework and since Mom worked long hours, when Dad came, he pitched in to bring me up to date. I believe it made trouble for him in his homelife with Aunt Adelheid. He came often and didn't let his wife dictate to him what he could and what he couldn't do with or for his first family.

My brothers and I were the only children Dad had. He and Adelheid lost two babies. The loss must have been sad, sad for both of them. It was no wonder that Dad loved us as much as he did. Dad took the trouble his second wife gave him with much patience, he came to hug me and to support Mom in the long wait to hear from Edgar and Erwin. Every day we waited but nothing came.

It was cold and it got colder and colder all the time. There was a short cut over a field I could use, coming home from school. I was always pressed for time since I had chores to do. I used this shortcut often and so I did this day, When I used this way to get home, I had not any idea that it would scare the life out of me. The road led through the middle of the field and on the left side about ten or so American soldiers with a bunch of shepherd dogs erected what looked like a radio tower.

I walked along and for some reason, they sent the dogs after me. The dogs circled around me, showing me their teeth. I stood very still not moving but I was scared to death. I heard the laughing from these soldiers and even though they were Americans, I knew they were not my friends. To them I was a German girl and was still seen as their enemy. This must be it, they saw me not as a full grown up enemy, but as a half grown up one. And to these soldiers, the enemy was the enemy no matter what their size or their age was. It was the only explanation I had while I was standing there being so afraid that the dogs would bite me.

They played a game with me by calling the dogs back and forth, laughing the whole time as I tried to make my way home. I was fighting back tears by the time I reached the end of the field, that's when they decided to leave me alone. I entered the railroad community and made a run for home. Birkenweg #3 was it and I was glad when I got there. Running through the garden, opening and shutting the front door of the house behind me, now I felt safe. I laid my school things on the kitchen table and said a thank you prayer that I was home and I was safe.

Getting home I got busy and made the fire in the kitchen stove, I cleaned and refilled the oil lamp that was hanging on a hook down from the ceiling. I did the homework I had brought back from school and waited for Mom. I had so much to tell her. When she got home and I told her about the awful day I had, she was very upset. She gave me strict orders never to take the shortcut home again. She said to take the long way and come in the other way to the railroad community. She said she had another saying we needed to go by. "It was better to be safe than sorry." I wanted to remember this every time I was tempted to take the short cut. This experience taught me it was better to be safe than to be sorry.

I learned another of the lessons life teaches; there is good and bad in all people. I had come across some that had more bad inside of them than good. I would remember this day. It placed a fear in me for every large dog that crossed my path. Even if they were on a leash, I went out of their way if at all possible.

There was another such event that scared me a week later. I was on an errand for Mom and walked on a side road that had a lot of trees and shrubs. A horse platoon from the nearby Ranch Dueppel came galloping down the sandy road. To get out of the way of the running horses, I hid behind one of the large trees. But I was seen when I hid myself away.

One of the riders brought his horse around and made it rear up on its hind legs. The hooves of the horse missing me by inches. The rider saw I was a small girl, turned the horse away from me and raced after the other riders. I again had a close call and could have been hurt and was so lucky that I was not. I again told Mom and she warned me to be more and more careful. Happenings like this after World War II we called normal. Every day something sad was happening. The saddest of all was the shooting of a four-year-old girl. She and her twin sister were on a walk on a nice day. They were a part of a group of kids living at an orphan's home. There were many such homes as the war separated families. She ran away from the group and came close to the camp for German war prisoners. The fence had a warning sign that anyone coming close to it would be shot.

Before the young girl that was the caregiver of this group of children could catch this little runaway, the guard in the watchtower shot. He was a twenty-year-old and he shot and killed a four-year-old little girl. A child that was not old enough to read the warning signs posted. There was a woman put in charge of a number of children and she was not fast enough to do anything about what happened. It was such a sad time for the kids in this orphan's home and all their caregivers. We were all taken back and saddened by what had happened. All in the orphanage grieved and the railroad community we lived in grieved for this small child.

The American government took a hand in this by sending officers to the home. The funeral for this tiny one was paid for by the Americans. An honor guard stood at her grave. But all this would not make her live again.

The Americans took charge over taking care of this children's home. Kids in this place wore better clothing and had from now on had very good food to eat. All this because a four-year-old lost her life. The little twin sister did not do well since she was now alone. The home started to look for foster parents for this cute little girl.

Our neighbors, Mr. and Mrs. Leder, took this cute little girl into their home. It took a while to turn her around and get her to smile again. If anyone could, it would be the Leder family. They were wonderful people. We knew them as neighbors and friends with a heart filled with love. This was the medicine needed to make this little one live and smile again. The death of her sister had turned her heart to stone. When you looked and spoke to her, her eyes showed how sad she was. I always wanted to hug her but was afraid to touch her. Mr. Leder said she was shy and wanted to be left alone.

One evening I was outside pumping water to wash the dishes I needed to clean before Mom came home from the Unra Lager. She now worked for a Jewish family, the Pfeigenbaums, after her regular work schedule. They paid her well and the extra money she got from them allowed us to buy at the black-market somethings we needed.

So, here I was at the pump being busy. The garden pump stood close enough to the Leder's open kitchen window, I heard voices and laughter. Marianne and Hildegard were at play in the kitchen. Then I heard giggling and this did not come from my two friends. It came from this little one that was now a part of their family. The Leder family managed to get her back to being the sweet girl she was meant to be. The wall of hurt that she had around her heart came down.

She stayed with the Leder family for a long time. Her parents, that the twins became separated from during the war, found her and took her home. Mrs. Leder told us the hardest of all for them was to go to the cemetery to say hello and goodbye to the other one. They found a daughter and lost a daughter all in the same day. Mom and I could not imagine what it would be like to feel happy and unhappy all at the same time.

The name of this little girl and her twin I have forgotten. What I remember of her are the large brown eyes and long brown hair she had. This will always be in my memory, she was so tiny and cute. An angel of a little girl. I went, after pumping my pail full of water, inside to wait for Mom, eager to tell her of the giggling I overheard coming from the Leder's kitchen window.

When Mom came home tonight, she was of course, tired from work and a bit cranky. All I had to do was to look at her face to see if she had a good or a bad day at work. If it was a bad one, I tried to keep my distance from her. This was hard to accomplish in the small living space we had. If it happened to be a good one, I could cut up and joke around with her. This was the right time and hour for me to be close to her. When I told of the good news about our tiny next-door neighbor, she smiled a big, big smile. She was as happy as I was to hear good news after a hard day at work.

Chapter Twenty-Five

Going to sleep not interrupted by sirens was a blessing. For Mom, the long hours she worked started to show in her behavior. She came home tired and she let her feelings out on me. She climbed all over me for every little thing. She found something to fuss about, even when there was nothing to fuss about. These times were not good for either one of us. When Dad came, I had a chance to tell him about it. He tried to be the middleman and help me and mom. After him talking with me, I saw how hard it was to be a grown up. Somehow it made me think I didn't want to grow up. However, I knew I couldn't stay a little girl forever. Right now, I was Dad's little girl, and needed to be mom's big girl. Oh, how confusing all this was for me.

Mom was a cigarette smoker and when she ran short or was empty handed, one wrong word from me would set her on a warpath. She told me to have a cigarette made her feel full and less hungry. We did not agree on any of this when she substituted smoking for not eating. But I believed she did this for me, when she ate less it left more for me.

When she was home for the weekend and there was not any money to buy the smokes, she sent me riding a bike to look for thrown away cigarette ends on the street. I was embarrassed doing this but I did it for her. She snapped out of being cranky in a hurry if I brought home a good find. She had a small pipe she used, taking off the paper and filling it with the tobacco from my find.

The American soldiers had the habit of walking along the streets of Berlin, taking a puff or two, and throwing the cigarette away. Maybe they knew a needy smoker would pick up the thrown away leftover. Mom and

I followed such a gift giver one day. It must have been a Saturday or on a Sunday, any other day Mom would be at work. We knew walking a ways behind, he was getting ready to fling the smoke away (meaning by smoke, he threw the cigarette away). Mom signaled me to be ready to go. Oh, I was ready and set to make a dash for it but hadn't noticed the lady with a small dog on a leash behind us.

The moment came when the soldier let go of the cigarette and stepped on it. He went on his way without giving us that followed him a glance. I was not fast enough to outrun this small dog coming from behind me. The lady walking behind us trained her small companion to do for her what I did for Mom. The surprise to see this was ours. The woman with the dog did not pay attention to us. She took from the dog what he brought to her, calling him or her a good dog. The dog was happy, the woman was happier and they went on their way. Leaving us standing there looking so surprised at what just happened, but laughing hard and loud at what we had seen. Our laughter must have followed her and the tiny dog all the way down the street. She never turned around to look at us. She turned at the corner and was gone.

Mom and I went looking for more throwaways. We walked on a very uneven sidewalk full of holes. I kept my eyes on the ground, not to miss anything. To find cigarette butts was the reason Mom and I were out and about in the first place. When I looked at Mom, I saw she had a grin on her face and I wanted to know why. She chuckled and said, "It was good the soldier stepped on the cigarette before the little dog picked it up. What would this little thing have done if it was still glimmering?" He would have barked arf, arf, arf and arf for sure.

Now it was my turn to grin. In my imagination I saw this tiny fur ball jumping up and down, barking at the object till the glimmer was gone. Then it would pick it up and take it to the lady, getting the petting and the words 'good, good dog'. Or whatever it was she was mumbling when she rewarded this tiny helper.

Mom and I found ways to be happy, just like Dad and I did. Each one of my parents had a special way in reaching my heart. The times we lived in were difficult, but it made us aware of how important it was to love one another. We did this very well in our small family. Nothing was more important than to show our love. Love for God and each other.

After such a walk, it was nice to get back to the tiny place we called home. We sat down to talk and relax. We talked about the dog and were amused by this. We also talked about relatives, friend and neighbors. Most of the time we spoke about Edgar and Erwin. Not knowing anything of them was a great concern for my parents. When Dad came for a visit, it was all I heard them talk about. But the month went by and nothing was heard from my two brothers.

Chapter Twenty-Six

It was getting close to Christmas. My friends in class were excited, as some still believed there was a Santa Claus. Or they pretended to believe, because it was fun to pretend. I did not believe but said nothing, it was not for me to spoil their fun in the game they played or take away their belief that there was a Santa Claus.

On the 24th of December it was a school day for me and a work day for Mom. Came 6 p.m. that evening, it became a special night for all of Germany. The night before Christmas Day was celebrated as Holy Eve. And it would for all of us be the Holy Eve because the war was over. Not any bombs would be dropped on this special "Holy Night". For the first time in five years, there was a "Peace on Earth". The people that had the means for it, had a Christmas tree. We did not. Mom and I had each other and this was wonderful. I looked forward to sitting with Mom tonight, talking about Dad and thinking of Edgar and Erwin. I knew Dad had Aunt Adelheid and us. Mom and I prayed that someone would be good on Christmas to my two big brothers. We believed they were alive in a war prisoners camp celebrating Christmas far away from us, but thinking of us.

Many thoughts went through my eleven-year-old head and they had nothing to do with school work. The kids around me were like me, not thinking of school but excited what the evening would be like. Miss Kutner our teacher knew we were caught up in the holiday spirit and she made it easy for us. Us being excited must have spilled over on her, because she told stories of how it was when she was a young girl and we sang Christmas songs. It was a nice, nice, extra special day for all in this class.

Come 3 p.m., time to go home, she approached me asking for a favor. A big favor was what she called it. She told me there was a Christmas program some of my class was involved in. One of the girls had gotten sick and she wanted for me to take her place. It was a last-minute request but she knew I could do it. She knew mom was not at home when I got out of school and this way, I was able to be the fill in for the girl that was sick. I said yes, I was glad to help out and with the other kids that were in this program, I was taken to a church in Berlin - Schlachtensee.

The walk from the school to the church was very cold. My coat was not the best and I shivered all the way there. The outside of this church showed the evidence of having gone through a war. But the inside the back rooms were heated and we could defrost. We were in the room for the Clergy and their gowns were hanging in the lockers, along with the angel gowns and silver halos for us kids.

A bushel basket of apples stood on the table and it was meant for us. Miss Kutner handed each of us one, told us to eat and we could talk, but not too loud. We were in a church and not in the classroom. We sat on the floor munching the apple and wanting to celebrate the Holy Eve in this church. This was the first Christmas after a five-year war. It was for all of us a silent and holy night. Silent because the dropping of bombs stopped and it was holy because it was Christmas.

Over the years we had been taught by parents and grandparents it was the birthday of Jesus and he was the Son of God. We had two important reasons to celebrate this special night. The birth of God's son and peace for Germany and the other countries that fought a war against us. Here I sat with my friends in church. I was hoping Mom would understand, should she get off work early, that it

147

must be something very important that stopped me from being there before she was. And I could explain it all when I got home.

Miss Kutner helped to put the angel outfits on us and gave us white candles to hold. She would light them at 6 p.m. and we needed to be careful with them. She told us when the church bells started to ring, this was the clue to enter the sanctuary, find our places sitting around the altar steps and let Holy Eve unfold.

My hair was brushed by Miss Kutner more than my mom brushed it and she let it hang loose down my back. The same was done with all the other girls. The boys' hair was easy taken care of. All of us wore a silver halo, even the boys, and we felt festive. I was picked by Miss Kutner to be the lead angel. This alone made me feel special.

I thought of Mom and wished she was there to see me. The kids all told me that their parents sat in the sanctuary. I knew mine was at work and couldn't help it that she couldn't be there for me. Besides, not anyone, including my teacher, had told me about having this special Church program for this night of all nights. Maybe I was not told because she knew of my poor circumstances. The sewing of the angel costume and all, none of it we had the money for or the time to do. When my classmate got sick it gave me the opportunity to take her place and wear what her mom had made for her. Her mother did a beautiful job dressing her daughter to be an angel. With me being her substitute now I felt pretty wearing something that was meant for her but was now mine. The whole event made me feel special. When I got home, I wanted to tell Mom all about it.

It was time, 6 p.m. was here. The church bells in the steeple of the church were ringing. Ding – Dong – Ding –

Dong was their wonderful sound. For most of the time during the war they kept silent. Now Ding – Dong – Ding – Dong they were free to speak. On this Holy Eve they spoke loud and clear. Germany was celebrating Christmas with the rest of the world. I wanted to tell Mom every little detail of this special night when I got home. Then when Dad came, I would repeat my story. He would want to know, too.

The bells stopped and the organ played. This was the clue that we needed to enter the sanctuary and as instructed take the place sitting around the altar. Miss Kutner opened the heavy doors and with the lit candles in hand, slowly we made our way to find our place. The church was filled with people, every seat was taken. Someone made a place for Miss Kutner in the front row. She was to give me and the other four girls a sign to get up and step forward to say the Christmas poem I had to learn in such a hurry.

Walking along I saw large decorated Christmas trees in the corners of this large hall. They glimmered and they glittered with tinsel and bulbs. I was amazed to see all this. But then I saw something I didn't like and it did not fit the picture I had in mind of peace in the world and good will towards all men. Soldiers with their hands hidden behind their back stood against every wall in this hall. All four nations, Russian, British, French and the American military stood against the walls of this church, with all the German people sitting on the pews in the middle.

This looked so very wrong to me. Soldiers should not be here and stand guard over us. This didn't seem right at all and right away I was filled with fear. I was eleven years old, had seen and heard so much bad before, during and after the war, that I did not trust soldiers here with us in this worship service. With holding their hands behind their backs, I was sure they had guns and they would do something terrible to everyone here.

My mind was going around and around and fear filled me from my head down into my toes. I had the thoughts of wanting to run away. I wanted to get home to Mom. But no one could get out of this place with all four nations in place and standing guard. I heard nothing of the message that night. I sat at the altar praying the man standing in the pulpit would speak for a long time. As long as he spoke, we would stay alive.

It was awful to feel this kind of fear again. I felt it when the bombs fell and we sat helpless in the air raid shelter. We could not run away from it then as we cannot run away from this tonight. All I could do was to pray and this is what I did then and did it tonight. I was praying for God to hear me and I wanted for him to answer my prayer. I wanted to be home with Mom. If I was taken away on this Holy Eve, Mom and Dad would be lonesome. Oh, so very lonesome without me. I prayed please, don't let this happen, but let me go home to Mom. I heard very little of what the man wearing a long, black gown in the pulpit was saying.

I watched my teacher in the front row, waiting to give the sign for us to stand up and say the poem. It didn't look like she or all the others were concerned about anything. I was starting to wonder if I was the only one seeing the military standing around us. When the sign came from Miss Kutner to do what she taught us to do, I got up and moved forward like a puppet on a string. We kids did what was required of us but my knees shook and scared I was the whole time. I was glad to sit down again. I was shaking with fear of what I thought would happen next. I closed my eyes, it was time for me to pray for a miracle.

This was Holy Eve and on such a night, miracles will be given. Miracles that lift the burden of a fearful heart and teaches to believe in all that is good. This happened for me on the first Christmas after World War II. The man in the pulpit stopped speaking, the organ was still playing and I, well I was praying. Please, God, don't let me get shot. I wanted to go home to Mom. Now the organ stopped playing.

Sitting next to my friends I kept my eyes closed. I heard the noise of a lot of talking and people moving around. But what I didn't hear and was waiting to hear were gunshots. I didn't dare to open my eyes till I felt a hand touch my shoulder. When I looked up, I looked into the eyes of an American soldier, he was smiling at me. He held a bag open and I was to take something from it. I did as he told me and when I pulled my hand back, I held a Christmas gift I could take home to Mom and share.

All the soldiers that stood leaning against the walls of this old church were moving about giving away Christmas gifts. They had bags full to give away and these bags must have been on the floor in front of them. I had not any way of seeing this from where I was sitting. They didn't have guns hid away that were meant to kill us, instead they had gifts for everyone. They were, for this Holy Night, Santa Claus in Russian, British, French and American uniforms. I was surprised and totally amazed by what happened. It was a magical night not just for me, but I believe it was magical for everyone that came to worship on the 24th of December in 1945.

Changing out of the angel costume and putting on my coat, Miss Kutner came to me to say to be very careful going home. I had to walk alone. My classmates had family there but I was on my own and it was dark outside. Everyone went in a different direction from me, but I was not afraid of anything at this moment. God had already granted me a miracle. Now, He would see to it that I got home to Mom.

It was cold walking from the school to the church. Now going back, the night air made it even colder. I said goodnight to everyone that stood outside and wished them a Merry Christmas. Since I didn't have gloves, I put my hands into the pockets of my coat. In one I had the gift. I wanted to make sure not to lose it. I walked a ways and ran a ways. Besides not having gloves, I did not have a hat and my ears, nose and my face were very cold. What I did have was a scarf. I pulled it out from under my coat and tied it over my head to cover up my ears. Now I was a little warmer.

I had to make it by a bomb crater that was used as a trash dump, this looked scary to me. I ran past it and came to the road leading home. Up the dirt road I ran. I noticed the light in the windows of many houses, and some of them had candles in them. Running and skipping along I was wondering how many homes had a decorated tree. We had the woods behind this railroad community – maybe the men in the families went and cut down a small tree. I knew we did not do this, we could have, but we did not think of it. When Dad cut down a tree it was only meant for firewood. It was Christmas and I wondered what he and Aunt Adelheid were doing right now. By now I was almost home, so I did not wonder for too long.

Standing by the garden gate, the light from the oil lamp in the kitchen was welcoming me home. When I got inside, Mom stood by the kitchen cabinet and had the Mom look on her face I knew so well. It said where have you been all this time? When she opened her mouth to speak with me, she said, you better explain yourself and do it fast. I have been very worried about you, do not ever do this again, do you hear me? Oh, I heard her all right and I saw in her face how concerned she had been. Now seeing I was home she calmed down and the relief showed in her face. She saw I was home safe and sound and apparently, I was very happy.

I was bubbling over with all I had to tell her. Mom put her hands over her ears telling me to slow down. I was talking much too fast. And before she took off my coat to hang it up, I pulled out of my pocket the gift I had. Small as it was, it was wrapped in pretty paper. It was something sweet to eat. It was a Hershey bar. The first chocolate I ever tasted and Mom and I shared it. It really was a Holy Eve for me and Mom.

We made the most out of this Holy Eve when we spoke of the people we loved and missed. My two brothers were our favorite topic. What we would do when they finally came home. We sat and ate the chocolate bar, happy to be alive and doing alright from one day to the next. This evening, this Holy Night, was a life changer for me. I made myself a promise that I meant to keep. I didn't want to forget the soldier that gave me such a sweet gift. And this promise I wanted to keep and honor for the rest of my life.

I knew then, that when one day I had my own home, this chocolate bar had a place under the Christmas tree. It would become a tradition in my home that when the tree was put up, a chocolate bar needed to be under it. Without it, the tree wouldn't blink its lights in my living room. Now I am eighty-four and a half years old and I have been keeping this promise ever since I made it.

Everyone that knows me, knows this special story. If God calls me away someday, this story I believe will be told from one family member to the other. How a kind hand and a chocolate bar helped a young girl believe that people are good. And she believed it to the day she died. Yes, the year 1945 – 1946 did this for me.

When Dad came to visit before the year ended, we had much to tell him. We said sorry when we told him about the chocolate. We did not keep any for him, the bar was so small. He smiled, puffed on his pipe, but he understood. After he warmed up a bit, he asked if I wanted to go with him to look for or cut some firewood. I said yes, of course I wanted to go. He needed my help to find or to cut it, because in the winter the wood was cold and wet. It needed to be dry before it burned and made a warm fire.

When we came back with two large sacks full of wet tree chunks and branches, Mom showed us she had a trick up her sleeve and she wanted to teach it to me.

Putting the wet wood in the old kitchen stove she poured oil from the lamp or lighter fluid on it. This made a fast burning fire. I watched how careful she was and I learned from her. Coming back from school I made the fire in the same way she did, so it was cozy in the house when she came from work. If I could manage ok without dropping the school books, when I found wood laying around, I tried to bring it home. I was Mom's housekeeper and I liked doing this for us. I almost had an accident with the oil, or was it lighter fluid? I threw a match in and the poof coming out from the oven door singed my eyebrows. I did not say anything about it and Mom didn't seem to notice it. Good for me. I felt foolish standing so close to the door from the stove and being so careless.

Chapter Twenty-Seven

The new year was starting and we looked forward to the changes it would bring. We hoped and prayed for it to be better for all of Germany. Dad came to see us more and more. It was not going well between him and his wife Adelheid. We became the haven of rest when he came to visit. He gathered smiles and laughter from us and took this back with him when he left. We started to be concerned for him. Mom looked at me and said, I could have told him this would happen between him and her. But then he would not have listened to me. She was much too young for your dad. Now it is too late for him to change anything, but I must say I do not like seeing your Dad hurting like this. Hearing my mother's words about Dad made me think she still loved him. I thought she cared and will always love him. Knowing this made me sad for mom and knowing about Dad made me sad for both of them. I knew there was not anything I could do to help. I needed to be their big girl, listen to what they had to say and stand by them.

From my two brothers we had not one sign of life. When the mail came, we looked if we had a card from the Red Cross. Neighbors had news in this way but nothing like this came to our mailbox. We never gave up hope. My parents said they felt in their heart my brothers would return home.

We started spring planting in the garden. The neighbors helped by sharing packets of seed. It was my job to turn the soil and get it ready. I did this in the evenings when all my other work was done. On weekends with Mom at home, we raked and planted. It was fun to work with Mom in the garden.

The newspapers gave us much to think about. Write ups about the death of Adolf Hitler, Eva Braun and others were the topics. War trials started and stories of many terrible things circled around. A wonderful radio station was broadcasting German and American music. The people that had a radio learned about country music, American films and Walt Disney. Of great importance was the meeting in Potsdam of the leaders of the Three nations. They had to talk about Germany and what to do with Berlin.

In Berlin, the black market was flourishing. The people bought and traded and paid high prices for everything. Mom sent me to such a place to buy flour for soups and making gravy. When I returned with what she wanted, we found we had been cheated. My bag was half salt and the top half was flour. I cried, but not because somebody had done us wrong. I cried for Mom, she worked after working hours to make the money to buy what we needed. She was tired and worn out, sick at times. She was out her hard-earned money and didn't have enough flour for soups or gravies. What we had was plenty of salt.

Mom comforted me by saying this was not my fault. This could have happened to her if she had gone. When Dad came, he told me the same. So, we got up every morning and did what we needed to do. Mom kept working hard every day she worked overtime and I cleaned our home and did well in school. I was among the best students in my class and this made my parents proud.

Time to get together with Marianne and Hildegard slipped away from me. I had way too much to do to play games like other kids my age. Marianne helped her Mom like I did mine and Hildegard was spoiled by all, but always a nice friend to me. We repaired the hole in the fence, we had not any need for the path leading to the air raid shelter anymore. Mom and Mrs. Leder talked when they worked in the garden and so did we girls. Mom and I had picked a name for these talks between her and her friend. I always asked Mom when we got inside, if she wanted to share something from the "Over the fence talks" she and Mrs. Leder had. Sometimes mom passed on things to me and other times she was closed lipped. Hildegard and I shared the bond of sitting in class together and had the privilege to be friends and neighbors. This was all we needed to continue our friendship.

When I had extra time, I buried my nose in a book. I liked to dream about far-away places and someday, maybe travel to see them. I do believe I was not the only one to have such dreams. Germany was renewing itself. Out of the ashes of the past, a new and a better country would arise and take its place in the world. We, the people, needed to work hard and be steadfast in what we did and how we went about everything. We needed to get the world to believe that we wanted to change and that we did change.

Hitler's propaganda films, showing the military doing the goose step at public functions, this must become a thing of Germany's past. Something to learn from by looking at films and reading the history pages of a book. What happened in Germany should never be repeated. However, as shameful as it was, it must be talked and taught in the schools. It should never raise up its ugly head and be allowed to make a come-back in Germany or elsewhere in this world.

There were writings in the Morgenpost, the daily newspaper of Harry S. Truman, Prime Minister Winston Churchill and Joseph Stalin. I think we read of a Frenchman by the name of De Gaulle. What was said or written about him, I am not sure about anymore. But I remember that the three main power figures had a meeting in Potsdam. Germany's fate was decided by drawing matches out of a hat or a bowl, so I read or maybe someone told me. Which one of the three picked the larger match would get the bigger portion of German soil. It so happened that Joseph Stalin won. I do think it must have pleased him to be the winner.

After their meeting, my hometown Berlin became known as the divided city. Divided into four parts. The British, the American, the Russian and the French sector, this was the new Berlin. Mom and I had the good fortune to live in the American sector of Berlin. But not far away from us was the Russian sector.

We were kept apart from it by railroad tracks and a long stretch of barbwire fence. All of us knew this was the divider between the West and the East. Some people we knew had family living on the other side and went visiting over there. When they came back, they told us we were lucky not to live under the East government.

Brandenburg Gate, 1945

Chapter Twenty-Eight

The weather turned warmer. What we had planted in the garden started to grow. Time it was for me to pump water and help the growing to come along better and faster. We could look forward to have a nice garden this year, this was Mom's opinion. If she came home from work early enough and it was still light outside, she liked to stroll through the garden and look at things. She loved to see things growing. The first little green coming out of the soil, to see it gave her pleasure. Walking down the garden path, from the screeching gate to the front door of the house, she looked at the coming in bloom flowers. We had multi-colored tulips all the way down the path and other pretty flowers. Mom's favorite of them all was the dainty daisy and the lilac. Double lilac was what she liked and loved. And I, well, I liked what she liked so much. But to be honest I loved all flowers, most of all the yellow sunflowers with their brown faces. We had a few of them by the gate.

It was a Saturday, Mom and I sat by the kitchen window, when the garden gate opened. We thought it was Dad but it was not. It was Mom's sister Berta bringing us the sad news that Mom's mother and the only Grandma I had passed away the night before.

The relatives I had on Dad's side all died before I was born. I still had aunts and uncles from Dad's family in the Rheinland. But from them I knew only two. Uncle Paul and Greta Weiss. We visited them during the war, before Adolf Hitler put my Dad into prison. Meeting them was nice and I loved the time we spent with them. The visit we had was much too short but it was sweet. Then it was back to Berlin and hoping that one day we could and would make this trip to see them again.

Here I sat, looking at Mom and her sister having a very serious talk. I was surprised it was only Aunt Berta sobbing. Mom did not, she kept her emotions in check. For some reason my Mom did not cry. I was very surprised by the way she behaved and thought she might cry after her sister left. I thought I better prepare myself for it.

When Aunt Berta left, she had told all there was to tell. She gave Mom information about the funeral and how her Dad was dealing with the loss of his wife of many years.

When Mom did talk with me, the surprise again was all mine. She shared that the Franz Weiss family was never a part of her mom's inner circle. She held other family in her heart, but she held us at a distance. Mom said she believed Grandma cared for us but not enough to let us into her heart. Mom said she believed this happened when she married Dad against her parents' wishes. Then twenty years later came the divorce and he remarried. All this could be the reason Grandma put a guard up around her heart.

Mom said she was sorry to tell me this but I should know why she was not able to cry like Aunt Berta had done. While Grandma was living, she had hope that one day Grandma's heart had a sign stating a room was for rent. Mom said she would have loved to rent us the room. But with Grandma's death, this was not meant to be for the Franz Weiss family.

This was so sad to hear from my Mom. Now I had the answers to how come we didn't visit as often with the grandparents like the others did. We only saw them on their birthdays and not often in the in-between times. My special day was also Grandma's. I would think of her when my birthday came around, because it was her birthday like it was mine. But unlike what she did with me and my brothers, I would keep her not at a distance but always in my heart. I had a chance to say goodbye to my grandma standing next to her bed before she was taken away. She was my and my cousins' grandma, we would remember her and always love her.

The day of the funeral came and was sad for all of us. At the church, seeing my grandpa sitting in the middle of his family, brought tears to my eyes. His son, my Uncle Emil was sitting next to him. Grandpa looked so tiny and lost sitting next to his son.

It was Grandpa's neighbors living a floor below him that owned a funeral home. They gave a helping hand in taking care of Grandma's last needs. The whole family was grateful for their help in reaching out to Grandpa. Here we sat in church, all of us having our own thoughts of how much we had lost.

I looked at Mom at my side when Grandma's favorite song was played. It was Ave Maria. Now Mom had the tears in her eyes that had been missing up till now. Again, I looked over to see Grandpa and wondered how he would get along without Grandma. It was hard to imagine him without having her at his side. To me, he had always looked so tall and powerful. He was broad in the shoulders from years of brick laying. A man with clear grey eyes and a will of steel.

This man was gone. He died when Grandma died. How would he go on with only having their children to look in on him? He had this and the memories of their long marriage but would this be enough to keep his spirits up and keep him going?

We got the answer to this question when a week after the funeral Grandpa came to see us. He was asking us to move in with him. He needed our help. His offer came at the right time as Mom's sister Friedchen was able to return home. And she needed her house back as soon as possible.

It was right for her to come back to what belonged to her. With it she also claimed the fruit of our labor, all that we had planted in the garden. We hoped that she was willing to share some of it with us. This would only be fair. Fair and very nice of her.

Now Mom and I would be homeless again but we had Grandpa's wonderful offer to move in with him. He needed us as much as we needed him and we said yes to the move. We had found a place to call home. I thought of Mom's saying that God was looking out for us, and yes, I too believed that this was it. Every time we had trouble coming our way, He provided us with a way out of it. I thought this was awesome and we were grateful for his help.

When we moved in with Grandpa Sauer, there was not a way we could have known he would only live eight weeks after Grandma. He missed being with her so much, he followed her to heaven. Like it was done for Grandma, the neighbors below us did the same for Grandpa.

I felt sad losing him and not getting to know him well. I had my chance to do this but lost it and this was my own fault. I felt guilty losing this God-given opportunity to get to know someone special. I was the one that should have come home to him after school. Mom still worked late hours and she could not. I did this a few times coming home early and the way he acted when I was with him scared me. He slept a lot and, in his sleep, he talked. He was talking to Grandma as if she was still with him. He talked about the children they had as if they were small and he was holding them on his lap and close to him. This somehow frightened me and instead of going home to him, I went to Mom's workplace. We came home to take care of him together. He was alone because I was so afraid to be left alone with him. When I told mom about this, she said that my grandpa lived in a world we couldn't be a part of. But it was real to him and him alone. He was reliving raising his children and being with his wife. And when he dreamed, all this it meant he was happy. I said when he woke up, he must be disappointed because it was only us he saw. Mom said yes, maybe this was right. I remember looking at mom saying, no wonder he likes to sleep so much, because it keeps him together with the family that God took home. Talking of this, thinking of this, somehow all this was a bit too much for me. It really frightened me.

Mom saw to it that a neighbor lady took my place to take care of him. She came to fix the lunch mom prepared ahead of time. And she checked on him a couple of times in the afternoon. Mom made sure he was taken care of because I was such a scared girl. I, by doing this, missed out on so much. I had a chance to get to know my Grandpa Hermann Sauer. I could have hugged him, loved him and got much love in return. I let my fear rob me of this. And now, a little too late, I felt shame and guilt to have acted this way.

When Mom and I came home on the day of Grandpa's passing, the good neighbor Mrs. Haag stopped us in the stairwell, telling us Grandpa stepped into eternity this afternoon. She said she was sure that he wanted to be with Grandma and she didn't have to wait long for him to join her.

She believed he got up from the sofa in the kitchen to get something and he fell. Then when she came to check on him and saw what happened, she called for her husband to come to help her. He came up the stairs and they managed to take grandpa from the kitchen to the bedroom. Then all that was left for them to do was to wait for our return. They were sorry to give us such sad news. I heard mom say thank you for all the help they gave us. And they told us how much they liked grandpa and they were glad that they could be of help. Again, mom said thank you and told them we did not want to stay home this night. After Mom and I went upstairs she was the one going to the bedroom to see her Dad. I waited in the kitchen for her. Then we turned around, got on the train to Berlin, Zehlendorf to be with Mom's sister Berta. Eight weeks ago, she came to tell us we had lost Grandma. Not too much later we stood at her door telling her and the family about losing the other one.

Tears flowed but this time all of us sat and cried. I cried after going to bed. I had to sleep with my cousin Waltraut. We both cried till we fell asleep. Mom and Aunt Berta talked into the wee hours of the night. Both loved their Dad and tomorrow they needed to let the rest of the family know. For the Sauer's kids, all six of them, sad times continued.

Chapter Twenty-Nine

The service for Grandpa was just as nice and meaningful as it was for Grandma. Grandma's favorite song "Ave Maria" sounded as beautiful for him as it did for her. Again, we were thankful to the neighbors that gave us so much help. We had a family living on the floor below us and next to Mr. and Mrs. Haag that owned a funeral home. They pitched in for Grandpa with Grandma and now for Mom taking care of her dad. We had helping hands all around us. And in times after the war this was a blessing to have. The neighbors that gave us help knew the Sauers family, better than Mom and I did. Sitting all the years in a bomb shelter under the house together made them not just neighbors They had become close friends. One cared for the other one. And in our time of need they came to us with open hands. They showed their love and respect for their neighbor and their family. We were fortunate to be looked after this well by all of them. Leaving the small Chapel, the family met at the cemetery in Berlin, Kreuzberg. Grandpa found his resting place there, right next to his wife Emilie Sauer. We knew he would be happy to be reunited and this for all eternity.

With the family standing there hugging and talking, Aunt Erna, Mom's youngest sister, walked down the road to look at the names on each tombstone. On one she found her first name. She called my mom to show her. She said to her, "Look, Ellie, here is my name. I think it means I might be next to die."

She didn't know how true this was. At the age of thirty-six and the youngest in the Sauer family, she was next to leave and to be missed. She was young, pretty, fun to have around, full of life and she had not any children.

She wanted to have children. For some reason that only God knew about, she was not able to carry a baby full term She was the aunt to nephews and nieces that loved her. We would remember her for the fun and all the love she gave us. Her smile, her laughter was catching and being with her meant to catch up on all the smiles we didn't smile when we could or should have smiled. When she passed, she was cremated and shared the cemetery plot with her parents. She was the last to be born in this family but, after the death of her parents, the first to join them.

In the days, the month before her untimely death, when Aunt Erna came to visit, it was noticed she could not see well. The small dog she had was leading her around. Instead of her taking him out for a walk, the dog was taking her for the walk. She depended on the small dog to be her seeing-eye dog. Going for the eye examinations more than just once, they found a tumor pressing on the nerve of her eyes. They removed it and the surgery was done by a well-known doctor. His name was Professor Doctor Sauerbruch. He couldn't give her the eyesight back, but it took care of the pressure that was building up in her head. A plate needed to be placed into her head after such a surgery. Actually, only half of her skull was removed, however nothing she needed was available after the war. She and everyone in the family knew it was only a matter of time and she joined her parents.

It was her brother that had the means to take care of her. Meaning Emil and Lene Sauer agreed to be her caregivers and they did it with love and devotion till God called her away. Now she and her parents rested in the same plot at the cemetery in Berlin, Kreuzberg. Being the youngest in the Sauer family she had a close relationship with her parents. It was right for her to rest with them. She had the feeling or is it called a premonition, when they all stood together at the cemetery that she would be next. And with this too, she was right.

We thought it was odd that Aunt Erna had the strong feeling she would die young. Because after Grandpa's graveside service she found her first name Erna on a marker not far from his grave. She came back grabbed my mom by the arm and showed it to her and me. Saying lightly, that maybe she would be next. Now after this service for her, we went looking for Erna's name just a few graves away from my grandparents. We looked and looked, not on any of the markers left or right or around the corner could Mom and I find her name. We went from one row to the other and couldn't find it. It was like it had never been there in the first place. None of the adjoining graves showed signs of disturbance of any kind. They all looked like they have been there for a long time. Mom looked at me after the search and said, we must have imagined it was there! On the way home, I was deep in thought, but did not tell my mother what I was thinking. No, we didn't imagine anything, her name had been there. There was not any explaining this, but I knew it had been there.

Strange things happened in our family after the death of my grandparents. This with Aunt Erna was just one happening we all believed was odd. Every one of Mom's family had their own story to tell. I was listening and believed all of them.

On the marker for my grandparents was carved "Hermann and Emilie Sauer and daughter Erna Kraemer. May they rest in peace." Their birth dates and the dates when they died was carved in the stone. When we came visiting, we always went looking for the other Erna. But she was gone and she stayed gone.

Living in town only fifteen minutes away from the cemetery, we went there often. Always in the evening after Mom's working hours. A flower vendor stood at the gate and when we had money to spare, we bought a bundle. It became a ritual looking for the other Erna we knew should be there but wasn't. We couldn't find her. Only our Erna was there next to Grandpa and Grandma. The other Erna's name was not found, no matter how hard we searched for her. And believe me that Mom and I did not give up looking. Checking the records, it showed that our Erna was the only one resting in this area of the cemetery. Odd, we thought, odd and very, very strange.

Uncle Emil came for a visit, he told Mom something incredible that happened to him and his wife after Grandpa's funeral service. He told mom that he woke up at night and heard the front door to their apartment open. He heard a choir sing a song and the name of it was "Mir ist erbarmung wiederfahren, erbarmung derer Ich nicht wert. In translation "I was given forgiveness." Forgiveness that I didn't deserve. Uncle Emil said he didn't get up to see about this. This happening, as unnatural as it was for him, it seemed natural to hear this. The next morning, he wanted to talk with Aunt Lene his wife about it. He wanted to know if she heard what he did. He asked if she heard anything unusual in the middle of the night. She answered, yes, she did. He asked if she heard the choir singing this song. She shook her head no, she didn't. But what she heard and my Uncle didn't. She heard the front door to their apartment open and footsteps of many people entering it. But unlike Uncle Emil, she didn't hear the song. The stories my family told were amazing to hear. And I believed all of them. For me it had one wonderful meaning. My Grandpa Hermann Sauer was in heaven and was doing fine. Because for whatever he needed the forgiveness for, God gave it to him.

Chapter Thirty

Time moved on. I had to switch schools and make new friends. I needed to go to school close to our apartment. And now that we have left Berlin - Schlachtensee because Aunt Friedchen and family came back, our new address was at Berlin - Friedenaú, Handjerystrasse 62. All the way up to the fourth floor then make a left turn and this was our permanent address and home from now on. From my brothers, there was still not one sign of life. Dad and his second wife divorced. I felt very sorry for him but glad he was free of her. I never knew or understood what he saw in her. Mom kept her feelings about all this to herself. But if she would say anything it might be, "Franz, I could have told you so."

Dad moved out of the apartment he had shared and rented a small room. He stayed in the East sector of Berlin. This proved itself, with the passing of time, to be a big mistake. A huge mistake.

I was now a teenager. I looked like one, my braids had been cut and I did what other teenagers did. I wanted to wear a little makeup and Mom said no to all of it. But in time, I won her over to my side and she let me use lipstick and mascara for my eyes. I was always a good student with responsibilities at home and had very little free time to myself. I acted out like kids my age did at times and because of it, she put me in my place right away, always letting me know she was the boss. I did not get away with giving her a lip. No matter how old I was, Mom would give me a slap or sometimes two. She said it was her right to correct me, because she was my mom.

When the weather was nice in spring, summer, or fall, we liked going for long evening walks. When we went by a burned down building and we saw a flower growing among all the rubble, we stopped to look and Mom said "New life is sprouting up. We are all going to make it." And make it, we did. On the walks we took, we still passed by many ruins of burned down buildings. It was taking time to clear the evidence of this five-year war away. It was hard work with having to borrow money from other Nations to rebuild this city. Or to rebuild all of the country. After that, Germany needed to get busy and repay the loan to them. This too would take a long time. Mom and I had long serious conversations, trying to reason things out. Sometimes, we had silly conversations, like what would we do if we had lots of money? She and I could come up with lots of things to do if we were fortunate to be rich. This kind of talk between me and my Mom was fun, because both of us had a vivid imagination. I loved these kinds of walks and talks with her and wanted to have more of them. But she worked all the time and not often did we get to take such interesting and fun walks together.

One day the long-awaited Red Cross card came to the mailbox, telling us that Erwin was alive and the past years he was a war prisoner in Russia. He wrote he hoped to be released one day (but he didn't know when that would be) and return home. The card had been censored and a lot of his writing was marked out in black ink. But praise God, we knew about one of my brothers. Now we were waiting and praying to hear from Edgar.

The days went by and Mom, Dad and I lived for what the mailman dropped through the mail slot. Much on the card coming from Erwin was blacked out. We tried many ways to find a way to read what was under the black marking but we couldn't. We held it up to the light bulb to decipher what was blacked out. Holding it over light steam from the tea kettle was another way we tried, then gently wiping it. Nothing would let us see what was under the black ink. We gave up and read only what the card allowed for us to read. All the while, there was still not any sign from Edgar.

West Berlin was slowly coming to life and developing a new heart beat. Ruins from the war were there but restaurants played music. Germany started to make after-the-war films. Coca-Cola was a favorite drink. Ice cream parlors did good business in the west part of Berlin. Amusement parks with roller coaster rides and other fun things opened up. They came out of nowhere to Berlin. Where have they been hiding all this time?

American soldiers dated German girls. In the British-French sector of town it was the same. The other side called the East side looked different. It was like night and day. The West was coming out from under and it looked like the people living in the East were still looking to find a way to come out from under. We in the West had hope, while in the East they were still waiting and praying for it.

Dad lived over there in the east part and started to work for a newspaper. He could give us bits and pieces of information before the news came out over the radio or in print. We only shook our head because there was such a difference between the West and the East.

Dad was earning money but I do not think he gave Mom any of it. She might not have asked him for any. She always worked and was always depending on what she by herself could earn. But working this hard made her sick. It was the middle of the night when I went for help. At the end of the street was a doctor. It was the same doctor

Grandpa had called when Grandma was sick. He made house calls.

I ran over to his apartment house; the large door was not locked even though it was in the night. I made it up the stairs, rang the doorbell and told him about Mom. He got dressed and came with me. Mom was very sick and he told me she needed hospital care right away. He left me and made sure an ambulance came and took Mom away.

We had a friendly neighbor. We called her Mrs. Lichtenberg. She rented a room down at the end of the hall from us. She got out of bed and we took a trolley to try to follow the ambulance to the hospital. We couldn't follow as the ambulance drove faster and didn't need to make stops at a trolley station to pick up other passengers. Why we couldn't ride with them was what we were asking ourselves. But this is neither here nor there, the point I am trying to make is they didn't take us along. I didn't have any money. Mrs. Lichtenberg did not just pay for her fare, she also paid for mine. She asked if I would be alright with Mom being in the hospital. I told her yes, that I could manage. I was not about to show her I was afraid. I just said when Dad came by, we would figure it out together and I knew he would be there for Mom and for me.

She just answered, "I hope you are right but if you need anything, knock on my door. I will help you if I can." I promised I would but I was thinking I hope I wouldn't have to do this. I believed she had already done much for us in this one night. She was elderly, in her mid-70th and out with me on a very cold night. I would be the one wanting to check on her in the next few days instead of it being the other way around. I owed her and I knew it. I was so grateful to have had her help. I was depending on Dad to stop by, but with him working for the newspaper I didn't know when his next visit would be. I hoped it would be soon because we needed him.

Chapter Thirty-One

I did not think of going to the school to let the teacher know why I would have to miss coming. All I knew and wanted to do was to take care of my mom. We were in deep, deep trouble. It was the time of year when the weather got cold. Before leaving Mom at the hospital I was told Mom had double pneumonia. She was very sick and her fever was high and she would go through a crisis. She would either live or she could die. All I prayed for was for her to live.

I was informed by one of the hospitals staff that I was to help with meals for her. Whatever I could bring was appreciated as the hospital's kitchen didn't function 100%. I panicked when I heard this, as our kitchen at home also didn't function at 100% capacity. Mom and I had to find ways to make do and stretch what little we had. Or to do without till we found a way around this problem. Surprisingly we always managed somehow. Mom's saying was, only with the help from above did we manage. I thought of this when I was told I was to bring food for Mom to the hospital. I felt desperate and really prayed desperately for the help from above.

The little storage room next to the kitchen had hardly any wood and coal. Living in town, we couldn't go out like we did living at Aunt Friedchen's house, and go to the woods and cutdown a tree. When we had zero to do with and not any money for buying, we stayed at zero, wishing and dreaming for a warm apartment and food to eat. This was the way it was when my mother got sick. When I got home that night and said thank you and good night to Mrs. Lichtenberg, I checked the cupboards.

I found that I had a loaf of bread, margarine and some sugar. On top of the kitchen stove stood a two-burner small gas stove. This became my helper in my time of need. In the room next to the kitchen, I found a large enough tin can. I placed it over the flame of one of the gas burners and it gave me heat. If I stayed to the front part of the room, it did very well. By the window it was cold. So cold that any liquid left in a cup overnight by morning turned to ice.

I kept the door to the bedroom closed and slept on a sofa Mom had by the kitchen wall. The same one Grandpa slept on when he moved us in with him. I had overcome my fear knowing both of my grandparents died in this apartment. Mom had worked in it, turning it into our home by changing a few things around. She told me my grandparents are wanting for us to live in their place and are now watching over us. Watching over us as our guardian angels.

Hearing this and believing it, took the fear away from me and some of the guilt I felt when I left him to stay all alone. That I did this really put a guilt complex on me. Staying with Mom at her work instead of being with my Grandpa when I could have, after he passed made me feel so bad and so sad. Mom later told me that he forgave me for having been so afraid. Now I was able be all alone and sleeping on the same sofa he used without any kind of fear at all. When I got up in the morning, I knew I need to hurry to visit Mom and bring her whatever we had to eat. I took a few slices of brown bread and spread margarine on top.

I wrapped this up in newspaper, there was nothing else to wrap it in. I put the iron skillet on top of one of the gas burners and melted sugar. When it cooled standing by the cold kitchen window, I broke it up with a hammer. It looked like pieces of brown broken glass but was like eating candy. I thought this would be good for her.

Now I needed to see, since I would be on foot, what I had to wear to keep me warm. My coat was flimsy. My shoes had holes on the bottom. Mom put paper inside to keep the wet away from my feet, if it was possible. It didn't help much. The paper took on the moisture and my feet got cold and wet anyways.

I looked and looked around and saw Mom's rabbit fur jacket she got from her mother hanging on a coat hook by the door leading to the storage room that should have held coal and firewood but didn't. I knew I needed to wear it. Mom was taller than me and her jacket made a nice coat for me. It would give me the warmth I needed to make the long walk to the hospital. Going through some things in the bedroom, I was delighted to find a pair of house shoes from my Grandma Emilie Sauer. They were made from a study material and with paper stuffing in the toes made me the nicest pair of boots to wear.

Before I left, I made sure the gas burner was turned off. Then with the goodies wrapped in newspaper, I was on the way to see Mom. For Dad, I left a note on the kitchen table so he would know to come and look for us. When he came to visit, he rang the doorbell even though he had a key. With us not opening to let him in, I was sure he would use the key and find the note. I really needed his help.

For me to go to his place of work or where he lived to tell him was almost impossible. It was too far away from our place to both places. Besides this, I was on foot. There was not any money for trolley fare to and from the hospital or other places. And I was not about to ask my nice neighbor for a hand out. She already paid one fare for me. I had to wait till dad came my way and I hoped I wouldn't have to wait for too long. Every time I saw Mom, I could see she was not getting any better. I stayed with her most of the day and left for home when it was dark. I wanted to make every second count being with her. The doctor said she needed a reason to want to live. And since my brothers couldn't be it, I needed to be the reason for her to want to go on. She needed to know how much I loved and needed her so she would fight for her life.

While I was with her, I sat next to her bed. If she would let me, I held her hand. We talked a little. She said, "Dad will come and if he does not, because of work, you must go to Aunt Berta." I knew she was worried about me and wanted for me to go and see her sister. I did not have the heart to say, "What money do I use?" I knew her purse was empty. She had gotten sick before the payday came around.

So, when the bell rang and a nurse came around to tell everybody to leave, I went home, avoiding patrol cars and other obstacles that can be harmful to a girl like me. I jumped into bomb craters. I hid in the ruins of burned down houses to avoid any kind of danger that could be waiting for a young girl like me. And with an angel that must have been sitting on my shoulder, I always reached home. I warmed the apartment in my usual way, tin can over one of the gas burners, wiped hands and face and brushed my teeth with hand soap. It all works when there isn't any toothpaste.

I ate a slice of bread or I cooked a soup with flour and sugar. Yes, grateful I was to have found some flour in a tin canister set. I learned from Mom how to do this and it was called Kriegs-suppe. In other words, a soup we cooked often going through the war, when food was limited. Wartime soup is the translation for what we ate often when the cupboard was bare. And when we sat down to eat it, Mom reminded me to be grateful for having it. And this is what I was, now for having found flour in the tin can.

The note for Dad was still on the kitchen table. He had not had the time to get away from his place of work. He would be surprised to find that Mom had to hospitalized and that I had to manage things on my own. When he came, he would know that we needed his help. I, for one, was waiting for him, eagerly waiting for him.

On this night before going to bed the doorbell rang. I went to open the door and expected to see my Dad standing there. But it was not him. Something, or better said, someone better than Dad stood outside the apartment door. Tall, slim and handsome, with a smile on his face and glad to be home stood my big brother Edgar. He was the right medicine our mom needed to get well. Seeing him would give her the strength to want to get well. In my heart I knew Edgar was the miracle Mom needed to want to live. And he was my miracle too. He was alive, he came home and he would know what we needed to do for mom. I was so happy to see him. I was so happy not to be alone anymore. Edgar went to bed in Mom's bed in the bedroom. I warned him that this room would be very cold. But he didn't care about this. He said the featherbed would keep him warm enough, I didn't have to worry about him. When I laid down on the sofa in the kitchen, I folded my hands and said, "Thank you."

Chapter Thirty-Two

Edgar didn't have any money; we both walked to the hospital the next day. Edgar said he would go to see dad and get some money from him to help us over the rough spots. Oh, my God, when Mom saw Edgar, her eyes lit up like the lights on a Christmas tree. They talked for a long time. He told us he was for two years a war prisoner in a French prison camp. France being so close to Germany he tried to get away four times, only to get caught and put back in again. The next break-out he did it. With the help of a train conductor, riding in the caboose, he made it all the way to Berlin. Just in time. I am not sure our mother would have made it with just me at home. She needed something extra and God supplied us with it when He helped Edgar to come home.

A few weeks later, she was released. The struggle to survive continued. She was not well enough to go back to work. More rest was needed. She got it because Edgar went to look for employment and found it. He knew how to drive a car, as during the war he was the driver for German officers. A hotel owner hired him to drive for him and important hotel guests.

Now there was Mom, Dad, Edgar and me in our family. But we were not complete because Erwin was still a prisoner in Russia. We waited for mail. Every Red Cross card was read over and over. Now it was Edgar holding it up to the light fixture in the kitchen. Studying the marked-out writing, searching for a secret sign that told us more about Erwin.

Whatever he wanted for us to know about him, the Russians marked through it with black ink. No matter how hard we tried to decipher what was under the black ink, we could not. We could only read what was allowed for us to read. After a while we got tired of staring at it and we gave up. When the next card came, we were at it again with always the same result. We were driving each other crazy trying to figure out what was under the black mark out. We told Edgar ever since the first card from Erwin we have been trying the impossible. Now he was home and doing it with us, but it got us nowhere and left us all with a headache.

Oh, before our mother was released from the hospital, I had to stay with Aunt Berta for a while. Edgar, after coming home and seeing Mom, went to visit Dad and only came back to me for one day. He gave me some money Dad must have given him. This gave me trolley or train money. He told me that till Mom came home, he wanted to stay with Dad. This was alright with me because I believed they had much to talk about. I guess they did not worry about me, as I was by this time a bit over thirteen years old. I still had to make the daily visits with Mom and I kept after it. I kept after it 'til I ran out of sugar to make the skillet candy. I ran out of flour to make the wartime soup that kept me going.

Then the hospital was forced to do for Mom what I couldn't do any more. When this happened, Mom told me it was time for me to go and see her sister Berta and family. I was to tell her about mom's hospital stay and Edgar's coming home and staying with Dad. I listened to her and was now doing as I was told. I remember I took the train to Berlin - Zehlendorf to see my Aunt Berta and her family.

It was so good sitting in a warm kitchen and see my cousins Traudel and Ischa and Uncle Werner. I didn't ask if I could stay with them, but when it was time for me to leave for home, I stood up and could not walk very well. I fell on my face and I needed help to get up. After removing Grandma's house shoes, Aunt Berta saw how discolored my feet looked. She said I was not going home. I needed help. Looking at my feet and what I saw looked so bad it even scared me. After seeing this, I wanted to stay.

Every day, I took a foot bath in lamp oil till my feet looked normal. My Aunt went to see Mom and she took care of things. I was a happy girl knowing all was getting better and the credit belonged to my aunt and her family. She took good care of me till Mom was ready to come home and take over.

All this time I didn't think of school and the consequences I would have to face. I was absent and this was something not allowed without the signature letter by a parent or guardian. There was a price to pay for not attending. Someone from the school office came by the apartment the day after all of us got home. We did have some explaining to do. I was told not to delay but get to school as soon as possible. This I did not have a problem with at all. And the circumstances we had gave me the excuse why I stayed away for so long.

Dressed and cleaned up nice, being on my best behavior I went and faced my homeroom teacher and the principal in his office. A note from Mom was a great help. I think that my teacher and the principal understood how difficult this has been for our family. They gave me all the help I needed to catch up. I brought home arm loads of homework every single day. I was not good in math but Dad was. He pitched in and between the two of us, I brought home a good grade. Thankful was I to have such smart and helpful parents. And Edgar was there. What they didn't help me with, he could and would.

The time came when Mom went back to work. Edgar helped with the income every month. Dad did whatever he could, whenever he could. And my brother Edgar did what was best for him. He liked his job and he liked meeting with important people. Because he drove for this hotel in Berlin - Wannsee he had the chance to meet all kinds of people, from actors to prize fighters and so forth. He made friends and of course he had girlfriends. When he had a weekend to himself you would find him on the dance floor, swinging a pretty young lady around.

At home, he told us about his social adventures but he was not interested in any of the young ladies he met. The only interest he showed was in having a pretty dancing partner. When a young lady got to serious with him, he came by to pick me up. He had me fix my long hair in an older hairstyle, told me to wear some lipstick and in the boss's car he took me with him.

One of the girls worked at the laundry facility for this hotel. When Edgar dropped off the laundry, she opened the door. Edgar came out from there with a smile as she had questions for him. Who is this young girl in the car, was one of them. I asked, "Well, what did you say to her?" He gave me a smile and said, "You are the boss's daughter and I was to take you out for an afternoon drive." Whatever else followed between them, I did not want to know or hear about. I only knew he used me as the out when he thought a friendship was getting too serious for him. I felt sorry for the young lady but after the war, prison time served in France, my older brother was not ready to want to settle down. One day he would, but for right now he just wanted to enjoy his life.

Mom and I liked having him living with us. We enjoyed it when he told us about his friends and that he found favor with the young ladies. Because, like his mother in her younger years, he was fun and a terrific dancer. With all of this going on, another year went by and Christmas was around the corner.

Chapter Thirty-Three

From what we could see in West Berlin, the Christmas traffic was doing well. The stores we had started, ever so slowly, showing their goods. The store windows showed Christmas decorations looking so pretty that standing on the outside was fun. We walked from window to window and looked and looked but did not have the money for buying anything. It was a meager Christmas for the Weiss family.

Edgar, Mom and Dad did what they could but somehow, we needed more to cover the needs a family has. Came a bill collector to our door. The gas and electricity meters were in the hallway. It was the neighbor Mrs. Lichtenberg that let them in to read them. When they knocked on our kitchen door to collect the money we owed, if I was at home, I was not to open the door. We knew they would come back for a second time and we hoped to have the money by then to pay them.

Since I came home from school between three and four p.m. and the family came around six p.m. for Edgar and sometimes way later for Mom, I had the job I disliked so much. It was for me to keep the door and my mouth shut. How often did I stand behind this door, holding my breath, wishing I was older and able to go to work? I wanted to help with the household finances. When I voiced it to my mother, she said not to wish my life away. Enjoy your young years. Other responsibilities you will have to carry on your shoulders soon enough. I understood the truth in her words but at the moment this didn't help us much.

I heard kids in my class talking and daring to make a wish list for Christmas. I was not one of them. If I could have written one, it had as number one, Erwin home with us. A warm fire in the kitchen stove and food to stretch over the holidays, till the end of the month.

The clothing we wore we bought at a thrift store, including Dad's and Edgar's. When I looked at my brother, he wore what he had with flare. No matter what he wore, he always looked tall, and with his dark hair and light eyes, very handsome. So handsome, that one fine day a photographer stopped him on the street. He asked to take his picture and wanted to display it in his store window. For this he was given a free eight by ten photo of himself. Edgar was game and obliged the man. Sure enough, a few days later we stood in front of the store window and Edgar's photo was looking at us from behind the glass. Edgar went inside and came out with the promised photo in his hand. My handsome brother was grinning from ear to ear. He looked mighty pleased with himself.

When the date showed it was the 24th day of December, we had nothing and only each other. It's hard to believe with everyone working, we had so little. It was a struggle for us to make ends meet. I heard my brother say he needed to move on. It was not right for him to be still living at home with his mom and little sister.

When, on the 24th of December at 6 p.m., the church bells proclaimed it was Holy Eve, Mom took the axe to two of the kitchen chairs and made firewood out of them. If we needed, we would do the same with the other two. For the next days after Christmas, a tin can over one of the gas burners would provide the warmth we needed. I did it when Mom was in the hospital and it could be done again. It kept at least the kitchen warm for us.

For Christmas dinner, we ate a few jars of applesauce. Dad was responsible for this Christmas meal. He bought a few boxes of applesauce in the East sector and planned on selling them in the West sector at the black market for more money. With the money he made from it, he was then able to buy other needed items. He brought them to us and stored them in the storage room of the kitchen. With us being so hungry, we took from him a few jars and hoped he would understand why we did it. His pockets had less money when we ate six jars of what he wanted to sell. However, we were sure, knowing how hungry we were, he would not mind that we helped us to a full tummy. After all, was it not Holy Eve?

After we ate, we sat by the warm stove waiting for Dad to come. When he didn't show up by 8 p.m., we knew he would come on Christmas day. It was a custom in my hometown, to put candles in the windows for the ones that were still missing because of World War II. Edgar, Mom and I bundled up to brave the cold winter air while walking through the dark streets. We didn't need the light of the few street lamps at Handjerystrasse 62. They didn't burn as bright as all the candles in every window. It was beautiful, yet a sad sight to see.

Mom said it was Germany's hope that in the coming years the candles would get less and less as the loved ones returned home. She said all families wanted for their husbands, sons and fathers to return home. It was our wish this included Erwin for our family. Mom again spoke. She said it was also a sad fact that some continued to place candles till they came to the realization that their family member was gone forever.

For such families, with all hope gone, not any candles will grace the windows anymore. But another candle might replace it. It will burn like the eternal flame and forever light up their heart. Love and memories will keep this flame burning bright. Then Edgar, Mom and I took a long look at the windows. We turned around and, cold as it was, walked slowly home. We thought of Erwin and maybe the next Holy Eve, our window would be dark because he came home from Russia.

Christmas day Dad came. In his hand was the Red Cross card from Erwin. The Christmas greeting went to his address. Erwin knew he would bring it to us. Mom, after all of us read it, tucked it in between the Christmas branches in a vase. This was our tree. Besides a few bulbs and tinsel, Erwin's card was the best decoration.

We didn't have cookies or cake but Dad bought some bread and in both of his coat pockets, he had a few potatoes. His briefcase had a pound of flour, sugar and coffee. He must have made a stop at the black market on the way to see us. The stores closed for Christmas but the black market did not believe in taking a holiday.

Dad spent some of his money and was our Santa Claus. He pulled the potatoes out of the coat pockets, and handed them to mom. Grinning he said, he didn't want to put them in the case with the paperwork in it. Mom grinned too saying, first washing them would have helped. Dad grinned back at her and lit up his pipe. He was home with us and there was food on the table, thanks to Dad.

We sat on Christmas day with a cup of afternoon coffee, looking out of the kitchen window at the tall church steeple that we knew was built by Hermann Sauer, Mom's dad and my grandpa. It was peaceful and we had hope of better things to come for this family with the incoming new year.

New Year's Eve went by with just Mom, Dad and I sitting together. Edgar went to a dance. At the hotel where he worked was a New Year's Eve party. He had the invite from his employer to come and have fun. Besides this, he told us he was making plans to leave. He wanted to be on his own. He needed more from life and did not see this happening for him in Berlin. He had not set a date yet for his departure, but I knew already how much we would miss him.

Chapter Thirty-Four

Berlin went through unrest with politics, groups in street fights and snatchings of people from the West to the East sector of Berlin. All of it was seen as the after results from World War II. My birthday came and went by. Not much to do was made over me being one year older. I continued to do well in school and not much fuss was made over this. It was expected of me to do well.

On one such morning, my brother dressed, came out of the bedroom with a suitcase in hand telling us he was leaving. He was going back to France to hire on in the coal mines. He heard from a friend this job paid well. If he could make it over there, he would help us by sending some money.

The surprise showed in Mom's face because his going away must have been a spur of the moment decision. She was definitely not happy with the way he was leaving us. And for me, with his going, he took also some of the fun away I was having. I would miss him so very much. He wouldn't come anymore to pick me up so I could pretend to be the boss's daughter. Together we scared his unwanted girlfriends away. It was fun to pretend I was older then what I really was. Yes, with his leaving, I would have less fun from now on. But there were other things I would miss about him. The fun fights he had with mom over little things that made her mad and later they laughed about it. He could get our Mom going with what he spouted off to her. Mom asked him what money he would use to get back to France. He laughed and said, "Mom, I go back in the same I came to Berlin. Jumping on the train and hiding away in the caboose." As he came, the same way Edgar left again. All that was required of us, was to say God bless you and to wish him good luck on his next adventure. We had to let my big brother go to live his life the way he was meant to live it. His sudden departure was hard on Mom. I am not sure about Dad. But Edgar was close to 30 years old, Dad might say he needed to strike out on his own.

Now we three waited to hear from him to have a safe arrival in France. After a few weeks a letter came. He made it and found work in the mines. His address was Faulquemont, France. Knowing him the way we did, he was a go getter and would be alright.

We thought of Erwin, when would the Russians let him go? For us in Berlin, bad times reared their ugly head again. The Russians had closed the borders, cutting off all food supply for West Berlin. We knew it was to put pressure on the Western Nations, to get from them whatever it was they had in mind. A way had to be found to get food for 2.5 million West Berliners. This was not an easy task and it was the topic on the table for the big guys.

It was President Harry S. Truman that came up with a solution to the problem. He was the feisty one in the group of important people and he would not let the Russians scare him. He started, with the help and agreement of the others, the so well-known Berlin Airlift. It started in 1948. Much was always on the table when dealing with the Russian government. The Western Nations were always kept on their toes by them. But they found ways out of a difficult situation and, by doing this, avoided what could be another war.

A lot of talk was going around among the people of what could or should have been done different. But the West Berliners came around in their thinking that the Western Powers did what was right for them. They had the admirations of almost 2.5 million people. Mom and I were cheering them on all the way, from the first day the Airlift started.

Chapter Thirty-Five

Living on the fourth floor, right under the roof, when the first planes roared over the top, Mom and I fell to the kitchen floor, face down. The war came to mind for both of us. We thought bombs would drop and with the noise of the planes, it transported us back in a hurry to the World War Two.

For only a few seconds we stayed face down to the floor. Then we realized the planes were not killing machines but they were the help that was given to us, to keep us alive. We got up and said there was nothing we needed to be afraid of anymore. Once we were enemies, now we needed to be friends. Every five minutes a plane flew over the roof in the direction of Tempelhof Airport.

Many people found work by unloading the planes and also doing fast repair work on the runways. Women poured tar into the holes to keep the planes coming and going. It was an enormous sacrifice made by everyone working together on the Berlin Airlift.

Berliners unloading coal and flour at Templehof. 1948

Again, we formed lines in front of stores. Again, we had to pull the belt tight. For Mom and I this was not a hardship. We had not had the luxury like others, to loosen the belt. For us, it was some more of the same.

Dad came by as always to visit. Nothing changed there. My parents shared the news with each other that came out of Russia. From Edgar, we got mail about once a month. He was not a letter writer but he did it, to keep us clued in with what he was doing. He wrote he was working and found a room to rent in Faulquemont with a family he liked. What was of interest to us three, the Geib family had a pretty daughter and, in his letters, he spoke of her. Money that he wanted to help us with never got to our mailbox.

And by now, we had made adjustments. We were good at adjusting to difficult circumstances. And when we did it well, we felt kind of proud that we managed for one more time.

The next mail we got from Edgar shocked us, a nurse had to write it for him. He had an accident at work. When he drilled, some of the coal went into his eyes. He must not have had protective eye covering. He said in the letter not to worry, he has not lost his eyesight. He needed to heal and the Geib family and the nurses at the hospital in St. Avold treated him well. If we had the money to visit him, we would have wanted to go there and Edgar knew this of us. Even if we had to hide away in a caboose like he did to get there, we would have wanted to try to be with him somehow. But with the Russians acting up, the only way out of Berlin was by plane. And we really did not have the means for this.

We wrote a letter back to him and said to please be more careful. We let him know in our mail that nothing had changed for Erwin. He was still kept by the Ruskies in mother Russia. We wrote 'much to our hurting heart' he was still there. We also wrote we still tried to decipher what was under the black markings of the Red Cross card when we got one. Crazy for us, but we kept trying and getting zero result.

The Airlift was in full swing. The pilots flew their planes around the clock. We had gotten used to the noise day and night. It became music to the ears of every West Berliner. Living under the roof on the fourth floor, we had a little space out by the kitchen window I could stand on it. It was kind of like a small balcony but open not closed in. I did this whenever I felt like it. And me standing out there, it scared my mom a little.

The planes flew so close coming in for a landing at Airport Tempelhof, that you could almost make out the faces of the pilots. Mom fussed at me when I did this as the noise was deafening and the house shook a little. The dust came down from the ceiling that Grandpa had covered up with plyboards. And you better not leave anything uncovered standing on the table. Dust, dust would fall over everything.

Mom and I used the dust cloth every day and we had a hard time keeping the apartment clean. But grateful was all of West Berlin to the Western Nations. To take care of 2.5 million people was an enormous undertaking and it cost almost 70 lives. English and American pilots and the crews gave their lives for their one time enemy. One plane crashed not far away from us into the apartment building. We heard the noise and knew immediately something terrible had happened. The papers reported every bit of news and we mourned the loss of lives.

Every time that is difficult and is recorded in history, has its heroes. One man became this for us children of West Berlin. His name and rank in 1948 were Lt Gail S. Halvorsen. He became best known as Berlin's Chocolate Pilot. Another name for him was The Candy Bomber. And the name I liked more was Uncle Wiggly Wings.

This name was appropriate as Lt. Halvorsen promised to wiggle the wings of his plane before releasing a flood of parachutes from his aircraft with candy attached. The children at Airport Tempelhof waited every day for this from the first moment they met him. Their meeting was meant to be, this is my belief.

What I learned about this meeting between him and the Berlin of children is this: Flying to Berlin, coming from Frankfurt, he was having a bit of free time on his hands. He made his way over to the kids he saw standing behind a barbwire fence. He met them and admired them for not begging anything from him. Later he said that to have freedom meant more to them than anything he could have given them. This was the belief of Lt. Halvorsen at the time of meeting these boys and girls.

Walking away from them, he remembered the two sticks of gum he had in his pockets. He took them out and went back to give this to them. He wished he had more, but this was all he had and he wanted for them to have it. He divided the gum up into four pieces up and gave it to them. He showed them it was something for them to stick in their mouth. They pinched pieces of off it and handed them from one to the other And, when all of it was gone with nothing but the silver wrappings left, they handed this from one to the other to smell it. He made himself understood that the next day he would bring more to give them. They should come back and wait for his plane. To know it was his plane and there would be a candy drop, he gave them to understand he would wiggle the wings of his plane. With this gesture of a kind heart, it started a love story between the children of Berlin and this American pilot. In 1948, a Lt. Halvorsen, with the children of West Berlin, walked together into history.

June 1948. First and original picture of children at fence at Tempelhof.

The news picked up the story of the pilot and the crew. He was called by the ones in rank above him, to give answers to them. What was he doing and why was he doing it? He thought he would be reprimanded and he was pleasantly surprised when they gave him their support. Candy companies in the U.S.A gave a big helping hand and soon what he was doing was given a name. It was called "Operation Little Vittles." It had the right name. The parachutes dropped from his plane became gifts of love from the American people for the children of West Berlin.

1948 C-54 Dropping candy on Berlin.

Chapter Thirty-Six

Being older, I was 14 years old, and reading all the news I could lay my hands on. When there was a new article in the paper about all the children gathering in Tempelhof, Mom just said our friend is being talked about again. There are times when I shut myself away from the real world. It was hard for me to see other families prosper when my family was at a standstill. I think I was envious of what others had and could do, when we couldn't do a smidgen of what they did. When I brought it up to Mom, she reminded me what I was doing was not nice. I knew she was right in correcting me the way she did. When I tried talking with her about my feelings, she seemed to turn a deaf ear to me many times.

Then I approached my dad. My Papa as I called him. He would listen to me with both ears wide open. He seemed always to be there for me when my mom couldn't. When he answered me, he said, "You know, you telling all this to your mother might make her feel bad. Because she is working so hard in your behalf and even mine," he said. "Then when one of us complains, this must really be upsetting for her." My goodness that I couldn't think of this and Dad needed to tell me this, it made me again feeling ashamed of myself. I wanted to be careful and watch what I said from now on. My mom deserved better than what I gave her. Somehow, I wanted to find a way to make it up to her. If I only knew what I could do for her. Apologize was first on my list, hugging her if she lets me was second. Mom was not brought up getting a lot of hugs from her parents. This was the reason she didn't give out many. Dad was the all-time hugger and I inherited the liking for hugs from him. Coming home one night, she said they were let go from their jobs

She was now among the many jobless getting unemployment checks. The money was not enough to live on and not small enough to die from. I seriously wanted to stop going to school and enter the workforce. I had not thought about what a girl of my age could do but I believed the employment office had advice for someone like me. Every time I started this conversation with my parents, they said a firm no.

In this, I found Dad was in Mom's corner and it threw me a little because most of the time I could bring Dad around to my way of thinking. But not this time. I was at odds with both of them. The minute I tried to open my mouth, both of them said, "Don't start with us. You already know the answer."

Without being able to talk with my parents, I crawled into my dream world more and more. In this world was not any cold or hunger with bill collectors knocking on the door. This world became my world and I hid in it often. In it, I was a young girl, wearing pretty clothes and was also allowed to wear makeup. Whatever job I had paid well and my family and I had nothing to worry about.

In the real world around me, Mom treated me to money to see a movie now and then. The leading ladies like Jane Russell, Betty Grable, Esther Williams and so on and so on became my and every German girl's role models. We imitated them and, like the Hollywood star Marlene Dietrich, we shaved the eyebrows off. We put bright red lipstick on to look more like Debbie Reynolds. We German girls wanted to give the Hollywood stars a run for their money.

This was my dream world and to shaving my brows and wearing lipstick, Mom said no. She said we did not have the money for such things, all of this was only foolishness. I heard what Mom said, but I kept on dreaming that I was somebody else. I wanted to be someone else but not be Dagmar Weiss anymore. Growing up was hard and it became harder and harder for me to live in the real world. Because in it I had to face the real me. The girl that had holes on the bottom of her shoes and wore clothes bought in the hand me down stores. In my dream world I was pretty. I had pretty clothes to wear, I used makeup like all the other girls. And more important than all the other things, I had a job that earned money Yes, I liked living in this world that became more real to me than the world that was around me.

My mom must have had an extra good day and was in a good mood. She surprised me by giving me a library card. I was in heaven and I went there often to pick out many good books. I really didn't have too much time for reading. It had to be done after my homework and household chores. When we sat down to our evening meal, a stew or a soup of some kind, Mom and I read while we ate. Spooning the food into our mouths, both of us had our nose in a book. Looking at my mom sitting across the table from me the thought hit me. Maybe, she too needed to escape the real world now and then. Maybe even more than I did. Nothing was made easy for her, it was always work and more work for her. And here I sat worrying about the shoes and clothes and not having what my friends had. I was ashamed of myself when I looked at her and saw the strands of grey in her hair. The rough hands she had from all the hard work she had done. Again, I had the wishful thinking that she should say yes and let me go to work and help out a little.

Instead, I learned from the library books about romance between two people that liked each other. I learned about the Wild West, Indians and cowboys. Sheriffs keeping the law, going after the outlaws and bringing them to justice. I was amazed by what I could learn from books. The Cold War was raging in Berlin and we read about other things not pleasant at all. This brought me and my family back to the realization we are in the years after World War II. And nothing was going well.

The bright spot for me was the name Lt. Gail S. Halvorsen and that he became the Ambassador of Goodwill with the candy parachute drops he continued to make. Mom and I thought of him as the Easter Bunny or Santa Claus wearing a military uniform. What a blessing he was to all the children that waited daily for him at Airport Tempelhof. I, however, was not one of them. Too many responsibilities kept me away.

On a sunny day, it must have been a weekend, Mom sent me on an errand. It was a nice warm day with the sun shining in my eyes. It blinded me and I blinked a lot; the matter of fact, the sun was so bright I had a hard time keeping my eyes open. I walked by the house on Handjerystrasse that was the crash site of the plane and its crew. I stopped there for a few minutes and said a prayer for all flying the Berlin Airlift. With my eyes down to the sidewalk, I continued the walk, walking towards West Berlin City Park and the city hall.

In Schoenberg's city hall the Freedom Bell was hanging. Chiming every hour on the hour. A gift from the U.S.A. to the people, the brave people of West Berlin. With the help of the Western Nations, we could be brave because they, too, were brave. We had no choice but to be brave. So, again, we stood in line outside the stores. Again, we heard it said, "Sorry, we sold out. Please come back tomorrow." Yes, times were tough but we, the citizens of West Berlin, we had to be tougher.

I walked slowly down the sidewalk and was enjoying the sunshine and hanging after my own thoughts when I noticed that a way up from me, something was laying on the ground. Coming close to it, I saw it was a parachute that still had something sweet attached to it. The chute was stepped on and dirty. I didn't care about that but kept my eyes on the sweet gift that was mine for the taking. It was chocolate and in the process of melting because of the warm sun.

I stood there looking at it and knew who had dropped it from his airplane. None other than Lt. Halvorsen and his crew. A gust of wind must have carried it in my direction. I knew what was laying on the sidewalk was meant for me. Looking around, I saw I was all alone and no one was watching me from the apartment windows. Not at all shy, I bent down and helped myself to this special treat. Knowing that a Lt. Gail S. Halvorsen and his flight crew had dropped it to the street made me smile. It made me extremely happy that I was the finder of something this special. I was eager to do the errand for Mom, then rush home and tell her all about this.

For me, this was the second time I was given chocolate by an American, in the most unusual way. The first time was right after the war, in the old church in Schlachtensee on Holy Eve. It was the miracle story I told everyone about since 1945. Now, I had a second miracle story to add to the first. And this one, none other than the well-known Berlin Chocolate Pilot and his crew was responsible for.

I was standing in the sunshine, loving the taste of chocolate in my mouth, I made up my mind never to forget how I was introduced, and by whom, to the sweet taste of chocolate. I thought in the coming years I could remember this kindness. I wanted somehow to make it a tradition in my home, when I was old enough to have one of my own, to give away chocolate as a gift. This would help me to remember the hard times my family had and how they had to work to make it better. It would be a constant reminder of the many helping hands God provided Germany in our time of need.

I stood there, thinking all of this, I could hear the planes fly above me, one by one, delivering food, medicine, coal or whatever to the Airport Tempelhof. Among them was the plane of Lt. Gail. S. Halvorson and I just ate and enjoyed his gift, that was meant to be mine. I thought, "God, bless all the helping hands and give the pilots and crews safe landings.

A few minutes before my find of the parachute, I stood by the house and the damage talked to me of precious lives lost that did their duty to help us West Berliners. I slowly continued on my walk. I think it was to check on apartments and the cost of them at West Berlin City Hall. We had my grandparents' and were lucky to have it. However, it was in bad shape with the roof damage from the war. If we could, we needed to try to better ourselves. This is what Mom wanted for me to check on.

I went to one of the offices at City Hall, I was shown a list of all the people looking for apartments and I knew we didn't have a chance. The name Weiss, starting with the letter W, placed us to the bottom of the listing for apartments. Besides, I saw that the monthly income required for something new made this not possible for Mom and for me.

I was disappointed and knew Mom would be too. Being faced with this made me wish to leave school and to pitch in to better our situation. Why would Mom and Dad not show themselves reasonable about this? This was so frustrating for me. I knew if I looked around, there had to be a job for a girl like me. With all these wants and wishes in my head, I reached home.

Taking two steps up at a time, I made it to the fourth floor and leaned on the doorbell. Mom opened and I pushed past her into the kitchen. I had so much to tell her, it was all bubbling out of me, nonstop. When I told her about my find on the sidewalk, she was glad for me. I was waiting to hear her scold me because I picked it off the dirty pavement and ate it. But, no, she didn't do this.

Chapter Thirty-Seven

Now, every day, Mom, Dad and I read about the progress that was made by our allied friends. They flew in everything for West Berlin using three airways. Gatow, Tegel and Tempelhof. Tons and tons were their planes' cargo. They did not give up on us. And, come hell or high water, the West Berliners didn't give up on them.

Dad was told by me about my adventure on this sunny day and, like Mom, he was pleased. Dad came more often to see us. He was my biggest support when it came to any school projects. He was good in math and I could always rely on his help. I only needed to wait for him to come by at the right time to be able to assist me. When this did not happen, I got a lesser grade. Dad would grin and say anyone is allowed to make mistakes now and then. Yes, but we should not allow for it to happen often.

It always made an impression on me that Dad remained cool, calm and collected whenever I messed up. However, Mom was not like this. She lost it and got very upset with me. Mom also was a cigarette smoker and when she was out of them, she became very irritated. I was the one around to have to put up with it. Later, Mom was sorry and would try to smooth it over with me. I understood her. I always did understand what was going on with her. Everything she did was for somebody else, not much did she do for herself, except to smoke these awful smelling cigarettes. The way I saw it, it was the only gift she gave herself. I understood that the way I needed food, the same way she needed cigarettes. Back then I didn't have a word for why she smoked so much. Today I call it addiction. I did not care if she was irritated, cranky, unreasonable or whatever she was without the smokes, I loved my Mom.

I understood she needed the cigarette like I needed food, water, sunshine and fresh air. Dad smoked a pipe. When he came, he shared his tobacco and she rolled her own cigarettes with paper on a small machine she had. She also had a small pipe just made for ladies. It always made me smile seeing her puff on this tiny thing.

The up and down days we went through finally made Mom think about my offer to stop going to school. She was now ready to take me up on it. My teachers made us aware of me leaving without a grade card of my school years completed, I would have nothing to show that I had been their so-called super star student. I was alright with it. What we went through on a daily basis needed to stop.

The Cold War continued. We stood in food lines getting food or leaving empty handed. The planes flew every five minutes over the rooftops of West Berlin. Every West Berliner being grateful to hear the roaring noise of them coming and going. And I knew that somewhere way up there, my hero was continuing his flying "Operation Little Vittles." Now, it was time for us to think of how to put vittles on our table.

I found a place at Biering's Restaurant working in the kitchen as a helper for the cook. Sixty D-Marks a month was what I earned. I started my shift at noon and I worked till 10 p.m. A meal was included as my pay. I was happy I could pay the apartment rent, it was forty a month, and Mom had twenty extra for household use. I was paid fifteen D-Marks every end of the week. Now I knew I was not a little girl anymore. I was Dagmar Weiss, a grown-up young lady and holding my own end up in our small family. This I wanted to do for a long time, to make it a little easier on my mother.

When I mentioned this to Mom she said, "Why are you so determined to be a grown up? You will still have a ways to go to fill the grown-up shoes you are so anxious to wear. Just you wait and see." And with this, our talk about my employment at Biering's was over. With what Mom said, she cut me down to size when I got too big for my britches. My work started on a Monday, being the underage worker, I was having Saturdays and Sundays off.

Mom and I were making use of this Saturday before I started a job to do fun things. Meaning visiting with family and window shopping. Well, window looking for us. We still had to leave the going shopping to others. We didn't mind. We hoped that one day in the near future, we too would be among the shoppers.

We made it a long Saturday and left the apartment early. We visited in Schlachtensee with Mom's sister Friedchen. We saw what she did with the house and the garden around it. We visited with the Leder family next door and other neighbors who had been in hiding under the rooftop with us after the war. All of them were doing well and going on with their life. The little twin Mr. and Mrs. Leder foster parented was found by her parents and Mr. and Mrs. Leder kept in touch with them.

On the way home toward the evening, Mom got off the train at Wilmersdorf and we strolled home. Coming down Handjerystrasse, Mom passed by the house to make a stop at the corner bakery shop. Maybe they did not sell out and still had a loaf left for us. We stopped and we were so fortunate we did not have to leave empty handed. We got there around closing time and this must have been 6 or 6:30 p.m. But lucky for us, the baker was not all sold out.

Chapter Thirty-Eight

With our evening meal wrapped in wax paper and a smile on our faces, Mom and I entered the house Handjerystrasse 62 and started the climb of many, many steps up to the fourth floor. We didn't turn on the light. The evening sun was giving us enough light through the long stairwell windows to see. As we made our way up, someone was making his or her way down. The steps coming down sounded slow and heavy. Mom and I came up to the second-floor window, that's when we saw him.

There, in a ray of the evening sunlight stood a tall, slender figure. My brother Erwin, the son and brother Mom and I had been praying for, for such a long time. He was home. I will never forget this, the evening sun behind him framed his tall, handsome figure and the Russian fur cap he wore made him look even taller. Not saying a word, standing like a shadow figure in the sun, stood the one we have been waiting for since 1945. He was home. Oh, he was really, really home.

I had to grab my Mom as she looked not steady on her feet. We both made it up the extra steps to hug him hello. Tears filled Erwin's eyes and Mom and I shed rivers of tears. Grateful tears because the unwilling wanderer was released from the Russian war prisoner camp to be home with his family. Dad would know as soon as he stopped by. What a surprise this would be for him. And Edgar would right away get a letter saying come home if you can, because your brother Erwin is here.

Climbing up the rest of the stairs was not easy. I clutched the loaf of bread under one arm holding onto Mom with the other. She was shaking so bad that Erwin had to take her arm and I stepped behind her. With him holding onto her and me guiding her from behind, we got her to the fourth floor. When we got to the inside, we turned the light on and looked at Erwin. There he stood dressed very poorly. He had a heavy coat over his clothing and wore the large fur hat he called a babushka. He was thin in his face and body and with the wooden soled shoes, he looked very, very frail and tall.

The wonderful smile on his face to be home said it all. What Mom and I felt cannot in any way be put into words. Mom's boy, my handsome brother, was home. We felt that God blessed us not to lose anyone in World War II.

This Christmas, Mom and I didn't have to walk the street to see the candles in all the windows for the ones that are still missing. Our family was blessed to have each other. The window of the Weiss family would this Christmas show not any candle light. On the inside of our small place, it would tell a different story. Candles in white and red are placed between the evergreen branches of tinsel and pretty Christmas bulbs. The red candles for family love and the white showed us grateful for the miracles God gave the Franz and Elisabeth Weiss family.

We might have suffered loss of our possessions, but many had suffered such losses. We were rich, very, very rich because after the war we were still one whole family. I had so many thoughts going through my head while I was looking at my brother. The last family member that had been missing in the family circle for many years. He was now home. What a blessing, what a miracle this was for us to experience.

Erwin went into the cold bedroom to clean up a bit by sponge bathing. We all had to do this kind of clean up, as we didn't have a tub. We couldn't worry about this. This we called having small concerns. All this falls into place when a family works together as a team. When we mentioned to him it was kind of cold in the bedroom and we should go there so he could strip down and wash in the warm kitchen he laughed and said, no, no. He said, after mastering the Russian winters, washing down in a cold bedroom was child's play. Coming out all clean and still smiling, Erwin saw the cupboards in the kitchen looked kind of bare. This didn't matter to him or us. We had a loaf of bread we bought at the store and after Mom blessed the bread by making the sign of the cross with a knife on the back of it, we sat with Erwin under the kitchen light at the table. Like always, we thought tomorrow would take care of itself as far as food was concerned. And with the Lord's help, it always did.

We ate our first meal with him. The first with for us in four years. A couple of slices of bread and a couple of cups of coffee, Erwin said, made this meal served by his mother's hands a feast for him. We had all day Sunday to talk and he needed to fill us in on the past years.

I was glad I had a job starting this Monday. All of this came at the right time. Erwin would go looking for work but first he needed some loving and tender care from Mom. It would take a while before he could go to work. His mental state and his body needed help.

The following day, Sunday afternoon when Dad came, Mom let him come in not saying a word about Erwin. The look on Dad's face when he saw Erwin was amazing. I would call it priceless. First, he looked like he wanted to cry. Then he looked like he wanted smile but he didn't dare. The third look was of unbelief that he saw what he saw. He wiped his eyes with his hands and took one more look. When he realized that what he saw was for real, there was no holding him. He went to his son and placed his arms around him saying, "Welcome home. I am so glad you made it home." We saw that Dad was all choked up and very emotional to have his boy home at last.

Like he always did, Mom and I saw him reach for his pipe, filling and smoking it. One thumb was placed through the suspenders, the other was holding the old, worn out pipe. Smoking and smiling, our dad walked back and forth in the small kitchen. He was smiling as he puffed and walked, happy with the world around him. The son that was gone and seemed lost to him and Mom was home to stay.

Erwin survived the war prisoners' camps in Russia and little by little he shared the survival story with us. He told us leaving us behind in Rietschutz and making it back to his unit was done with many unexpected detours. When he got there all was in an uproar and total confusion. It was clear that the war was over with everyone wanting to go their own way.

He said all he wanted was to get back to us if he could. But what he was facing with all the others was to become a prisoner. He didn't want it to be the Russians but rather wanted the Americans to be his prison guards. It was for him to find a way from Warsaw back to the American lines. He found as his only and welcome transportation a grey donkey and a cart. He and his grey friend traveled at night. In the day time they found a place to hide and rest a while.

How he and the donkey managed to eat and drink in this time, we didn't ask about. Come to think of it, we didn't ask Erwin about any of this. And Erwin, as far as I can remember, never saw a need to say something to us about it. He and the donkey must have lived off the land or gotten handouts from farm people. Germans that wanted to help a young soldier make it home to his family.

He was on foot, traveling only by night, and a day came along when he had a decision to make. To move on or to stay. He decided to stay. Erwin heard noises coming from a crater a bomb had made. Someone was down there and was hurt. Looking down in this hole in the ground, he found a wounded soldier. He knew he and the donkey had reached the end of the line. He crawled down into the hole to be company for a wounded comrade.

Looking at him he knew he could not do anything for him. Only talk with him and hope talking with him helped somehow. Erwin felt if this soldier was going to die, he should not be left all alone. And if help came, it was help for both of them. The donkey and cart were now in plain view, standing at the top of the bomb crater. It should get some attention from someone. Either from the Russian or from the American side. Preferred by my brother was the American, of course.

When help arrived, all of them wore the American uniform. His wounded buddy was brought up first and got medical help. After he was well taken care of, it was Erwin's turn. Crawling up out of the hole in the ground, trying to hold his hands behind his head, he gave up and became a war prisoner. He felt alright being in American hands. Now knowing he made it all the way to the American lines, he felt better.

We now wanted to know, at least I did, what happened to the donkey? My brother laughed and said, he was taken prisoner too but after looking him over and finding him not to be the enemy, he was set free. He had the good fortune to be fed and water given and maybe had a warm stall to sleep in. Or maybe he was given to a German farmer that still had a barn standing and this became his home. Erwin said he wanted the best for his grey four-legged friend.

Then he was taken to join the others standing behind the barbed wire fences. All of them wondering what was going to happen to them. Soon Erwin found out. However, what was in store for him was not good. He was set apart from the other prisoners and was told since he wore the SS uniform and fought against Russia, he needed to be turned over to them. This, for my brother walking all the kilometers to reach the American lines, was bad news.

When he told us about this we agreed, it was a scary outcome for Erwin, who tried by donkey and cart to reach the American lines. It made the kilometers he and the four-legged friend placed behind them into nothing. He might as well have stayed where he was at in the first place.

After a few days being held and sheltered by the Americans, the march started for many prisoners to the train that transported them away from home. Erwin explained what poor conditions they were in. Sick, not able to hold their head up or walk, they were moved along the road under guard. What I am not sure of anymore are what kind of guards? American or Russian guards? Because what happened next surly didn't happen with having Americans to guard them. Surely not! He said so many fell and needed help from the one walking next to them. If no one could be of help, shots were heard. Everyone knew one of theirs just died.

Erwin said while shaking his head, a war can tell an ugly story, a very, very sad one. The ones able to walk knew there was only so much they could do. It was their goal to stay alive, to make it. When they made it to the train, they were treated like cattle. It was a cattle train that hauled them to Russia. When they arrived under difficulty, they called this place a suitable name. It was called Hell.

No one knew for how long they would be there. For some, it was meant to come home like my brother Erwin did. And many, he said, many of them never did. He was one that, for some reason only God knew, made it back to family and waiting friends. Friends that made it through the war like he did. We learned after searching for them, they lived in the East sector of Berlin under the Russian rule book.

Chapter Thirty-Nine

I started my new job at Biering's and I liked working. Erwin gained back some strength and looked for employment and for his old friends. He found both. With the Airlift in full swing, he hired on unloading the incoming planes. Time off he met with his friend Hans Leus to exchange views on the situations in East and West Berlin and what they thought was Berlin's future.

When I found the time to visit with them, I loved the stories about what they did as boys and how much trouble they got into being policemen's brats. They made their dads' hair stand up on end, so they told me. A fun time I had when I heard this. Some of it was news for our Mom. Too much news for Mom's too sensitive ears. I heard her say over and over, "Erwin, how did this pass by me? I didn't know you boys did all of this and you got away with it."

Hearing this made Erwin laugh. He said, "Mom, you have not any idea what Edgar and I and the gang did. Policeman's kids got away with much in those days, till our dads got wind of it. Then we all were called on the carpet and we paid for it." I believed my brother's story. He and Edgar pulled a few with me. Like putting a string around my loose tooth and fasten it to the kitchen door handle. When someone yanked the door open, it was to pull out my tooth. I screamed and screamed tied to the handle and the two of them standing on the other side laughed and laughed. Oh, yes, I remembered how they laughed and I cried and cried.

Or, when I woke up from sleep in a dark room and at the foot end of my bed a bright light moved around and booing sounds made me wet my PJ's. I thought I had a ghost in my room. Yes, ghosts by the name of Edgar and Erwin with a large flashlight in their hands. These two scared me so bad that I lost my voice and wet my pants. I remembered it well. Yes, I believed every single story he told us about the boyhood pranks. Now, being twenty-seven or twenty-eight years old, it was much too late for Mom to spank them.

Erwin worked, Dad worked, Mom picked work up here and there. Nothing was steady work, at the end of it an unemployment check was always waiting. As for me, I liked being a working girl. I was liked by everyone I worked with except by one important person. The boss's wife. From the time she met me, she had something against me. It must have been my youth. She criticized me every chance she had. The way I looked, the way I walked, talked and worked. I could not do anything right, no matter how much I tried to please her. I was to get off work at ten pm, but it was more like midnight when I left the restaurant for home. Mr. Biering entertained friends after he closed the front door. Most of the time, they wanted something from the kitchen to eat. The Cook always left on time. But I was handy to stay later living so close by. Without questioning, I worked for Mr. Biering and his guests.

When I came home from work, Mom was still awake, but my brother went to bed. He had to be at Tempelhof Airport very early for his shift. Mom put her hands to work to surprise me, two aprons for me. Two nice, hand-sewn aprons to keep me clean from the dirty work in the restaurant kitchen. I liked them and was proud of what Mom made for me. She did a fine job stitching them out of leftover material she had.

The cook often tried to help me by talking with Mrs. Biering and getting her thoughts going in another direction. Sometimes it worked, other times it didn't. When my employer's wife saw me wearing my new aprons, she promptly started in on me.

Mrs. Biering made fun of me and made me cry. I tried to hide it from her that she got to me. Sometimes, in this small kitchen, there was not any getting away from her. I was aware of how little we had. This was the reason I came to work for Biering's. I thought, "Alright, next time she starts it again, I will try to speak up. Maybe I could say the cook's outer wear was provided by the restaurant and maybe mine should be too." Mom and I would always appreciate such a help. Then see what comes from it.

Telling Erwin and my mother about this, they stood behind me, they said to show her a stiff upper lip. If anyone could do it, they said it was me. I told them that it was embarrassing the way this woman talked with me. She has a way of looking at me and with her words and actions was always putting me down.

The days went by and the cook and I became a team. When she left the kitchen for a moment, the cook told me to let it roll off me and not take it so hard. Everyone knew that for some reason she was after me. I think Mr. Biering knew it too but didn't do anything about it. To top it off, he started to let me walk his wife home before my work at the restaurant was over. He didn't want for his wife to walk the dark streets of Berlin home at 10:00 p.m. at night while he at midnight closed up the place. But I, a fourteen-year-old girl, was alright to walk around in the dark. What an odd way to think and do for an employer with his young employee.

I was so glad to earn money; I would do what it takes to keep my job. So, if it meant to walk a fussy person home at night, I saw it as part of my job. I was getting paid for it. The walks worked out well for me. Mrs. Biering opened up to me. I saw how very unhappy she was. She and Mr. Biering never had children and now over sixty some years old, Mr. Biering had a much younger girlfriend. He let me walk his wife home instead of her waiting on him and then for them to go home together. He closed the place and then visited his girlfriend. I started to feel sorry for Mrs. Biering. I understood she was hurt and why she must dislike young people. On these walks we became friends. She let up on me and from this moment she became a welcome visitor in the busy kitchen. If she didn't show up, the cook and I missed her.

Chapter Forty

Then one morning Erwin told us about his most embarrassing time or moment in Russia. My work started at noon and it gave me time to have a talk with my brother. We heard the planes fly overhead every five minutes on their way to the Airport Tempelhof. This morning Erwin was not there to help to unload them. He had to see a doctor to get much needed help.

Since he came home his tall, thin build had changed. He looked more like a heavyweight boxer. He was bloated looking and all of it was water. When pinching his leg, it left a hole in the skin that stayed for a while. This meant his body carried fluids. He needed to see the doctor that has always taken care of us. He came to help my grandparents and my mom when she got sick. We called him our family doctor.

The doctor saw him and said the water from his body needed to be withdrawn. He came home from Russia extremely undernourished, even the smallest amount of food more than what he got in there worked against him. If it was not withdrawn, it could go up to his heart and kill him. The same killed Grandpa Hermann Sauer in 1945-1946. Eight weeks before Grandpa, our Grandma died. But she passed from something besides water in her system. As if it was in our hands to decide about it, but we didn't want to have any more death in our family. It was for Erwin to listen to the doctor and us. He was told by Mom to grit his teeth and fight the good fight. He must want to win it, he was home with us. He needed to shake off Russia and overcome. God sent him home, surely to do well and to go on living his life.

Erwin asked me to sit down a few minutes what he wanted to tell me wouldn't take very long. So before taking of for work I relaxed a few minutes to hear what my brother wanted to share with me. I watched when he slurped the awful tasting cup of coffee. It had plenty of sugar in it but was still pretty awful. He said with a little smile he knew this doctor would do better with him than the woman doctor that checked the prisoners in good old "Mother Russia". He looked at me and said it was not fun to have to stand undressed in long rows in front of her and she walked by pinching their backside. I said what? She pinched your backside? You must be kidding! But no, my brother was not kidding me.

He said all of them worked for farmers or had mine work in Russia. Working for a farmer was the better of the two jobs. In the mines, when someone was sick, they cut off a toe or finger to get hospital care. They knew that the woman doctor, by pinching their behind, would declare them fit to work if they were or not. Erwin grinned when he explained, to have a soft or flabby backside in Russia gave the prisoners much needed bedrest.

He knew the doctor he saw this morning would do well by him. Tomorrow he would be at work at Airport Tempelhof doing his part for the Berlin Airlift. The Western Nations and the Berlin citizens were hard at work to show Stalin and Russia what they were made of. And with this combined effort, it established a bond of friendship and mutual respect. The West Berliners hoped it would last for a lifetime.

It took some time for Erwin to be totally himself. But little by little, Erwin let go of the memories he had of Russia. At my place of work, everyone wanted to hear his story. On the way to take Mrs. Biering back to her home, she squeezed me like a lemon to hear what my brother had to say. She cried, walking next to me, when I told her that at meal time the prisoners drilled each other's addresses into their head and heart. If one of them was fortunate to be released to go home, it was his mission to visit the family of the table partner he had in Russia. This was a solemn promise they all gave to each other.

Well, Erwin said, he sat at a meal, when all of the sudden his partner's head dropped into the bowl. This man died sitting next to him and was, like many others, buried in Russian soil. When this happened, my brother told us that he realized something had taken its toll on him on the inside. Instead of being sad that his buddy died, he was angry. Because with him, all the information died that my brother gave to him.

Erwin said he felt upset that this man dared to die. With him he took Erwin's hope of getting information to us should he be set free before he was. This made him very upset. He told me when he realized what feelings he had, his heart had turned hard and the only thing still working was his brain. It told him he needed to do what it took to survive Russia and come home. If this happened, he wanted to visit this man's family. He said he remembered his address and it was something he still needed to do. Well, he did it before during the war years, when he came to Berlin to face a fallen friend's family. Now he needed to do it one more time and bring sad news to a waiting family. It was a hard duty to perform but it would bring closure to this family. A lot of families didn't get this. They waited and hoped and wondered. It is best when a family finds closure and to a degree moves on by knowing the truth.

Reaching Mrs. Biering's house, I told her the rest of my brother's story. Erwin said that he asked God to help him to pray. Since he came to Russia and Russia was a place called Hell, no one prayed. At least no one told him that they prayed. It was their belief since they entered Hell, God had forgotten about them. Hell was a place that God couldn't enter. He only entered Paradise.

Erwin seemed to remember the Bible teachings about this. Then another realization hit him. The realization that they all lived in a man-made Hell and only prayer could deliver all the prisoners from this. Every day he turned his thoughts into a prayer and slowly he started to hope.

By this time, Mrs. Biering was crying and I was too. She told me to tell my brother she was glad his ordeal was behind him and she wished him the very best. Now that I saw my employer's wife safely home, I turned around, wiped my tears away and ran through the dimly lit streets home. Tomorrow was another work day. Maybe by then I had some more to tell her of my brother Erwin's journey back from Hell.

Chapter Forty-One

When the family came by for a visit, Erwin and I were usually at work. We didn't get to see them often but they never showed up empty handed. They left us with veggies and fruit from their gardens. By eating much better, we knew Mom's brother Emil or her sister Friedchen came by for a visit.

It seemed that Dad had more money in his pocket, yet we knew he hadn't changed jobs. Nor did he tell us of any promotion. Mom and he came to Biering's when I was at work. The cook and I fixed them a meal. A meal they ordered from the daily menu. I learned to decorate the plates before they left the kitchen. For my parents I decorated them extra nice. Maybe by giving the plate more fresh parsley with a lemon slice, or cucumber with tomato slices. It all depended what they ordered in the way I decorated their plates. When my folks sat at a small table, they liked the view to the kitchen door. This way when they saw me, I waved at them and they waved back. They waited for me to get off work, then we walked the short way around the corner to the house together. Going home, Mom and Dad were feeling well. They had a full tummy because of the good the meal they ate. And with it they each had at least two glasses of wine. Well maybe three but then who was counting?

Our Dad really did have more money in his pockets and he said he earned it by working for a friend. We learned later, much later, that he worked in secret writing propaganda leaflets for the newspaper he worked for. When Erwin and I visited him on a Saturday afternoon, we found him being kept under lock and key in one of the paper's secret rooms. Yes, now we knew why his job paid well.

Dad was part of a circle of people the paper used to set people straight about the goings on in the East part of Berlin. We only went to see him one time and we never went back again. The less information we had, the better it was for us.

When Mom ran out of money before it was my payday, she came by the back door of the restaurant. Then I needed to get a head start on my weekly pay. She ran short on money pretty often. Her being a heavy smoker did not help much, but what could I say to my mom about this? Not much I was able to say, not much I able to do about this habit she had. My brother Erwin also smoked. So did Edgar when he was home. Dad smoked a pipe and the only non-smoker was me, and I wanted to keep it this way.

To help mom, I started to clean the ashtrays at work and took the cigarettes, the butts, home. She could open them and smoke the tobacco in the small pipe she had. Again, I was embarrassed by this, just like I was when we walked behind someone on a street waiting for this someone to fling the cigarette away so I could hurry and pick it up. I wanted to get away from having to do this. But when would this time come for me? Come to think of it, I had a lot of nasty work to do while I worked at Biering's.

It was my duty before going home from work, to clean the kitchen and the restrooms. Cleaning the restrooms was enough for me to lose the dinner I ate earlier. Then there were the people that made snide remarks to a young girl like me. I told myself all this was happening because I worked in a place like this. In this place I met all kinds of people. They were either friendly or over the top unfriendly. The friendly I liked. The unfriendly I learned to ignore. I told myself I was lucky to have this job after all it is our own fault; didn't Mom and I pick it? We walked with our eyes wide open into this job situation. So, at times, I had to put up with bad behavior from someone that had too way much to drink.

I was not yet sixteen years old when my boss, Mr. Biering, had to tell his grabby friends to leave me alone. When I signed on to work, it was with our understanding I was to learn about the restaurant business so one day I was able to open a place of my own. I had not any want in me to be the owner of such an establishment. To own or to waitress or be the hostess in a place like this was not my cup of tea.

I kept telling myself when my ship came in, I would know it. I would leave all this behind me, but hang on tight and sail into the sunset. Or better yet, I would sail the seven seas to see the world. This was my dream, to travel and see the world from one end to the other. It was not a dream of mine to take care of people that delighted in drinking too much. I learned while working in a place like this, it would never be in the cards for me to want to own a restaurant. No, no, none of this was for me.

In all the days that followed, we kept our noses to the grindstone. Erwin worked at Tempelhof unloading the planes. I kept my hands in the dishwater and working on being grateful and being cheerful. Dad came by after he had a payday and made Mom's purse richer by extra numbers of D Marks. He knew that she was still getting the on and off again unemployment checks, we only didn't know for how much longer. Besides, she still looked frail and sick. She should not even think of wanting to work. But this was Mom, she was the eternal go-getter.

Chapter Forty-Two

When we needed new clothing, the second-hand store got the money. The clothes we bought were not new, they were used clothing, but they were new for us. Erwin boasted he gave the store free and good advertising. He wore the shirts, pants and jackets with such elegance and flare. Not to forget to add charm to the mix. I can say this with all honesty, I thought of my brother as being movie star handsome. So was Edgar, the tall, dark and handsome Romeo of the Weiss family. Edgar wrote whenever got a vacation he was planning to make it home to have the reunion with his brother. He looked forward to seeing us again. Well, it goes without saying, so did we.

Hand in hand we worked through the days. Having hope and strength renewed as the Western Powers fought for the City of Berlin, West Berlin with its 2.5 million people. On the 12th of May 1949 the Soviet Union ended its blockade of West Berlin. They instigated it on the 24th of June, 1948 and ended it on the 12th of May in 1949.

So, the roaring of propellers stopped and the silence that followed was very welcome. It took a while to get used to the silence in the sky, but we did get used to it. What was hard to deal with that, after the blockade was lifted, the Cold War continued. With this we went toward another Holy Eve on the 24th of December and the 25th was Christmas day.

Christmas was the perfect time to sit together with Erwin telling us of the miracle that came his way when he didn't believe in miracles any more. We sat, Mom, Dad and I, to listen how he learned in Russia to pray and believe again. Here is what he shared with us:

He said it was a shock when the man that sat next to him for many weeks died right in front of him. Everything they talked about in case one went home before the other did died with him. Erwin needed to look for another partner and start with him from the beginning. He said he felt angry that the man slipped away quietly and died. With thoughts like this came the realization there was something very wrong with him to feel this way.

He knew way deep down inside of him, that to act this way when someone passed away was wrong. He said the way he felt made him feel ashamed and he wanted to make a change and this change needed to be made this very minute. He thought he needed to believe and to pray again, like he did when he was a boy. And maybe there were others wanting to do the same. He realized that the prison years in Russia did damage to him to the point that he wanted to give up and throw in the towel. But he said his head and what was still left of his heart told him this was wrong to do. It was the worst he could do.

The key to get home was by prayer. He talked with the others and they all meant to say a prayer every day. Erwin thought that with this kind of help in his corner, he might find his way back to believing again. He forgot what he believed in when he was a boy and he needed to get back to it. Starting by praying to someone who has always been in charge over the human race was a stepping stone for him. He became a praying man for him and the others that wanted to survive Russia and make it home. In this Russian prison camp, he started a prayer chain that made all of them believe it was going to bring them home.

Erwin spoke slow when he said, we all knew when we came to Russia that we lived in a man-made Hell. But it was man made and not like the other in the Bible. There was not any way to get out of the Bible kind of hell. But with the man-made Hell, there was a chance the door could open. And prayer was the key that fit the lock. Erwin said they had nothing to lose and they had much to gain by giving prayers. It all started with him and caught on with all the other prisoners. They were all homesick for their families. Prayer may be the ticket to set them free and bring them home.

After a while, Erwin got up and sat down on the wooden box that held coal and wood for the stove in the kitchen. He placed both elbows on his knees, pressing his fists against the face. He looked at the floor as he continued to speak. Saying food got less and less and if something fell down from the ceiling, it was seen as added meat.

When the camp got smaller and smaller, they were transferred to another camp. After one of those transfers, all had to work in a mine. Erwin said it was odd, there was not a place for them to escape to, but they had to wear ankle bracelets while working underground. Soon he saw that they worked together with Russian workers and they, of course, were free men, working a long day with German war prisoners as partners.

It was one of the Russian men that came up to him and gave him to understand that he knew him. He knew him and wanted to help him. And help him he did by feeding Erwin raw potatoes every day. He brought them with him in the pockets of the work jacket he wore. Erwin learned to depend on the kindness of this young Russian as a coworker and as a friend. To Erwin, this young man was a God send. A God sent helper working next to him under the ground.

We asked Erwin how could this Russian know you? With a tiny smile Erwin went on to say this young man was part of the group that hid in a cave in Finland. After several failed tries from the SS for them to give up, it was Erwin that made the last effort and it worked. If they had not listened, a flame thrower was to kill all of them. Erwin said they came out with their hands held up, a sign of surrendering. He then offered them a cigarette and kind of tapped them on the shoulders as he went from one to the other. Then they were taken away.

For this Erwin was decorated with the Iron Cross Second Class. He said he was proud of this medal that he received for saving lives. The other medal on his uniform made him shiver. It was the Hand-to-Hand Combat Medal and he earned it for staying alive when his opponent died.

Erwin looked at us and said how in the world could he know when he saved this young man in Finland, that at the end of the war they would change places. They would meet working under the ground, the Russian as a free man and he would be the prisoner. Now this young man, day by day, returned the favor of feeding Erwin whatever he had to keep him going.

Not every day did they work next to each other, other times he had a different partner. Erwin said when this happened, he could count on his friend Ivan to find him. Still smiling when he told us about his friend Ivan he said, "You see? God hears all prayers. Help came to me in a dark place when I and other prisoners entered the mine." Ivan for him was the light at the end of the tunnel. He represented the God light for my brother Erwin and all the others.

Coming from this place, he was released to come home. Erwin looked at us and said in a low sounding voice, "I would have like to have thanked Ivan for what he did for me but I didn't have the chance. I went to work with Ivan and he, all this time, he fed me. Then one day the trucks rolled into camp and took me and others away. All of us had not any idea that we would be leaving or that we had the good fortune to go home."

He said he was sure that Ivan would ask about what happened to him and get some answers. Erwin nodded when he said we were two men so different from one another but yet in many ways so much alike. We spoke a different language and to communicate was by hand signals. But we understood each other very well He said, smiling and thinking of Ivan, we the one-time enemies by the circumstances we were in, we became very good friends.

Chapter Forty-Three

We sat with Erwin for a long time. Thinking of what he just shared with us, we didn't speak a word. What he had said took a hold in our minds and hearts. We too believed that the Lord hears every prayer. When Erwin and all the others started to pray, he sent Ivan to Erwin as his instrument to show compassion and love. Erwin had many such stories to tell. He found in us good listeners and I made up my mind not to forget any of them.

I was grateful that he made it home from Russia. This place, this Hell as he called it, was now behind him. A long time we sat next to Erwin, it was getting dark outside. All of us having thoughts of how amazing it was that he was sitting next to us this Christmas. Not a candle we placed in the window this year for the still missing. Ours came home. In a little while we put coats and jackets on and walk the street to look up at each window that held a candle. Now we prayed that God would help them, like he helped both of my brothers to return to their homeland, family and friends.

Here at home we West Berliners had another war to fight and to win. It was called the Cold War. Every day we kept busy, helping the Western Powers fight this war. For our family, and most of all for Erwin, life became more normal. Every day we had a routine to go through and it was up and at it and get ready for another work day.

While meeting with friends, Erwin met a young lady and they took a liking to each other. She was a window having lost her husband at the end of the war. She had not any children and alone like she was, she was free to love again. Her name was Hildegard Treulieb and she and

Erwin became a couple. They didn't have in mind to marry but wanted to support each other.

She had a nice place to live and Erwin moved in with Hildegard. Her husband must have been the same size as my brother. Whatever clothing she had of him, she gave to Erwin. When they stopped by for a visit, we saw a nice-looking couple standing in front of us. A very happy looking couple. Now with the Airlift over, many people had to find other employment. Erwin too was on the lookout for something suitable for him. He wanted to learn a trade. Going at age 18 into the military didn't give him much of a chance to do this. Berlin being a city in ruins gave many the opportunity just to clear away the rubble and to earn a wage this way. But it didn't teach anything for later use. Erwin wanted to learn and be stable in having a trade. We agreed with him, it was time for him and right for him or anyone to make plans. We were in his corner or better yet, we stood behind him.

Mom wrote letters to Edgar about Erwin and Hildegard and Edgar wrote back he had married his pretty French girl and wanted to come visit so we could meet her. Her name was Huguette. It used to be Huguette Geib and now she was my sister-in-law Huguette Weiss. Soon Edgar wrote Mom would be a grandma and I would be Aunt Dagmar. I was very excited with what was happening in the family.

Now with everything looking so much better, Mom, Dad and I needed to continue to do what was best for us. I worked hard at Biering's. Mom took little jobs here and there and Dad, when he got paid, put extra D Marks in her hands.

Erwin had a friend that helped him find a job after the Airlift was over. It was learning a trade that would support him well. It was laying floors in houses, apartments, theaters and so forth. Erwin jumped at this chance and was now in training. With the rebuilding of a town like Berlin, there was much work to do.

I had a birthday coming up and was all of sixteen years old. Working at Biering's gave us money every week but I disliked this place of employment more and more. Young and older men paid me attention and thought they could get away with it. I spoke to Mom about it and she said it was all part of me growing up. She wanted for me to ignore this, hold my head up high and walk away from all these nasty people. She said it was Mr. Biering's place as my employer to help me.

When I came from the kitchen and was walking through the restaurant to go home, these men standing at the bar wanted to buy me drinks. Mr. Biering was not of any help at all by saying sit down, one drink will not hurt you. It was not any wonder that I started to dislike him too. However, Mom and I needed the income and because of this I learned to put up with unacceptable behavior.

When I was leaving and made it to the front door of the place, getting to the outside I took a deep breath and ran all the way home. I ran up the long flight of the stairs to the fourth floor. A long ring a ding leaning on the doorbell, waiting to hear footsteps coming to open up. I was home with Mom. The saying is true for all of us. It states, there is no place like home. Our home looked war damaged, with the ceilings covered with cardboard. But when Mom was able to have a fire going in the kitchen stove and she had scrubbed the kitchen floors sparkling clean, the apartment had a glow we all liked. It also had a special smell of cleaning materials Mom used. Oh, what I really mean, it was home because loving hands made it a home for us.

At my work place, it was not made easy. I was liked by everyone I worked with and way too much by the patrons of such a place. I was wondering what I could do to find other and better employment and make more money. Since I did not have to be at work till noon, I went to the employment office to see what they had to offer. I saw that since I worked in such an establishment, they wanted for me to continue in it.

One step up would be to become a hostess in clubs and more fancy places in West Berlin. Mom went with me to check on a place for a hostess position. The money was more than right but the place for me to make such money was not right. I continued working in the kitchen at Biering's and rushed home to Mom every night. Glad to have the day behind me and facing a new day with God's help.

The good man upstairs, as Mom like to call Him, had a way in working in the Weiss family. After the war, the church doors opened wide to anyone that wanted to worship. Our family did not participate in any of this. Each one of us had our own way of believing in the power of God.

Mom, who was raised as a Protestant, had the God voice in her ear and it gave her the guidance she needed. Dad, raised a Catholic, saw God as a chess player who had all the moves planned and his opponent didn't have a chance to be a winner. Erwin, my brother, renewed whatever belief he had in Russia. And my brother Edgar came in touch with Him in France.

After overcoming his fear, he saw him in the friendly faces of the American soldiers that exchanged the SS uniform he wore to the army uniform from a fallen German soldier. Then they turned him over for prison time under the Americans instead of having Russian prison guards.

And, for me, well I was believing in what my family saw and knew about Him. I was still finding my own way to Him. Or was He the one that was looking for me? Anyway, I think all of us were a work in progress in the way we saw and believed. Sometimes the foundation of faith shook and wanted to crumble. But it didn't. We always found the cement to fill in the cracks to keep it together. Not that we read the scriptures every day, none of us did. What we had in the heart as small as it was, it carried us over the rough spots. The Franz and Elisabeth Weiss family had faith as small as a mustard seed. And we know what a mustard seed is able to do. It can move mountains. God moved many mountains for us, because He is an amazing helper, Father and Lord.

Chapter Forty-Four

I remember it was a cold night when I left Biering's, my Dad was waiting for me outside. He knew it was time for me to go home and he waited, standing in the doorway of the house. He was all shaken up and I had never seen him like this. He did not have a key to the front door of our house. When he came to visit us, he always came in the day time and left in the evening. He never needed a key and he never asked for one.

Him standing outside from my place of work was a surprise for me and to see him in the shape he was in concerned me. His outer clothing was wet and he was shivering. I held his arm as we both hurried home. He waited for me down stairs in the hallway. He wanted for me to prepare Mom for his late visit and him wanting to stay. Taking two stair steps at a time, I reached the top floor. Mom let me in and when I told her about Dad, without hesitating she said for him to come up and to get warm. We both knew something serious must have happened. We wanted to know what it was and how we could help him.

Dad, in the wet clothing, was slow in making it up the stairs and was glad when he got into the warm kitchen. Mom still had some of her dad's things handy and my dad changed into something dry. Mom hung his wet clothing on hangers in the small room off the kitchen. By morning they too would be dry.

Now, with a hot cup of coffee, Dad sat on the wood and coal box next to the kitchen stove. For all of us the coal box next to the warm stove was a favorite spot to sit. Erwin sat on this box, telling us how he was released from Russia to come home. Now Dad sat there telling us how he had to flee from the Russian sector to the American sector of West

Berlin because the Russians wanted him to work for them. He refused over and over and they sent the East German Police after him.

My poor Dad sitting there, holding a cup of steaming coffee, told us the most amazing story. The story why he needed to be a refugee of West Berlin. He said that the job he held at the newspaper was a special kind of job. It required special training and talents, this is why it paid so much money. Money he shared with us pretty often.

My brother and I knew, by one of the visits we made, that he was kept under lock and key at his place of employment. We didn't want to question Dad and left it up to him to explain but he never did. We never saw Dad without the briefcase, a camera or a set of binoculars. I teased him calling them his spy glasses. I didn't know how close to the truth I was because this was exactly what he used them for.

He was sent to photograph incoming Russian planes at an airport in East Berlin. He also helped Russian military men to defect, bringing them to West Berlin. Now it was out in the open at last, my dad was a spy! Oh, my goodness, this would surprise Erwin to hear this.

I and Mom had a hard time with this, but the money he had was more than a regular job would pay. This alone convinced us of the truth of his story. We asked why did he want to give it up. He said the changes in the people he worked with told him it was the right time to stop. When he spoke with the person in charge, he was allowed to step away from it all.

He then started to apply for the work he was suited for and this was in the Radio Branches. He did this by going to the employment office and they moved him from one company to the other offering him good positions.

Good paying positions and he refused to take them. When he was asked why, he said no, he was not working on helping to get ready for another war.

It was airplanes and missiles they wanted him to help design. He stood in front of every willing employer and giving them a strong no. After so many times saying no to good offers, a warrant for his arrest was issued. The Russian or East German government had gotten tired of my dad saying 'no, thank you'.

The arresting officer that came to Dad's apartment recognized him, as he had served under my dad when Dad was still in the Police Department. He told Dad he would leave and come back in one hour and he wanted for him to be gone and never come back. With his briefcase, camera and the binoculars he couldn't do without, Dad worked his way from East to West.

It was early in the evening when all this took place. Dad said he knew I left work at ten p.m. And sometimes later than ten p.m. It was for him to get from the East to the West in this amount of time. He could not take the regular routes because the police were by now searching for him. In a roundabout way, he made his way to the river Spree. He knew of a shallow place across the river and wanted to make it to the West from there.

After having to make detours because he thought danger was waiting for him, he walked by a Catholic Church. For some reason he wanted to stop there, knock and talk with the Priest. He was raised a Catholic and he thought since he was in trouble, this was the right place to speak with someone or ask for their help.

He rang the doorbell and was honest with the man that opened the door. He told him he was wanted by the East German Police and by the Russian government. He was ringing the doorbell because he needed to talk and was asking for help. He was told to wait and the man that answered the door would be right back.

Dad said he waited and waited till he couldn't wait any longer then he moved on. He told us he felt, for some unknown reason, God had turned his back on him. And never would he ask for this kind of help again. Somehow, in a very, very roundabout way, he made it to the river Spree. He found the bridge he knew had a low water flow and from there walked through the shallow part under the support beams across.

Holding the briefcase, camera and the binoculars over his head he made it to West Berlin. Now he was safe. He was soaking wet but he felt safe. Shivering and shaking, he made it to my work place. He said thank God he didn't have to wait long till I came out.

Now he sat with Mom and me telling us this incredible story. Mom told him he could sleep on the sofa in the kitchen for as long as he needed to stay with us. I took the second bed in the bedroom. The room Mom had gotten used to having all to herself after Erwin moved away. We made Dad comfortable on my sofa and we had time to talk some more in the morning. We needed to help figure out what Dad had to do to be accepted as a refugee of West Berlin. We though he would not have any trouble at all. But we were wrong, trouble was just starting. And the more trouble he encountered, the more Dad moved away from God.

Steadfast we were in purchasing clothing in the second-hand store and the cigarette butts I brought home for Mom from Biering's, helped also fill Dad's pipe. Erwin and his girlfriend Hildegard liked coming to visit. They too lent a helping hand with Dad. We wrote Edgar that Dad was staying with us. And he wrote it would be a crowded apartment when they came for a visit. But they wanted to come and together we needed to keep our chin up. It was a tough time we live in, we needed to be tougher and come out better for it. We tried but it was easier said than done.

We saw Dad going from office to office to be recognized as a refugee. And I, well I worked at Biering's and tried to ignore the intoxicated men and women. This included my employer Mr. Biering. He could be hand full when he drank too much. I knew I wanted to get away from there and find other employment. But how could I leave, when the little money I made was still better than any other job would pay. Young girls like me most of the time worked toward an education. I was not. I was just out there earning any kind of money. There was a big difference between me and other girls that had the chance to become somebody. I gave up willingly my education to go to work. Now, I saw clearly what my teachers meant when they came to see Mom and me. Asking me to stay in school. Somehow, I still believed everything would fall into place and it would work out. Not just for me, but for all of us.

Chapter Forty-Five

Coming home from work one night, Dad was not sleeping on the sofa in the kitchen any more. Mom told me he was ordered to claim a bed in one of the refugee places in West Berlin. In the day, he could be with us, by ten p.m. he needed to sleep with all the other runaways from East Berlin in this to him assigned place.

The man that gave him the orders on how he was to live from now on said it might help him to get approved faster. Dad was willing to do anything to belong and so were the many others that like him waited for approval from the West Berlin government.

Thinking of West and East Berlin was like speaking of night and day. The west part of town was rebuilding, the stores showed things to buy. The attitude of the West Berliner was different. East Berlin seemed to be standing still, very little of any kind of improvement was seen. Change for the East Berliner was slow in coming.

In the West, the Americans went out with German girls. Or the other way around, the German girls went out with the Americans. It was not a big surprise that some pushed baby carriages around. The shuttle buses going by and the American soldier whistling at every pretty girl. West Berlin was indeed alive and doing much better than its other half.

American music became popular and was played on the radio, in restaurants and in clubs. The carnival and the circus came to town. The West Berliner that had money could take advantage of what was offered. We had good as well as bad news to read about or hear about. Newspaper stands on every corner gave the world news. Magazines showed popular fashions and we had the first beauty pageant in West Berlin. There was exciting news happening all around us.

The bad of course always comes along with the good. Political groups started to make trouble. Abductions from the West over into East Berlin was written and talked about. Killings of private citizens in hallways of apartment complexes shocked West Berlin. When talking with Dad, he said none of this shocked him.

The abductions had to do with the need the East had of intelligent people. The people that, like he did, said no to what was offered to them. He said, not that he thought of himself as in the same class with any of them, but he thought of being in the same boat as they were and he needed to have eyes in the back of his head. Over and over he tried to be recognized as a West Berliner, no matter what he did or where he went, it was always a dead end. He made one more big, big effort and wrote a letter to the First Mayor of West Berlin. He was so sure if anyone would understand and be of help, it was Ernst Reuter. When my dad heard back, he said to Mom and me he was told in writing he was too lazy to want to work and should return to East Berlin. He was told to make amends, to make it right and go to work. Dad said can you believe this? Didn't this man read in my letter what I didn't want to work for? It was for another war in the making. All of us Germans shouldn't want to help work for something like this.

Going back to the East sector like Ernst Reuter suggest for him to do was out of the question. Impossible for him to do. In the first place, he would be arrested if he went back and sent to heaven only knows where. The Russians did not forgive or forget easily and neither did the East German Police. If he went back, he wouldn't be seen or heard from again.

The next letter Dad wrote to Mayor Reuter was straightforward and direct. With the result that the return letter was also straightforward and direct. Dad was to be examined and questioned about his sanity by doctors and others. By mail, Dad and the Mayor would get the results of these tests.

Of course, Mom and I worried about all of this, but Dad was so calm about it, it was almost funny to watch him. Dad took everything in stride and jokingly said the Mayor may be more eager to read the doctor's results than he was. I was there when the letter came and Dad said for Mom to open it and read it to us.

She tore it open and smiled as she read the result of Dad's examination. Dad was declared sane. The only fault they found him guilty of he was three times declared to be a genius. Dad hearing this smoked his pipe and chuckled. Then he said "Where do I go from here?" On this night at the refugee camp, Dad must have slept well. He was a winner. He won the say so against the Mayor of West Berlin. No one could or would send him back to live in East Berlin. What a blessing, what a win this was for him.

However, it did not give him citizenship right in West Berlin. The Mayor now, so we believe, kept looking at Dad. He made it hard on him. Not being a citizen meant he couldn't be employed. Dad used charm, wit, talent and know-how to survive. We Weiss' knew how to fight. Days turned into weeks, months and a year was gone. Dad couldn't stay forever at the refugee camp. It didn't change anything for him that others found acceptance in West Berlin but not my Dad. Dad was the last man standing at this camp with entrance papers to West Berlin denied to him. He needed to find his own way. And he did. He didn't return to live with us but he found a way to take care of his needs.

He managed to get by, I do not know how he did it but he was able to rent a room in Berlin - Schoneberg. Could be Mom lend him the first rent money and he took it from there. On the wings of a prayer he wanted to make it. His place was not too far of a walk from us. Mom also picked up work here and there and since she was a fine cook, she worked as household help for a butcher and his family. Now she ate her main meal of the day with them and I got my good portion from the cook at Biering's. Two of us had one good meal a day. When Dad came by to see us, he was welcome to eat what we had. This much we could do for him. What was ours was also his.

Dad came on weekends for dinner and all in all we thought we were doing so much better. My brother Edgar wrote he and Huguette had their sweet baby girl and they name her Blandine Weiss. This little girl was the French doll in our family. When Dad heard he was a grandpa he looked at Mom and said let us hope it will not be too long before we get to meet Mademoiselle Blandine Weiss and her Mom. We all wanted so much to meet Edgar's family and for him to be together with Erwin again.

We didn't know that the year 1950 had many changes in store for our family. Starting with my brother Erwin and his girlfriend Hildegard Treulieb. More often he came to visit without her. He and Mom had long talks but not any of it was shared with me. I, wanting to be a good sister and not a nosy one, I kept my nose out of their private lives. But a blind person could see that the two love birds were flying away from each other. One wanted to fly south and the other north. Or the other way around. Whichever way this was, it was clear that they were drifting apart.

Being aware of it, for me it meant soon they would go their separate ways. Erwin would pack his few belongings and move back home for a while. Another two weeks went by and, suitcase in hand, Erwin was glad to be back with Mom and me. In the early morning hours on Saturdays or Sundays we had the best talks. This was the time when I found out why my brother left his pretty girlfriend.

He explained that she craved attention from everyone all of the time and it became too much for him to put up with. If there was a get together of friends, she made sure she was always in the middle of it. She had a need to always want to be the center of attention. Should any of their friends, woman friends, want to talk with him she became angry and upset and would pout for days. He talked with her about their trouble and how they could avoid it but she wouldn't listen. Being the social-butterfly she wanted to be, meant for him to leave her and come home.

He still had a hard time of it. Hildegard, realizing what she had lost, wanted to win him back. She showed up at his place of work or at his favorite restaurant wanting to talk with him. He and friends went to have a beer after work and Hildegard knew how to find him. He remained steady in not giving in to her. For him, when it was over it was over. I felt sad for Hildegard but I knew that my brother knew what he was doing and would do what he thought was best for not just him but for both of them. To us he said, it took all this for him to learn that he was not meant for her. In time he hoped she would realize that being apart was right for both of them. And he hoped she would find the right person to be with. In other words, he wished her well. We respected his wishes and feelings and tried not to mention her name any more.

Our dad continued the fight to become a working citizen of West Berlin and his best help in his effort was always our mom.

Chapter Forty-six

To work at Biering's I was having to grit my teeth and bite my tongue much of the time. I wanted to get out of this working environment but the need for money made it impossible. With this in mind, I smiled when I so much wanted to cry or even scream. I kept on working, washing dishes, mopping floors and decorating dinner plates for all of Biering's customers. Or is a better word for customers patrons? For me the word for them was a group of drunks. It was not very nice of me to think of them in such terms. But the regulars coming in and staying after closing all drank and drank. What else could I call of them? Maybe the next ugly word for them was freeloaders. I couldn't say if they paid for all the rounds they drank after closing time. I realized this was not for me to worry about. However, with them staying and the cook leaving on time, I was the one needing to stay late. They didn't only drink but they also ate while drinking. I was paid not by the hour so my check didn't increase by how late I worked. A real bummer this was for me, because we could always use the extra income.

When I hired on to work in such a place, I knew what to expect. But I didn't know how very bad it could get. Mr. Biering had a special table set up for his friends and they were verbal and annoying. Sometimes things got out of hand. Someone got into a fight over a girl when they had too much to drink. Getting up from the table they fell off their chair. Getting up from the floor, walking lopsided they messed around in the restroom.

I was the clean-up squad for every mess up and I thought, is this all I am meant to do? The only place I had to go from there, the way I saw it, was further down. I did not look forward to this and went home every night thinking, "May God help me." And help me he did.

It was the day we called Good Friday. Two days before Easter. When I went to work on this day, I did not know it would be for the last time. I came into the kitchen, put the apron around me to tackle the stack of lunch dishes. The cook was talking with the butcher that made a meat delivery.

When the butcher left, the cook told me that I had something besides the daily cigarette butts to take home tonight. The butcher had not cut off the ends of the sausages and since they could not be sold offered on a dinner plate, he was letting us take them home. I was happy because this would be added to the Weiss family Easter meal.

We had a busy day like always. I cleaned the ash trays, wrapping the cigarette butts up for mom in one of the restaurants dinner napkins. When it was time for the cook to go home, he divided the meat ends between him and me. I stayed longer than he did. It was my job to clean and close the kitchen and take care of the after guests for the boss as always. Getting ready to leave myself, I tucked everything away in my purse. Now I was ready to call it a day and go home.

Mr. Biering, not in the best of moods, came back to the kitchen. He had way too much to drink that evening. Maybe he had gotten into an argument with his wife or the girlfriend we all knew he had. I don't know what got into him. But he said, as my employer, he had the right to check my purse.

I must have turned red in my face because all I could think was 'oh, my God, he will now see all the cigarette butts I am bringing home for Mom'. I was so embarrassed that I did this, just like I was years ago when I picked them up from the sidewalk for my mother. I did not even think about the sausage ends the cook had given me.

Mr. Biering took my purse that was standing on a cabinet and tore it apart. Everything fell out of it, cigarette ends and the sausage pieces. It all fell out onto the kitchen table and the floor. I stood there watching, not knowing what to think or what to do. Everyone in the front of the restaurant must have heard him screaming at me and what he said to me hurt a lot. He called me a thief. And nothing but a thief. Then he said a few more words that I can and will not mention.

I was stunned by the way he behaved. Before I knew what happened or could say anything in my defense, he came around the table and slapped my face. It totally shocked, surprised and scared me. I took my now empty purse put back in my personal items and, as fast as my legs would carry me, I rushed well almost ran out of the restaurant. Getting home and by now I was sobbing. Coming in the kitchen, Mom and my brother could still see the redness from his hand on my cheek.

After I told them what Mr. Biering had done, in seconds, both were on their way to confront Mr. Biering. When they returned, both told me I was now among the many unemployed. Both were of the same mind, we may be poor but we did not have to put up with something like what happened tonight. In 1950 on Good Friday before Easter, I left Biering's for good. I see this Good Friday in 1950 as the day God rescued me and turned my life around.

On the next day, true to form, Mr. Biering had forgotten about the night before. When I did not show up for work, he sent someone to fetch me. Now the surprise was his. We said, "No, thank you. I will try to find better employment." and it would not be working in a restaurant anymore.

Chapter Forty-Seven

We stuck to it and I didn't return to Biering's, my ex-employer had the last laugh. When I went to the office to apply for unemployment compensation, I had a seven week wait before they would help me. The reason for it, my employer wanted me back and I was the one that refused to work for him. This was seen as my bad and not his. From this time forward any time the name Biering was mentioned by any of us, it left a taste like swallowing vinegar in my mouth. It shows how fast feelings can go from grateful to ungrateful. We were happy when I found employment in his establishment. Not any one else, because of my young age, wanted to give me a chance. Many months later, all this changed and I was ready to leave this place. Run from it was more the word for it. It was not right for me in the first place. But I can say it was the stepping stone to look for something more suitable for me. I stepped from step one working for Biering's, looking to find employment taking step two. Time would tell where I would wind up. When Mr. Biering slapped my face he lost a good worker. A worker that worked overtime hours for a small paycheck.

We bit our lip and I started looking at newspaper ads to find work. I did not have to wait too long. As luck would have it, but in my case, I would like to think as God arranged it, a new company looked to train workers. It was factory work promising good pay. I jumped at the opportunity and was standing at the door of the Juckel Company with many others to apply for work.

Again, I was among the lucky ones, or as I would like to think, God was looking out for me. I was hired on the spot. At the appointed time I showed up for training and now had work from eight to five. It was a job to make telephone cords that fit into the hand receiver. We were paid by how many we could put out in the work day.

My hands were willing to work hard and fast. Once I was trained, it would bring us a so much better income than I had before. After a while, the Juckel Company was willing to sign workers that worked at home. My mom signed on and worked a few hours every night to add even more to the family income.

I, being the go between, carried the load of cords that came in bundles of fifty back and forth. Being young and full of energy, this did not hurt me. The Weiss family was doing well for a change. It wasn't very long and I was promoted. No, this promotion didn't pay any more money. It was a different kind of promotion.

I was taken out of the large room that I worked together with many people and placed in a smaller group. It was a group of about fifteen girls and they were called the elite. I was the youngest and all the other girls acted like they were my mother. They were a wonderful bunch of young people and I liked all of them right away. Being the baby in this group they sort of protected me. I had fifteen or so big sisters that tried to teach me all they knew in more ways than one. All laughing because I would say to them oh no, I cannot believe you said or did this. This group spoiled me and I of course I took to it like the little fish in the big fish pond that I was.

Every day I looked forward to going to work and had much to tell my family when I came home that evening. It was so nice to go to work and not have to dread the day ahead of me. These girls laughed and they joked around most of the day. It was a nice working environment and I found my place in this group.

After the weekend, come Monday all the girls had stories to tell. None of them sat at home like I did. They had boyfriends or were engaged to soon be married. They went to movies with friends and went to clubs to dance. I found what they did interesting and fun but I had nothing of interest to tell them about me.

The money I earned, I turned over to Mom. I only kept enough in my pockets for transportation back and forth from work. If I really wanted anything, I was free to ask her for it. When the girls asked what I did for the weekend, I told them the truth. I worked in our small apartment, keeping it neat and tidy. I was always with my family and did not go out on my own.

Of course, I had to put up with a lot of teasing about this. I heard them say over and over they needed to do something to get me out from under my mother's overly protective eyes and hands. When the teasing got a little too much, I told them about the time when I was still working at Biering's. I told them that my Mom's eyes had a twinkle in them when she set me up with a blind date.

I really was not ready for something like this. But again, there was nothing I could say or do about this. Mom didn't give me the choice to say yes or no. She had a girlfriend and this friend had a son my age. This young man asked Mom if I would like to go to a movie with him. Mom didn't ask me, instead she said yes for me. The following weekend I went to the movies for the first time on sort of a date. We saw the George Gershwin story of his life and, when I came home, I was able to say it was fun and I enjoyed it.

After the first time going with him, this young man came around wanted a boyfriend/girlfriend relationship. Something I was not ready for at all.

My friends laughed when I told them what a hard time I had to get rid of Horst Podobinski. This was the name of the young man that gave me his attention. I wanted my mother to be the one to tell him I was not ready for playing the dating game. She was the one that played Cupid and started this. She needed to be the one to fix it by saying no. It was not up to me to get me out of it. Mom should have the responsibility to do this. Since this was her girlfriend's son, she laid it all right back on my shoulders. This was a bummer and so embarrassing to boot.

When I did what I needed to do, what we thought could happen did happen. It ended the friendship between Horst's mother and mine. They still spoke and greeted when they met on the street but did not visit anymore. On weekends when Dad did not come by, they used to get together for a cup of coffee and cake. All of this, because of me and Horst, was over between them and I was sure my mother would miss her friend. She didn't have many friends and when she did, she was careful in her selection of them. This was still a hazard left over from the WW II times when we couldn't trust anyone

She really had very few friends that she trusted but Tussy, Horst's mother, she trusted with everything just like girlfriends do. I told her how sorry I was that because of me she had lost her best friend. She assured me she was alright and I shouldn't worry about her. Now, telling all this my friends, I laughed when I said "See? I am not as much of a wallflower as what all of you thought I was."

That afternoon coming home from work, I told Mom I let the cat out of the bag about my short friendship with Horst Podobinski. I only did it because I wanted for the girls to stop teasing me so much. Mom smiled this little smile of hers and said, "I hope this will do it for you and if it starts up again, tell them 'All good things come to them that wait.' What is meant to be will come your way when the time is right." And with a grin she added, and "this time without any help from me." She kept her word and my friends at work stopped their teasing and they calmed down a lot.

Chapter Forty-Eight

In our family, things turned around. My brother came home late from work. He showed interest in one of the young women that worked in his favorite place to hang out. He told us her name was Erika and he wanted for us to get to know this young lady. He said she served time in Russia when the Russians, after the war, abducted her. But this was something he wanted for her to tell us about. All we needed to know was he was interested and serious about her. It looked like my brother found the woman he loved and her name was Erika.

Dad was fighting to become a citizen of West Berlin and on every corner, someone placed a stumbling stone. Of course, Dad blamed Ernst Reuter for all of it. Mom and I thought that he may be right. When Dad came across the stumbling stones, we his family, stumbled along with him because we needed to pitch in and help when help was needed.

Erwin gave household money and I gave all of mine except for what I needed for transportation to get to and from work. When the stumbling stones came our way, all of us had to give a little more. I took the trolley in the morning and in late afternoon. The ticket didn't cost much, but by not riding and walking home from work I saved the ticket money to buy Dad's pipe tobacco. I told myself every little bit was of help.

Mom smiled when she bought me a cheap umbrella at Hertie's. She said she didn't want the telephone cords to get wet in bad weather. I didn't believe this was the only reason why she bought this umbrella. Working as a family unit we always took care of each other. The umbrella was to protect me from the rain by keeping me dry so I wouldn't catch cold. It was not just bought to protect the work I brought home for her. It told me she was concerned for me.

One morning I came to work and our employer, Mrs. Juckel, gave us girls a big surprise. She put lockers in our workroom for our coats and purses. Not any more hanging coats and other on hooks in the outside hallway. We were pleased. All the girls, but not me, decorated their locker door with colorful hand towels. Only mine was white. I asked where did they buy these pretties, they only said they didn't buy them they were a gift. I didn't ask and no one explained who the gift giver of such pretties was. I should have asked. My towel being the only white one in color looked out of place among such pretties. But I wondered about it often enough, which store sold something like this? Then I dropped the thought in order not to appear nosy.

On another day when I opened my locker door, on the top shelf I found a vase with a rose in it. This started the teasing all over again. Now everyone said I had a secret admirer. They believed it was one of the guys working next door to us. He must have been watching me and found out which locker was mine. They said someone liked me. liked me much enough to leave a flower in my locker. Tease and tease was all I heard all day long. I laughed and, since nothing more like this happened after this, I forgot about it. Lucky for me, so did my friends.

It was a nice Sunday afternoon when my brother brought his girlfriend, Erika, to visit. I stood out in front of the apartment door to say welcome. Coming up the stairs, she was looking up and she was smiling. Now, standing in front of me, I saw she was small. My brother towered over her. She had light brown hair and light brown eyes, a wonderful smile and it showed her pearly whites. No wonder my brother was attracted to this nice lady. He would be crazy not to be.

Mom baked a coffee cake for this special occasion and we waited for Dad to show up. Around three p.m. it was coffee and cake time. All of us sat together at the kitchen table eating, drinking good coffee for a change, and getting to know one another.

The story of Erika's abduction by the Russians was a sad one. We had a hard time believing this happened to thousands of teenage girls after the war. Ericka said one of the girls wrote a book about this. Their life changed when they were taken away from their families. This woman that wrote the book, didn't want for this to be forgotten. She wanted for the world to remember it.

Erika was taken away sitting at the table in her family's home. They lived in a farming community. It was only her mom and younger siblings around the dinner table. Her dad was still among the war missing. She said without warning the front door was pushed open and the abductors came in and removed her from her family. Everyone she loved sat around the table calling out not to take her. But they did.

She said she, with the other young women that were taken away from their families like she was, lived through much. She did not speak of rape or other being inflicted but what she didn't say spoke louder than words. Years she was a prisoner in Russia, writing through the Red Cross cards to her family. She heard from her mother by return mail that her dad had made it home. All that was missing for the family to be complete was her.

Like my brother Erwin, the day came when she was released and sent home. To have work kept her in Berlin.

And, as luck would have it, or as Mom and I believed under divine guidance, Erwin and Erika Drews found each other.

A month after we met Erika, she became Erika Weiss. She was a pretty and welcome addition to the family. I went to work every day having something to brag about. I had two sisters-in-law in Huguette and Erika. I was the aunt to Blandine Weiss in France. Soon I would be the proud aunt to the baby on the way for Erwin and Erika.

Life was on the upswing for us. Erwin and Erika moved away by renting a room from a coworker. It was a very small room but when we visited, we saw the touch of Erika's hands. A pretty picture on the wall and flowers on the table. I could see that my brother was happy. In the mail we got from Edgar, it was the same for him.

We in Berlin walked at a steady pace. Dad continued in his anger against the Mayor of West Berlin and Mom was his best friend and support in all of this. Dad had a strong friendship for Mom and I saw it. Mom had love and friendship for Dad. This fact stared me in the face by watching her. I made up my mind that, if I ever fell in love and got married, it must be forever. I would do anything at all to avoid being a divorcee.

I saw how lonely my mother was at times. She showed it when she thought I was not looking. Listening to music on the radio and telling me that she and Dad used to dance to this tune. Or the way she ironed one of the shirts he liked to wear. There was still love in Mom's heart for Dad. But she gave him what he wanted and for him it was only friendship. She was committed in a friendship to Dad and having two hundred percent love for us kids. We had a very strong protector in family values, in our mother.

Chapter Forty-Nine

We made it through spring, summer, fall and this was November. The weather was cold. I still took the trolley to work and walked home after work. But with the change in the weather I needed warmer clothing. Mom said that we all needed to bundle up warmer and Mr. Werner's second-hand store was in need of some money from us.

For me it was not just a coat or a jacket. more than this I needed shoes. All the walking I did I needed a sturdy pair of winter shoes. Mom promised that with my next paycheck we would take care of it.

I still kept my eyes on the pretty towels my coworkers draped over the locker doors. Every now and then when the thought hit me, I asked where did they buy something as pretty as this? It was Inge Johl that told me they were bought at the PX. I asked "PX"? What kind of a store is this? I didn't recognize the name. I asked if it was a new store that opened up in West Berlin?

Inge shook her head no. She explained it was an all-American store and all the United States soldiers and their families did their shopping there. Its location was at Clayallee, right next door to a snack bar. I said alright, now please explain what is a snack bar? Inge said it was a nice eating place for the American soldiers, their families and girlfriends.

Inge laughed when she said, "I mean to say American and German girlfriends." I looked at Inge and understood what I didn't understand before. All the girls I am friends with had American soldiers as boyfriends. Not so with Inge, she said she was engaged to be married and when her fiancé went back to the States, they had the permission to get married. She said it would take a while till she started to pack a suitcase. Her fiancé just signed up for a few more years in Berlin. At least he hoped to finish his tour in Berlin. If not, she was willing to move with him to where ever they stationed him. She didn't want to be apart from him. She laughed and said she was very much in love and she would follow him to Timbuktu if she had too.

I was pleasantly surprised by all this news about my coworkers. I took extra big steps wanting to get home to tell Mom and Dad all about it. All the way on my fast walk home I thought it was not any wonder my friends looked so well taken care of. They had help from their boyfriends and in Inge's case, from her fiancé.

When I went to work tomorrow, I wanted to hear more. Much more. Tomorrow I wanted to be nosy. No, not nosy. I wanted to be inquisitive and get some answers from my dear friends. When they started to tell me what they did with their weekend, it was hard to hush them up. I got an earful of all the fun they had. Nobody was a stay at home or was a mom or dad's girl like I was. They went out and seemed to be everyone's girl. All of them were the kind that liked going to parties.

All of them partied except for Inge Johl, she had a small gold band on her ring finger and was true to a soldier. Ray was this young man's name.

Every day we packed our lunch. Like it did when I went to school, here at the Juckel company the lunch bell rang at noon. A few of the girls wanted to become hairdressers when this job was over. They asked what I wanted to be. I told them I really hadn't thought about it. Well they started messing around with my long hair. While one did this, the other worked on fixing my face up a bit more. I believed both thought I was behind the times with everything – clothing, makeup. They were aware that I didn't have the money for such things. But what they taught me by playing with my hair was to pay more attention to it. Some of the girls gave me face powder or a lipstick they didn't want any more. All my friends were really nice to me. Since I was the youngest, they started calling me baby.

When Mom saw they gave me makeup, she went to Kepa. A store that sold everything and bought me mascara. Kepa was a small store that sold inexpensive items. Using mascara, I saw I had long lashes. So here I was with holes in my shoes and still in need of clothing but I felt pretty. For the first time, my friends envied me. I had something they wanted and didn't have. Mother nature gave me long eyelashes.

My friend Inge came to work having three pairs of uniform pants from her fiancé to sell. She did not ask much for them and offered them to me. She said her landlady was willing to do any of the alterations needed for free. The pants would do the trick by helping to keep me warm. I did want to buy them but had to ask my mother first.

Coming home right away telling mom about it, she gave me permission to buy. But I needed to ask for an advance on my next paycheck. My heart was beating fast when I went to my employer's office. Mrs. Juckel said yes and wrote me a company check for the needed amount. It was the first week in November but for me, Christmas came early. I rushed back to the work room and showed Inge she and I were in business, we had a deal. Inge, not living far away from me, would set this up with her landlady and come get me when she was ready to sew.

I really thought I was coming up in the world. I wore powder, lipstick, eye make-up and now, like other young women, had slacks to wear. I forgot the purpose was to keep me warm. I thought I looked more modern and not so dowdy and this meant much to me.

I would never say it to my mother but there were times I didn't like what I wore. Like the warm, orange looking stockings or the one thumb gloves she bought at Kepa. I thought I looked hideous in it but wore it because it was all I had. Now, with my mother's permission, Mrs. Juckel's and Inge's landlady's help this would change. For me, Christmas had come a month early. I brought the uniform pants home and showed Mom and Dad my treasure.

Chapter Fifty

About two days later, around seven p.m., the doorbell rang and Inge came to get me. It was a short walk of 15-20 minutes from our house to hers. I holding on to my package tight. Inge unlocked the door leading into a long hallway. I was expecting to meet her landlady. Inge said we would do this after we had a cup of coffee and some cookies. She opened the door to her room and the surprise was mine.

I was to meet her fiancé Ray and he had brought a friend. I looked at Inge and she was smiling. It was the kind of smile that said, "hey, hey, the surprise is all yours. I got you." I was not sure what to think nor did I know what to say or do. I knew I had been had. She set me up. I thought oh no, I was in trouble in more ways than just one. What would my mother have to say when I told her about this? Or maybe I better not tell her any of this. All this was going around in my head while I was to drink coffee and eat cookies.

I was embarrassed the whole time I was there. How uncomfortable I was must have shown in my face. I didn't have much to say because the school English I learned was long forgotten. Inge did all the talking for me and I made use of the excuse, I did not understand one word of their entire conversation. I thought the whole time, 'Inge, when this is over, you and I needed to talk.' Somehow, I believe Inge knew what was on my mind and made herself ready for this friend with friend talk.

Glancing at Ray's friend I thought that he was handsome. He was blond and had blue eyes, a nice smile and had, like all Americans, pretty white teeth. I learned from Inge, he was called Gary. His whole name was Garrett

Dwain Monk and he was a corporal in the 6th Infantry Division. He had German grandparents and loved being in Berlin.

While Inge was telling me this, I thought this is way too much information for me. I will go home and forget about Inge's Ray and his friend Corporal Garrett Dwain Monk. This would be the end of it. Besides, what would a nice-looking military man want with a girl that looked like Cinderella before she went to the ball?

Inside, I was embarrassed about being tricked by Inge and about the way I thought I looked. I kept thinking 'why, oh why, is this happening? I did not ask for this and I didn't want this.' And I was afraid of the teasing tomorrow from the girls at work.

When time was up it was after ten p.m. Inge said her fiancé and friend needed to get back to camp and we would walk them to the trolley stop. I was so relieved to know it was over and I was free to go home. The pants that needed fixing stayed at Inge's. This would wait for the next visit. Then I would meet her landlady and be able to thank her for helping me.

Out the front door we four went. I was glad to feel the cold air in my face. Inge and Ray walked in front holding hands. All of a sudden, this young American walking next to me tried to hold my hand. I thought of this as being fresh. Being much to forward as we did not know each other. I pulled my hand away from his and gave his hand a hard slap. It was so hard and loud that Inge and Ray turned their heads to see what was going on behind them.

I pretended not to see them looking and kept on walking. So did the young soldier next to me. We both acted as if nothing had happened. Reaching the trolley stop, it was coming. I was so glad that this embarrassing evening was almost over. They got on the trolley with my friend Inge waving goodbye. I stood next to her, not smiling and not waving. With them gone I wanted to have a talk with my friend. Oh, my God, why did she do this? But my talk had to wait.

My mom stood at the other side of the street and saw everything. Now I had a very good reason to be concerned. Would she believe I did not know anything about this? We were not dealing with German boys here but with American soldiers. Inge saw the look on my face and said, "Don't you worry. I will explain everything to your mom." I thought she better do a good job of explaining to Mom. My mother would not take this situation lightly.

We walked over to my mother and Inge started talking. Mom listened and she believed her. I was in the clear. Mom came looking for me because it was after ten p.m. The down stairs doors after ten would be locked. I didn't take a key with me. I left without one because I did not have any reason to think I would be late getting home.

We said good-night to Inge. And I didn't thank her for the nice evening. I didn't have a reason for it. She tricked me into this and I was still angry with her. Now walking home, I tried telling Mom about the evening but she, to my surprise, did not have much to say in return. Before I went to bed and be up early for work, I said this was the last we would see of this American. The slap I gave him had sent him packing. With this thought, Mom and I went to bed to be up early and face another day.

I was not looking forward to the questions and the teasing I would get from the girls. Coming into the work room I saw my white towel on the locker was replaced by a pretty blue one. I pulled it down by saying this was not funny. I didn't have nor did I want to have an American boyfriend. I took the blue towel down and handed it to Inge. I knew she started this and had her fun with it. Fun at my expense, needless to say. I was slightly annoyed by this. But it didn't seem to bother my friend Inge. She kept smiling at me and avoiding the looks I gave her.

When I went for a bathroom break and came back, Inge again put the blue towel up. I pulled it off and she put it up. All the girls had a fun day at my expense. I grinned and finally decided to put up with it. It was all done in good fun. Before I left for home, Inge said in a few days her landlady had time to work on the pants. She would come and get me. I said, "Yes, Inge and please with not any more surprises waiting for me." She agreed and she and I were alright to be coworkers and good friends. Besides, Inge was a fun young woman. I could not stay annoyed with her forever. This would be silly of me and the girls would then call me a party pooper.

I made it home and handed Mom the work load I brought home for her every day. About three bundles of fifty phone cords to work with. Sometimes after we ate, I helped her and was able to take them back the next day. All gave us more money in our pockets. Even Dad, when he felt like it, we had trained to help.

Chapter Fifty-One

This evening I didn't get to take my coat off. The doorbell rang, outside stood Inge with a grin on her face, saying to Mother, "Mrs. Weiss, the American soldier came back and we are asking your permission to take Dagie to the movies and out to eat. May she go? Ray and I will watch out for her."

Mom gave me a gentle shove and without any further to do, she turned me over to Inge Johl. I couldn't believe it. Was this my mom? I wished my dad had been there when this happened. He might have said no. Where was Dad when I needed him? Nowhere in sight. I had a hard time understanding why this soldier wanted to see me. He had come back for more and he was asking for trouble. He needed to get it – to understand that not any of this was my idea.

I was out on a double date, that again was not my idea. On this date I learned about American movies and eating popcorn. This soldier that was my date dared to place his arm over the back of my seat during the movie. Me looking around, I saw they all did it so I thought this might be alright.

After the movie, we went to the snack bar for hamburgers and French fries. I felt very much out of place there. It was all much too fancy. People dressed so well, I did not fit in with such a crowd. Inge did but I thought I was an eyesore. I was intimidated by all of it and I felt bad about myself. In the snack bar the lights were bright and the hamburger was way too big for my mouth. I did not dare to pick it up thinking it would spill on me. Then I thought everyone sitting so close around us would look at clumsy me and laugh.

So, I asked Inge to excuse me from eating by saying the popcorn at the movies filled me up. This, of course, was not the truth, I was very hungry. I had not eaten anything since noon when we got the lunch hour. Again, I was glad when the evening was over. We took a taxicab back. I was the first to be dropped off at the house. Saying good night and getting out of the cab I thought, oh, God, now Corporal Monk knows where I live.

Before opening the front door, I managed to turn around to wave, then I rushed up the stairs to see Mom. She right away wanted to know if I had a nice time? If I had fun with my friends? I said I guess I did. I was not sure that I had fun. The movie was in English and I didn't understand one single word. Then I explained about going to the snack bar and being afraid to eat. To this, Mom said I was silly. I should eat and enjoy it. She went to the cupboard, knowing I was still hungry. She sliced bread, buttered it and gave it to me saying 'next time you eat.'

Smiling while eating I answered, "Mom, there will not be a next time." But again, I was wrong. This was only the beginning. The beginning of 'The love story of an American soldier and a German girl.' Every time Inge's fiancé and his friend got a pass to be out and about town, she came to get me.

My parents surprised me, that they were alright with it and let me go with them. It helped when I told them that this young American had German grandparents. Mom and Dad felt comfortable knowing this. From what little I was given to understand, Gary's grandfather came from a village somewhere by the North Sea. But only his grandfather did, not his grandmother. His grandparents came alone across the ocean. They met in America and then married. Gary didn't know the birthplace of his grandmother only his grandpa's was known to him. Well it didn't matter to us. We liked he had German ancestors.

In the meantime, Inge helped much with the language problem and told my young friend that if he wanted to know me, he needed to learn my language, then I would learn his. We both learned as we went along, now holding each other by the hand. He spouted words in German and for me some of the school English came back. I got used to eating popcorn at the movies and also ate the hamburger or a hotdog without having a problem with any of it.

However, the way I was dressed concerned me. I was very aware of being a second-hand Annie so to speak. In my family we all were second-hand Annie's or Charlie's. It could not be helped. We looked clean, starched and ironed but fashion? What was that? This was for others and not for our family.

My brother came by and we told him I was dating an American. He didn't have anything to say so I thought Erwin was alright with it. Edgar was told in the letters Mom wrote and he, like Erwin, did not say anything much about it. He only wrote us about his family living in a house in Faulquemont, instead of an apartment like we did in Berlin. For him, as well as for my brother Erwin, they were coming up in the world. We didn't have to have any concerns about them at all.

Dad, however, was another story. He had a constant struggle trying to make ends meet. It was good that he had us to help him. But like Mom always said, this is what family is for. Every so often Dad would mention how long it has been since he saw his own family in the Rheinland. He had a brother Paul and two half-brothers and three half-sisters living in West Germany.

He said the only way for him to visit them would be by air travel. He was sure the East Germans or the Russians would still have him on a wanted list. There was not any money to make such a visit possible for him. But like we all did, it was Dad's dream to see his family again. With the Airlift ended, traveling by plane was the best way to get out of or back into Berlin. Edgar wrote us as soon as he could, he wanted to bring his family to us. He was ready for all of us to meet and what a wonderful reunion this will be. We needed to save up some money till then to show them a little bit of a nice time. Erwin and Erika said let them come. We will work it out somehow because this is what a family is for. Well our family had to work extra hard to work things out. But knowing they were really coming, we could lay aside a little here and there. Hoping not to have to touch it in case of an emergency. Fingers off, this was the fund to keep Edgar and his family comfy when they came.

We did have to touch the fund because Dad got sick and Mom needed to call the doctor. It was good that this man had gotten to know us well or we would have been in more trouble than one can imagine. As always, Mom worked it out as she was always able to do. She needed to be the Weiss family miracle worker very often. If Dad had been recognized as a citizen of West Berlin there would not have been any trouble at all. But Dad was still fighting the system in the hope one day to win. The burden of some of the expenses fell into our hands to be held   responsible for. Mom said, with God's help we would manage it. And with the help he always gave us we did.

Chapter Fifty-Two

Finally came the time when my parents wanted to meet the young man that took me out almost every night. My friend Inge told Gary time was up and if he wanted to continue this boyfriend/girlfriend relationship, he needed to meet my parents. He was ready for it and he told me so.

One night coming back by taxi from seeing another movie, we said wish us luck to Inge and Ray and Gary climbed the flight of stairs to the fourth floor. Mom opened the door and at first sight fell in love with this young American. Dad was waiting in the kitchen, smoking his pipe and saying when we walked in welcome to my American boyfriend.

Dad used his English to converse with Gary and I was surprised how well they got along. Gary was not surprised by the poor condition from the war the apartment was in. We had a clean apartment thanks to Mom and her busy hands. I think Gary felt at home the minute he stepped inside. Now Ray and Inge did not have to watch us anymore. Gary picked me up and took me out after visiting a while with Mom and Dad. He managed to get a pass just about every night or every other night. Not always did we go out, Gary liked being around my parents.

During the visits, we learned a lot about his family in the States and all we heard of them was good news. He had a younger brother Eddie and lost a sister when he was only six years old. Her name was Joann and she died of scarlet fever. He told us, even though she passed away a long time ago, they were close as little ones and he is still missing her today. He said his mom was pregnant again and all the family hoped she would have a little girl. The times we did not go out but stayed at home with my parents, Gary brought popcorn to pop and for Dad and him some beer from the downstairs restaurant. That name of the place was Tante Anna's (Aunt Anna's). As the days went by Gary and Aunt Anna started a loyal and steady friendship. Gary would stop into Aunt Anna's often and bring up beer for him and Dad.

We all didn't realize that my handsome boyfriend started a second love affair and it was between him and beer. Gary did not mind stopping at Aunt Anna's first and bring beer for him and Dad upstairs. When he learned my Dad also enjoyed a glass of wine now and then he bought both.

I did not think much about it as in most German families the man of the house had a glass of beer after work before going home to eat the evening meal.

Dad and Gary sat and talked and when my brother Erwin got into the mix, they had what is called a party. The first time Gary met my brother, it was us coming home from a movie. Gary met Erwin standing outside wanting to get into the house. He told all of us later that he thought this may be a German boyfriend of mine. But he hoped it was a friend of our family instead of a boyfriend. When he learned this tall, young man was my brother, it showed how glad he was to be in the wrong.

Again, between my brother and Gary, like with my Mom, it was love at first sight. They were buddy – buddy from the start. Gary met my brother's wife Erika and was waiting for Edgar to come to Berlin to take part in the fun we were having. Edgar wrote it wouldn't be long and he and family would be there. We were all holding our breath and anxiously waiting for it to happen.

My friend Inge and her fiancé Ray became less and less a part of us and they seemed to be happy with not having to be our watch dogs anymore.

At my workplace I could chat along with the best of them because I was not the stay at home kind of girl anymore. The towel draped over my locker door looked as pretty as all the other girls' towels. I learned English from them and we all sang along with we worked, with the American radio station. Irene Good Night was among our favorite songs. We all loved country music and our American boyfriends.

This, of course, was disliked by all the German boys and they had a lot to say about it when given the opportunity. Walking next to someone on the street in uniform and having a German young man walking by, words could be heard that were not nice and would make my face turn red and my cheeks burn.

I was smart not to mention it to Gary as he would have turned around and went after such a troublemaker. Being Berlin occupation, even if my soldier boy got a whipping, he would have been the winner. The German police and the MP's would have been called and had a face off. Not good for either side.

I always pretended not to hear a bad comment or be aware of someone spitting on the ground after walking past us. I understood what these young men thought. The American soldiers had more to offer a girl than the German men had. And this and much more made the German young men angry. A German girl going with a soldier was viewed as a gold digger or a second-class citizen. It was taking a chance to be seen with them and many of us took this chance. Everyone had their own reason why they became a couple. Not everyone was a gold digger.

In my case, I got to meet Gary by accident and as time went by, I learned first to like him. He was the one saying to me that he loved me. Yes, he didn't say he liked me, but came straight out saying that he loved me. What was I to think or say about this? I waited a while before I said it back to him. I wanted to be sure that what I felt for this handsome, young man really was love. How would I know what love was when I never had been in love before?

The proof came when Gary had to accompany prisoners to Bremerhaven and was gone for over a week. Coming home from work I kept listening for his footsteps to come rushing up the stairs and then ringing the doorbell. I told myself, missing someone like I did could be nothing other than love.

For me it had nothing to do with him having more money or him being an American. I missed the young man with the nice smile, his sense of humor and the love he showed for us all. Not just for me, but he loved my family. Oh, well, to be totally honest, I might have missed the popcorn, too, he brought every night. So maybe we were gold diggers after all. It was a Sunday when Gary returned. Coming in saying hi to my family and then greeting me with a hug I said "Glad you are back. I missed you and I love you." You should have seen the smile on his face. Idle sunshine for him and me.

A few days after all this took place, Gary came back one evening, he had a talk with my parents. I was sent to wait in the bedroom so they could talk in private. When I was called to join them, I learned Gary asked to marry me. With moving a cigar band from one hand to the other, he demonstrated how serious he was about us. I saw on my parents' faces that they had nothing against this if I said yes. And yes, was my answer. I was very happy knowing he was serious about me, like I was about him. Making a proposal of marriage proved it to me that he meant every word he said to me. To my girlfriends at work I said not a word about this.

On another weekend, we went to a jewelry store located on Bundesallee and purchased for each other a simple golden band to wear on the left ring finger of our hands. Then we had a photo made of the two of us to send to Gary's family. I hoped they would like me. Gary said, "Honey, don't you worry. I love you and my family will love you."

Chapter Fifty-Three

When I came to work on Monday, I showed my friends the ring on my finger, all said it's time for them to party. At lunch one went out and smuggled a bottle of wine in. In coffee cups, they toasted Gary and my engagement. We didn't get caught and this was good for us, because drinking on the job could have cost us our jobs. I only had a little in my coffee cup. I really, really didn't like to drink. But since the girls were toasting my engagement, I thought it wasn't polite not to taste a small sip of it.

After the one bottle was empty, I couldn't believe it when one of them again snuck out to buy a second bottle. I did not participate in drinking this one. But I can tell you, our workroom was a loud and happy one. When it came to all of us singing American tunes, singing Irene Good Night at full lung capacity sounded fantastic.

Coming home and telling what happened, my parents had a good laugh. When I told them my friend Uschi threw up because she had not eaten well to have a foundation for the wine, they laughed even more. However, there was way more to Uschie's throwing up than we all knew. Come to find out, Uschie was pregnant. Her boyfriend was an officer and after she told him about the baby, he informed her that he was already married and he had children.

Finding out about this, her Mom insisted for Uschi to give up her baby after it was born. After a lot of back and forth between mother and daughter, my friend Uschie agreed to her mother's terms. She worked hard but the smile was gone from her face. For me, Uschie had good advice by saying, "Do not go the route I was on, it hurts too much. First get married, then think about having a family."

But did Gary and I listen to the well-meant advice? No, we did not. Gary reenlisted for another four years in Berlin and it was granted. He got a nice amount of money for reenlisting. Some of it he used to make a young lady out of the second-hand Annie I was. Since we were engaged, Mom allowed it for Gary to spend some of his money on me.

He got rid of the awful looking blue coat and orange stocking I wore. The coat we bought in a German store was a pale green. And for the first time, I wore nylons and black shoes with a heel. A small watch adorned my wrist and set off the golden band on the ring finger of my left hand.

When I saw me in the store mirror, I was not the same girl anymore. It was shocking even to me, to see the transformation that took place. I have to admit, even I thought I went from looking plain to being attractive. And it was Gary Monk, my handsome soldier, that brought about this change.

My change was not just on the outside but also on my inside. Under my heart I carried our baby. Gary was over the moon and back to be the dad for our baby. He went and talked with the American chaplain, or is it minister, and with his commanding officer. He brought us a stack of paperwork to be submitted that spelled the word marriage between an American and German citizen; making our baby at birth the American citizen but yes, having a German mom and a large German family in occupied Berlin.

After knowing we would be parents, we tried to find us our own place to live. But soon we saw how impossible it was at the time to find something. It was best for us to stay with mom. We used the bedroom as ours. Mom laid claim to the kitchen with the sofa that used to be mine. A small apartment it was with way too many people in it. But we stuck together like glue and the two small rooms we called our home was overflowing with the love we had for one another. I can tell you that it took a lot of love sometimes not to get on each other's nerves.

My parents did not get upset when they found out they were going to be grandparents. This was astonishing for me, but not so for Gary. He always thought they would be okay with their daughter, not being married, having a baby. And so were Gary's parents in Caney, Kansas. When they got our photo and saw the ring on my left hand, they thought we were already married. Gary told me he wouldn't tell them otherwise. Maybe sometime later he could explain it all to them, but not now. He informed me that in the U.S., a married couple wore the ring on their left ring finger instead of on the right, like we did in Germany. He laughed and said we wouldn't clear this up till we had to. Gary often teased and said since his parents lost a little girl in his sister Joann, they might hope for our baby to be a girl. Well, I couldn't promise it, I could only say our baby would be welcomed and would be loved. It was the first baby born here to our family in Berlin. The baby Erwin and Erika expected, they lost. Erika was sure it was due to the hardship she suffered when she was in Russia. But they would try again sometime later to have a family.

When I came to work my friend Uschi said, "Dagie, do you know how fortunate you are to have the support of your entire family?" "Yes," I told her. I knew and I wished it would have been the same for her. She had a hard time holding back tears when she hugged me.

It was in the middle of the week at work, Uschi started to have labor pains. Our employer, Mrs. Juckel, called the Ambulance to take her away. All of us looked down from the window and telling her all would be fine.

Ten days later she was back, trim and slim and minus her baby. She had a little girl, she was told this much but not anything more. She said she heard her little girl cry but the nurse nor the doctor nor her mother let her see or hold her baby. They thought they did what was in her best interest.

Uschi said she wouldn't allow this to happen again. Her mom would not have a say over her life. She applied for a visa to the U.S.A. and would become household help for a wealthy family. In the meantime, she would go out with the American military. She would target the officers, promising much, take all she could from them but give them nothing in return.

Our coworker and friend was not the same girl anymore. She was beautiful to look at but inside cold as ice. This experience had created a monster. Behind her back we gave her the nickname Ice Princess. We felt sorry for the man that went on a date with her. We girls had a talk with her but could see the Uschi we knew and loved was gone. Losing her baby and giving it up for someone else to raise changed her completely.

She got the Visa to enter the U.S.A. When we said goodbye, we wished her only the best. We wondered if Uschie would ever find herself again. The way it looked to all of us, we would never find out. Uschie was not planning to keep in touch with any of us. This was sad for us, we really liked the Uschie she once was and didn't want to be anymore.

Chapter Fifty-Four

The Company Juckel had a streak of bad luck and went out of business. All of us had to apply for unemployment. Here I was, not married, expecting a baby and having to look for a place of work. I found out fast not any of this was of my fiancé's liking. He fussed as the work offered to me was factory work as well as work in restaurants or fancy night clubs. This kind of work was not for me. Besides, being pregnant, how could I be a hostess in a club? It was silly to think of it or imagine it. I was clueless on what I should do.

It was Gary that came up with what he thought was a good solution. He asked me to step away from work and only take care of our baby and me. He said he was willing and perfectly able to take care of his family. I thought about it and talked it over with my parents. We thought it was amazing for a twenty-one- year-old to want to do this. It was really a good attitude for him to have. He was a young man not married yet but expecting a baby with his fiancé.

He wanted to take charge as if he was a married man. This showed my parents how serious he was about us two. I was younger than Gary and had to get a grip on it that at such a young age I would soon be a mother. It was kind of hard for me to believe I was having to look out for another life and not just my own.

I started to sew diapers and other odds and ends with the help of my mom for our little one. I withdrew from the employment office telling them I had plans to leave the country. It was taking a risk on my part as I had to rely on my fiancé for my upkeep and the wellbeing of our baby.

Gary seemed to be happy, never wavering and every first of the month there was the money in my mom's hands to buy groceries. Nothing was bought at the commissary by Gary. As long as I lived in Germany, we did as the Germans did. We favored the German stores and by doing it we helped build up the economy.

I did not want to have our baby born in a hospital but wanted to have it born at home. My mom had us three at home and I wanted to follow in her footsteps. I had regular doctor visits and from him got the name of a midwife. We went to see her and it was 250 D Marks for her to help me when the time came.

Mom and I worked on putting a bed together for the baby. We found one of Grandma Emilie's wash baskets to make into the cutest baby bed. Everything we had was homemade. Some things were given to us by my cousin Herbert Sauer and his wife Rosi. They took such good care of the things they had, we were glad to get them from them.

They had a baby carriage and all I had to do was add the pillow and blankets. I did this in pale green. It was the color used for a boy or a girl. It turned out looking so adorable. Mom and I were pleased with the work we did. Now all we needed was the baby. Boy or girl, we thought we were ready to hear the little voice of a baby cry in our small apartment.

On the 8th of November was the day he came into the world. The 8th of November, 1951 we named our son Danny Dean Weiss. We had to wait till we got married then in a flash with a stroke of a pen or typewriter the last name is changed to Monk.

When I was experiencing labor and was screaming my head off, I swore to myself never to do this again. But how soon we forget and much to Gary's delight, on the 11th of April 1953 we added Linda Sue Weiss to the family. Again, I had the full support of my family and I admired them and loved them for it. I was still only a fiancé and now the mom of two children.

Not any more money because of having two babies was added for additional household expenses, we kept it all the same. Instead, we asked Gary to buy Mom a small gas stove. The warm up of milk bottles and the cooking of food was this way made easier. We had a small two burner gas stove from Grandma Sauer but it gave up on us. Gary told Mom to look around and he would pay for a nicer gas stove. She was a happy woman when she found a white four-burner stove and it had a baking unit. Now she couldn't wait to bake cakes for family birthdays and the holidays. She was in heaven with having a new stove.

We let Gary's family know about having a granddaughter and they mailed big packages with cute dresses for Linda. They also packed things for Danny and some items for me. Never did we have things before that were this nice. And she baked a fruitcake that was yummy, yummy. My dad swore up and down it was not baked with milk, but Gary's mom used alcohol instead. He said write her to send more of this. This is a cake we cannot bake ourselves or buy in any bakery store.

Our baby doll Linda, unlike Danny, was born at the Kaiserin Vicktoria Hospital in Berlin - Kreuzberg. Family came by to see me almost every day. Gary came every other day and always brought one of his buddies along. He wanted to show off his family. Both of our babies had blond hair and blue eyes. Well, Danny had the blue ones, Linda had violet eyes. I could not take my eyes off of her when I held her in my arms, her eyes were so pretty.

Danny came with my dad to visit at the hospital a few times. Mom visited with me and Dad let him play around the grass area at the hospital. Danny was little and was not allowed to come in to see me. Therefore, he didn't get to see his baby sister till I brought her home. When we did, he paid not any attention when we pushed the carriage into the bedroom. He was busy playing with Dad and his toys. We snuck by him then Linda let her baby voice be heard. She was hungry and she let me know it. Hearing her cry made Danny perk up and take notice. I took his little hand and took him to the bedroom to show him who was making all this noise. He took one look at his sister and out of his mouth came the word 'Puppe.' It meant doll. I looked at my boy and agreed with him. I brought home a little baby doll we named Linda.

For Danny, she was never Linda. He called her Lindi. For as long as we stayed in Berlin, she would always be our Lindi girl and her Brother Danny's baby doll. Lindi's bed for the first few weeks was the baby carriage cousins Herbert and Rosi had given us for Danny. It worked fine till Gary said he wanted a new carriage and for Danny he wanted to buy a nice stroller.

We checked out the stores and came up with something nice for both of our children. Linda's was a pale grey and had a bumper like a car in the front. I couldn't believe how fancy it was. Danny's stroller was silver grey. In the middle it had wide dark blue stripes enhanced by shiny chrome. When the sun danced off the chrome it almost blinded me. Nothing came from the American stores located at Clayallee. All came from stores in our neighborhood.

Slowly we set in progress all the paperwork to get married. All this time we worked on being a loving couple. We saw many American / German relationships break apart. But we told ourselves ours would not be one of them. My parents divorced after close to twenty years of marriage. I prayed that something like this would never happen to us. To be married and stay married was the goal I set for me. Keeping my fingers crossed it was Gary's goal too. I knew my Mom, when angry, could hold onto it way too long. It was my thought I needed to be less in all she was more. Don't get me wrong, I love my Mom but, in some things, I didn't want to be like her.

I needed to be less argumentative than I thought my mom was, less angry and way more forgiving than she was. I thought if I kept these three principles in mind, Gary and I would have a good marriage. I was working these important principles from the time he placed a gold band on the ring finger of my left hand.

Chapter Fifty-Five

After we had Danny, Gary took more time to be around his buddies. They all met at a place called "Die Goldene Sonne". The Golden Sun and the owners were a woman called Edie and her mother. Gary had a friend called Cacey and often he sent him to pick me up instead of coming after me himself. Cacey was a good friend and did not seem to mind the extra duty put on him. In the workplace, Gary was his boss and he was a few ranks higher than Cacey.

Mom and I talked about this and both of us thought it was rude of Gary to send his friend Cacey as his substitute. By the time Cacey and I got to the Golden Sun, my fiancé had already way too much to drink and was on his way to happy land. Sometimes when I got there, he was on his way to unhappy land. This is when I had to use one, or two of the principles I set for me.

It was the principle of forgiveness combined with the love I had for him. When I came home from such a date, I closed the door to my bedroom. I looked at my two sleeping babies and had a good cry. My mom must have heard me and the next day wanted to know why I cried. When I told her what it was, she was angry with Gary and said she would give him a piece of her mind when he came.

However, when he did show up, she could never be angry with him. The truth is nobody could, including me. Gary, without anything to drink, could win anyone over to his side. So, my family and I gave him the excuse of being occupation in Germany. After all, as my mom was in the habit of saying, "Boys will be boys."

This was true, but this boy was now a dad and I, the young girl, was now a mom. In my way of thinking it was time to act like grownups. As the mother of two, I did not have play time. I didn't go with girlfriends and took time to have fun. My mom and dad saw to it that I did the work that a mother must do. It was for me to get the babies up and putting them to sleep. Keeping them clean, feeding them and most of all loving them. And if it helped when I put them to bed, I sang to them till they fell asleep. Brahms' Lullaby always worked and they both slept through the night. The next day Danny was hard at play again and his little sister started to show she had a cute personality.

Since my language was German, of course their language was German. Danny did not call his dad Daddy. He called him Papa. And Linda started her early years in Berlin on the same foundation.

We went out less and less and Gary took more time hanging out with his buddies. When it was weekends and we had a date, he came late or showed up early in the mornings. Sometimes he took the trolley instead of a taxi to our house, the conductor woke him up at the end of the line. The trolley changed hands as it continued driving over into the East sector. This was the Russian part of Berlin. Unsafe for an American soldier.

Gary was lucky the conductor woke him and got him off in time. Then he had to look to find a cab to get home to us. He thought it was extremely funny that he fell asleep on the trolley. We warned him that next time he may not be so lucky and a Russian soldier might wake him up. Then he wouldn't have anything to laugh about. I do believe my Gary did not worry about anything. He was young, handsome and acted like he didn't have a care in the world. I did the worrying for him. If he was intoxicated and somehow wound up in the east part of town, it would be taken seriously. With him sticking with friends more and more, we had reason to worry more and more. I was not the only one worried, my mom was the other.

I learned to write letters to Gary's parents and they answered with a letter or two a month. I saw in his mother's letters they cared about him and us. She had aunts, uncles and cousins sign their name to the bottom of the letter. This surprised me but it made me feel good. It looked to me and mine that we were wanted by Gary's family. All of the family, aunts, uncles and cousins included.

Mom and Dad saw the letters and by then I was good in translating them. They both knew by what I read to them we have a home in America with the Monk family. We were wanted and cared for. Mom was the one saying when the time came for us to leave, this alone would help her and Dad.

We still had some time left before this happened. We were not married yet and before leaving Berlin, I had to be Mrs. Garrett D. Monk. And our little cutie pies, even though they had the American citizenship because of their dad, they had till then a guardian. Till we married, their last name was my maiden name Weiss. After saying I do, their last name changed from Weiss to their legal name Monk. All the legal matters could become very confusing for someone like me.

I had difficulties many times to keep smiling and to show patience and love. Gary turned toward enjoying party time with his buddies that nicknamed him Papa. They teased him by calling him this name because he was such a young dad at only twenty-one. He enjoyed all the teasing and was good in returning it.

When we eventually went out for a walk, we met with older couples. They always said "how is Mama and Papa doing?" By this, meaning us and not my mom and dad. Gary answered, "Mama and Papa and babies are doing fine… but we want to know, how you kids are doing?" It always made the other couple laugh because they were older and we were the kids.

Now this was the kind of fun I liked. Sitting around in a place like the Golden Sun watching people get intoxicated and unruly was never to my liking. I had this when I worked for Biering's. And thinking of this place still leaves a bad taste in my mouth like vinegar.

It was not any fun for me to be sitting in a place like the Golden Sun or the 48 Club after a movie and see my fiancé get tipsy. Then he would act like a jealous person when one of his friends spoke with me or asked me for a dance. I always refused to dance and just sat there and enjoyed the music, watching other couples on the dance floor. Besides, I had never learned to dance. I didn't go anyplace till I met Gary. Gary didn't dance. This left me sitting at the table and watching other couples on the dance floor. But I liked listening to the music. The 48 Club had a wonderful band playing. They played all kinds of music and I liked the soft tunes. I called them music to dream by.

On the way home however, I was in hot water. Gary showed his jealous side and I bit my lip not to say anything. But the heartache was always mine. To be at home and not to go out at all was best for me. Gary has shown me that he has a jealous nature and this could become a trouble spot in our relationship. But only if I allowed it.

I was always taken back when my finance acted this way. If I gave him a reason for it then I could see why he was angry with me. But this was something I didn't understand because I did nothing to provoke it. If one of his friends stopped by the table just to say hello, this could become a difficulty for me on the way home. I thought to be home with our two babies, was the safest place for me to be.

By now I had lost most of my friends and all I had was my family and Gary's buddies and their girlfriends. The buddies I thought it was best for me to stay away from. And the girlfriends his buddies had took their loving someone lightly. I didn't like being around them. When we ventured out, we asked Erwin and Erika to accompany us. This way I was in good and safe company and dared to have a nice time. Going from place to place, we listened to music, ate something and taught Erwin and Erika to sing "Irene Good Night" in perfect English.

My parents never minded to babysit and when we came home, Gary always had a bottle of wine for Dad. The next day when Dad showed up, it was his pay for being such a good sitter and Grandpa. Mom enjoyed us telling her what we had been up to and urged us to get away more often. She was a good mom and knew I was young and had become a home body more than a nineteen-year-old girl should be.

My parents loved Gary and so did I, but we started to be concerned about his drinking. All of us thought it was due to being in Germany. Away from his family and his home in Kansas for so many years. When he went back to the U.S.A., surely it would stop. We loved him so much that we said very little of what we really thought. We were all guilty of accepting unacceptable behavior. And we enabled him to think what he was doing was alright. Alright, because we chose to put up with it.

Chapter Fifty-Six

A letter came to the mailbox from Edgar saying he was coming to visit. It was high time for us to meet his family. He wrote he was eager to see Erwin, Erika, my Gary and the babies. He told us their arrival date and asked if we thought his home town was ready for him. We wrote back we were not sure if Berlin was ready for him but we were. For them to hurry up and get here, we were impatient to see them. And we were and this included Gary. Till Edgar came, the days went by in the old familiar way. Doing laundry, cleaning, taking care of Danny, Linda and my dad, who was still not a citizen of West Berlin. We were wondering how to sleep three more people in our tiny apartment but it would work out. Mom and I would sleep in one bed, Edgar and Huguette would have the other. Danny and little Lindi had the baby bed. And Edgars daughter Blandine slept on the sofa in the kitchen. The problem was solved because Gary was still in the Barracks at Finckensteinallee. Erwin and Erika had theirs and Dad had his place. It would be a tight squeeze, but who cares? Our Edgar was going to be home for a few weeks.

In the evenings after Dad left, Mom and I waited to hear footsteps rushing up the stairs. Waiting for it to be Gary ringing the doorbell. Then when 1 opened instead of my mother, he stuck his head into the kitchen saying to my mom "hello, Mutti" However, he had trouble pronouncing Mutti so out of his mouth came "hello, Moodie". To hear it made both of us smile, it sounded cute. No one that looked at Gary could ever be mad at him.

If we listened for footsteps and they stopped at the floor below it was not him. We knew, instead of coming, he was with his buddies at the Golden Sun. If it happened to be a Saturday and not a week day, he would find his way to the door early in the morning. We worried when he was in this condition because often, he got into trouble that gave him thirty days restriction. Thirty days without a pass to be with us and the babies.

When this was the case, he gave me extra money to go to the corner phone booth and call him. Or I needed to take the trolley having Danny in a stroller, leaving the baby at home with my parents, and come to Finckensteinallee. He waited at the fence and we visited through the fence. Then home I went and told Mom about what we talked about.

When the days of restriction were behind him, he stuck his blond head and big smile through the kitchen door and said hi to his and my Moodie. All was always forgiven when the wayward wanderer had found his way home.

Berlin - Friedenaú, Handjerystrasse 62 four flights up, door to the left, was home for us till we left for America. This was to happen in 1954, when Gary's tour in my homeland and town was over. In the meantime, we went with the ups and downs that came our way, always trying to think positive. What we believed in helped so much. We believed that God gave us only what He knew we were able to handle.

Should the Weiss family lose their foothold somehow and life knocked us down, we only grew stronger. We made a fist, stood up, dusted us off and as a family unit having faith in God, we continued together. We always knew when God had us or one of us in His protection. He must have had Gary in his protection often. Mom had a saying that said, God protects small children and drunks. I really didn't like to think of Gary as a drunk. In my way of thinking drunks laid in the gutter and reeked of alcohol. This was not my Gary. I chose to think of him as a young man that liked to drink too much. This was better than to say he was a drunk, or on the way to becoming one. I had blindfolds on my eyes and didn't know it.

Talking of needing God's protection. So it was for when Dad, on his way to see us, got caught up in some kind of revolt or demonstration. It was the 17th of June 1953 when all hell broke loose. Dad, walking along peaceful, had to make a run for his life. He said bullets went by his ears and he had to run for shelter. He found it in a doorway of a house. Peeking out, he saw cars being turned over and fires being set. Tanks started to come down the street with people throwing stones at the tanks. As if stones could really hurt a tank!

Dad said the people were angry and it must be a political matter. People wanted freedom. Dad said he was not sure why this broke loose but East and West of our Berlin was on a collision course. He said this was serious with people getting hurt. With a bullet flying by him he could have been a victim of this uprising. To this we said oh, God, and we went about our daily duties not having any idea of what was going on. We heard sirens and so forth, but these are noises every large city has. There was nothing unusual about this till Dad came and told us he had been in the middle of an uprising.

There were fatalities. Nine coffins stood in front of West Berlin City Hall. Thank God, Dad was not in one of them. He was with many others the innocent bystander caught up in an angry mob. The 17th of June when my baby girl Linda was only two months old, would go down in history. The 17th of June 1953 was a terrifying day for the people of Berlin. When the newspaper reported what took place, we questioned how many other such days would this town have to face?

Chapter Fifty-Seven

After the storm of angry people was over, Edgar and family arrived. This was exciting. The plane coming from Frankfurt Main flew in at 8 p.m. Mom and I stood at the gate waiting. Dad stayed home, smoking his pipe, watching the grandkids and walking holes through the kitchen floor. He was as excited to see his son and family as Mom and I.

We could see the plane landing as we stood by the gate. We saw the bus going out to meet the passengers. When the bus came back and opened the doors, my tall brother was the first one to get out. Next to him was a beautiful, slender lady and a petite girl. Edgar brought Madame Hugnette and Mademoiselle Blandine Weiss to meet us. They greeted us by kissing us on both sides of the face like it is a French custom to do. We took a taxi home and they gave the same greeting to Dad and my children.

Small as our apartment was, we made them comfortable for a two-week stay. Hugnette liked to crochet. After buying pale green yarn, she got busy to make a dress and booties for Linda. She was fast. In hardly no time she had it done.

Edgar always said he wanted to marry someone attractive. Well, he outdid himself when he fell in love and married Huguette. She was French and so was petite Mademoiselle Blandine Weiss. When Erika met her sister-in-law, she gave both of us make up tips. She showed us how to get away not wearing nylons but looking like we had them on. She took the eyebrow pencil in black or brown and drew a seam (line) up the back of her legs. No one would have guessed she was barefoot in her in her shoes. Shoes with a high heel.

It was wonderful to have the French relatives with us and to hear about their life in Faulquemont and from Edgar how he felt about working under the ground. He lived his life as a coal miner and was a gardener, fisherman and motorcycle rider when he was not under the ground. He loved the outdoors. He was a good swimmer and loved soccer games. He was a soccer player as a young man and would remain to be one as he got older.

Erwin and Edgar had a high old time being together and my Gary was in the middle of it all. When we went out, he paid most of the bill saying "I want to show my to-be brothers-in-law a good time." I remember one incident when I caused what could have been trouble.

It was about seven or eight in the evening. A nice night and walking a way behind my brothers and their wives, a German passerby coming toward us spit in front of me. I called out to my brothers and they took care of it. Edgar went back and lifted this young man by the shoulders clear off the ground saying, "Don't you ever do this again. The American troops saved you from what came into Berlin before them. You better show some respect and show yourself grateful. Do you understand me?"

It didn't take long for a group of onlookers to gather around. All of them in agreement with my brother. When Edgar put this young man's feet on the ground, he understood as well as the onlookers, never again to spit in front of a girl walking alongside an American soldier. We walked away and heard the sound of clapping hands. It has only been four years since the Berlin Airlift came to an end. The West Berliner had not forgotten what it cost the Allied Forces to keep West Berlin going. Only a youngster like this young man was, would spit in front of an American soldier and his German girlfriend, or in my case fiancé's feet.

I understood it was a kind of jealousy on the young men's part, because attractive girls went with the American soldiers. Not saying that I thought of me as pretty or attractive. No, I never did have this notion. But my friends Inge Johl, Uschie, Sonja and her sister Georgia, they all fit this picture. When we walked away from this group that saw what my brother did with the German boy, we knew that the other people standing there gave him a piece of their minds. They were clearly continuing what my brother started, giving a lesson on why Berlin needed to be grateful.

With all the uproar of this incident behind us, Gary understood that my brother Edgar liked him. Liked him enough to stand up for him and me. He was looking out for us. Coming home we spilled over, telling it all to mom. She just smiled this little smile and said, "Why is this such a surprise? Gary is our family and is this not what family is for? When you and the children go to America, Gary's family will do the same for you, if it should be needed. We hope that you will not have any trouble over there." She continued saying, "This war has left many families heart broken. You and the babies might see and feel some of this sadness when you get to America. Then you must remember who you are and why you went with Gary to his homeland. It is love that got you there. It will be your love that will hold you up and together. When you work by stepping up to the plate together, you'll gain friendship and respect from the people around you."

Hearing Mom's words shook me up a little. I had not thought about it like she did. In one year, if all goes well, I would leave Germany and follow my husband to his homeland. All I have known, I would have to leave behind. Could I really do this? I have a deep love for my family and my birth place. The love I have for Gary, Danny and Linda I believed would help me do whatever it took to make America our home. I had, as far as I could read in the letter, Gary's family to back me up.

In 1954, it was for me and mine, "America, here we come." It was for me to make the most of my brothers' and families' visit while they were in Berlin. Time was speeding by while we were having fun. We enjoyed every day to the fullest knowing a year from now, we too will leave.

My dad's money was limited but every day he spent some to make pictures to give me memories in a photo album. He said if I should get home sick for them, all I had to do is look at the album. I knew when the time came and I got home sick, and I knew that I definitely would get homesick, one look at this crazy bunch in the photos would cheer me up. I pushed these thoughts aside. Right now, they were with me and I didn't want to think about the years ahead of me without them.

As much as we enjoyed the visitors, it was quite a task in this small apartment having so many people in it. Every morning one after the other, went into the bedroom to sponge bathe. Huguette, my sister-in-law, was always the first one ready. She went to the bakery to buy fresh baked bread for breakfast. Mom cooked one hot meal a day for our group. Should we have the feeling we needed something in between, we had odds and ends in the kitchen cupboard. We could fix up a plate and have at it.

When Edgar arrived, he asked Mom how much grocery money she needed and gave her the amount she quoted him. One morning she had to tell him she had underestimated and ran out of money. It was then that Edgar and family left Berlin. When Dad, Erwin and Erika showed up and later that evening Gary, they were surprised and sad to hear of their sudden departure. But this was very much like Edgar to do what he thought was best for him.

He did this when he left Mom and me to go to France and find work and the love of his life there. Mom and I left behind, we managed to do alright without him. Now we again had to do without him. Even more so because with him left Huguette and little Blandine. She was a little French doll. When she was out and about with us, people turned their heads to look after her. Her parents dressed her so cute. And a lot of the things she wore her Mom made for her. Edgar rationed the money for this trip and I believe, gave Mom what he could for their upkeep while they were with us. The rest must have been spending money for them to see West Berlin. He didn't have more to give to Mom, so it was time to pack and fly back to France. Dad was out of the little girl he practiced his French with when Blandine left with her parents. We had a short visit with them, but at least we saw them. I knew for me, Gary and our children it was the last time. If I could have one wish for this reason alone, I wanted for them to stay the full two weeks. It was wonderful to see them come, but so hard to let them leave again. Mom never mentioned to us any of her thoughts. But knowing her like I did, she felt bad she ran out of money so soon. She never mentioned her feelings to me. She didn't have to, no, she didn't have to.

When Gary showed up and I told him about it, he said he would have helped if we had phoned and told him. Gary was not ready to give Edgar and family up so soon. He went down to the restaurant next door and came up with pilsner beer, saying in his own way, Goodbye and Prost to

Edgar's going back to France. Gary, Dad and Erwin, but not Mom, Erika and I, drank the big container of beer. We drank cups of strong coffee instead.

I knew that I would miss my big, ornery brother. With Mom not voicing her thoughts, I watched when she checked for mail every day and was not happy till she had a letter from them. Again, I thought, this is what moms do. If I and the children left for America next year, she would wait for mail from us.

I always said if instead of when we went to America. Doing this, it upset Gary. He said, "What is this with you saying if we go? We all go or no one goes." It made me laugh to hear this from him. But it showed me how serious he was to keep our little family together.

We got busy with all the paperwork and had not any trouble to get approved by all the right authorities. The road was cleared to marry six months before Gary's return to the States. His departing Berlin was set for the spring and we would follow him in the fall. The Christmas and New Year's Eve of 1953 would be extra, extra special for the Weiss family. The other holidays I would spend as Mrs. Monk with Gary and his family in Caney, Kansas U.S.A. It was like a silent promise between all of us to make the remaining days, weeks and months count.

Chapter Fifty-Eight

Regardless of the weather, sunshine or slow rain, my parents took the kids with them wherever they went. In slow rain, the umbrella protected them. In sunny weather, we had an umbrella to protect the baby Linda from the sun rays.

Our big boy Danny shared all he could share with his sister Lindi. But when it came to caramel bonbons, he unwrapped them, took a nibble out first then handed the rest to Linda. He was the taste tester for what was good or not.

The money for the little adventures came from me. Gary always handed me telephone money without counting it. It was a generous amount and took care of more than just the daily calls between us.

For as long as we were not married, Gary's home was the camp at Berlin - Finckensteinallee. Only when he had a three-day pass, could he stay with us. So it was, that every day around noon I called him to tell him what was going on with all of us. Telling him of Danny throwing the new doll I bought for Linda into the duck pond at West Berlin's City Park.

A policeman came, catching my dad climbing over the fence to retrieve the doll, and he got away with getting only a warning. It helped that Dad could say he was retired from the police force. Doing this, the policeman became my dad's helper and Linda got her doll back. Slightly wet but still all in one piece. Linda was not laughing holding a wet doll, but Dad said her brother Danny thought it was funny and giggled and giggled non-stop.

A favorite hangout for this threesome of Grandpa and grandkids were the railroad stations. Danny loved seeing the trains coming and going. He and Dad played games of Danny being in charge over every train coming in and going out. Linda was too small yet for the game playing. She sat in the stroller munching on caramel bonbons. When they got home, she was a sticky mess. Sometimes so was Danny and her grandpa. Who says that grown-ups cannot enjoy caramels as much as kids do?

With Grandma, it was trolley rides and stopping for a hotdog from the street vendors.

For me, it was to take them to the ice cream parlor around the corner from us.

With their dad, it was for Danny to walk hand in hand to the newspaper stand for the paper for his grandparents. And not to forget, he went to see his first movie at the Outpost Theater at Clay Allee. Calamity Jane was playing starring Doris Day. She, besides Betty Grable, was his dad's favorite actress. The only interest Danny showed for this film was when it showed the train and, of course, he liked being treated to a bag of popcorn. He couldn't eat a whole bag all by himself, we helped him finish it. On the way out of the theater we bought a coke for all of us. Danny liked the way the fizzle from it or other drinks tickled his nose. He wrinkled it up and laughed. We were proud of our little boy when he sat for this two-hour movie between his dad and me like a good boy. We were sure eating popcorn and falling asleep for a tiny nap helped a lot.

In between times, Erwin and Erika came sharing the wonderful news that a baby was on the way. We thought Gary might not see their baby but I would. If all went well, they lost one before, I was asked to be this baby's godmother. I said yes. This made me really happy. My brother Erwin and Erika were godparents to Danny and

Linda. Now I was asked to be this for their little one. This was such happy news.

It was two months after Linda's birth, we had their baptism at the church in Berlin - Friedenaú, Die Kirche zúm Gúten Hirten, The Church to the Good Shepherd. It was their great grandfather Hermann Sauer that built the walk and the large door and the steeple of this church. Now his great grandchildren would be baptized there.

I remember it well. It was Easter Sunday, a sunny day when this took place. Linda was dressed in a dress Grandma Monk had sent and Danny in sailor suit from his American grandparents. Gary and I had a hard time to take care of Danny when the baptism took place. Our little boy spotted his grandpa among all the onlookers. Instead of Dad sitting with us, his family, he was sitting to the side and Danny wanted to go and sit by him.

But Gary and I could not let him go. The sprinkling of him, Linda and ten other children was taking place. Danny made a fuss because he didn't understand why a man in a dark robe wanted to sprinkle water on his and his baby sister's head.

It was quite a morning for us. My dad thought it was funny but Gary did not. Erwin and Erika, the godparents sided with Gary and so did I. My mom usually on our side this time took Dad's side. Mom and Dad had the opinion all this to do, this ceremony was too long for all the kids. They were all kind of wiggly and more so when Danny stepped up the game plan. My dad thought it was hilarious and so did, for some reason, my mom. We the parents and the godparents had the long faces. Glad when it was over, we walked slowly toward home.

Coming back from the church, a good meal was waiting that Mom started fixing the day before. We had a nice bottle of red wine to celebrate this special occasion. When it was empty, Gary went down to buy a container of beer. Our three men continued to celebrate till Gary had to leave for camp. This broke up the party. Erwin and Erika saw to it he got on the trolley or found a taxi cab for him to give him the ride back. By the time Gary left he was always more under the influence than Erwin or Dad. I had reason to be concerned. Mom always claimed he had a guardian angel watching him when he made it back to camp in one piece.

Many times, I wanted to speak with him about his drinking but always backed away from it. It was fear of being too outspoken could cost our children either their dad or mom. The children, since birth, were American citizens, but I was not. I thought I had reason to be afraid that if Gary left me behind, I would have a fight on my hand with him and the American government. A fight I might lose. I did not want to chance it and therefore bit down on my tongue and said not a word.

I held onto the belief that when Gary was in the States it would change. His drinking in Berlin was daily. I had to believe that this would stop when he was back home. The money would not be there for it. One dollar, or script as it was called in Germany, gave him four D Marks in exchange. In the U.S.A. a dollar was one dollar and I hoped this would stop the daily intake or the need for so much alcohol.

Whenever Gary showed up, and I mean whenever, because not always did he show up, we did the normal family things. In the summer we went for walks. In the fall, Gary like to walk through the falling leaves, shuffling his feet as he walked along. In the winter, he liked the snow and slid over the icy stretches on the sidewalk as if he wore ice skates. This was a happy playtime and fun for me to do with him. I enjoyed it when he turned loose and showed me the fun side of him.

The United States soldier he was had to stand inspection. For this special inspection he came to us to help him polish the brass on his uniform. This is what Danny and Linda knew of their dad; he was a man in uniform and they called him papa. When I took our children for a walk and Gary happened not to be with us, sometimes we had a funny situation happening.

A soldier and his girl walked in front of us and my Danny, recognizing the uniform, before I could stop him ran up to him and called him papa. I had some explaining to do to the young man's girlfriend because this made her turn around and look at him in disbelief. Then, after all was cleared up, I had something to tell Danny's real papa that evening.

Gary, the real dad or papa, thought it was funny and said, "Danny needs to look at me more. He needs to recognize the face of his dad and not only the uniform." Again, I did not say to Gary what I wanted. For him to come and be with us before the children's bedtime, this would help them and me. I thought I should point this out to him, but again I got fearful and didn't.

I thought of ways to help this situation that was so hard for me to grasp and get a grip of. I took a photo of him and showed it to our two saying, "See, this is your daddy, this is your papa. Tell him good morning or if it was their bedtime, tell him good night." Of course, all was said in German. I wanted to speak English with them when we left for the U.S.A. I thought as young as they were, they would learn quick when nothing but English was spoken. It never occurred to me this could be confusing to them. I thought of my little ones as being bright little ones. They, like I did when I met their dad, would learn and get along well in the United States.

Chapter Fifty-Nine

This last Christmas, Santa made it special for my parents. Pretty glassware and cartons of Chesterfield cigarettes for Mom. A new pipe and pipe tobacco for Dad. Not to forget the bottle of wine he liked to drink. When I saw the cartons of cigarettes for Mom, I was reminded of the times I had to pick them up from the sidewalk. This was only about seven years ago. Things changed. I didn't have to do this anymore. Today I didn't walk behind a man in uniform, I walked beside him because he was my fiancé, soon to be husband.

Gary's folks outdid themselves, and sent a box that held all kinds of good things. Odds and ends for the little ones and the best was the delicious fruit cake my to be mother-in-law baked. My dad and brother ate the most of it. They had the sweet tooth more than we women did. The letter in the big box was written with love, telling us how much they looked forward to meeting us. The last holidays we shared, we made the usual sentimental journey through the past years. Remembering, talking about it and being grateful for the way it turned out for our family. We agreed God, for some reason, saw to it that our family didn't suffer losing our loved ones.

At this time, I saw all the signs that my family wanted to make the clock stand still. The realization hit home that soon we were gone for good. No matter what they wanted, no one could make the time stand still. Tic-toc, tic-toc, it clicked down to Gary leaving Berlin and for us to follow him.

Following Christmas was the New Year's Eve party. Dad wanted to babysit the grandchildren. We took Mom to the 48 Club. Gary's friends asked her to dance and she enjoyed all the attention. She was a good dancer and did not have to sit at the table much nursing a drink. She had fun. Much fun to our and her delight.

For me it was special because my mom got Gary out on the dance floor, teaching him to slow dance. She laughed, telling him she did the same with my Dad when they first met. She said, "If I could teach him, I can teach you." This is what she did and got him and me out on the floor doing what all the other couples were doing. The last New Year's Eve was a fun time, with Gary not showing signs of becoming jealous. Mom was with us, maybe this made a difference. A happy New Year's Eve for me with my fiancé and my mom. Dad had the happy New Year's Eve he wanted to have. Looking after his grandchildren and playing with them. He was careful with having something to drink. New Year's Eve he would have a few glasses of wine or eggnog, after they drifted off to sleep. The sofa in the kitchen was there for him when he got tired. And since we were not home, he could use the bed in the bedroom if he wanted to be close to his grandkids.

When it was midnight, we saw my mother cry. I knew why she cried, next New Year, we were not there anymore. She might be going out with Erwin and Erika. By then their baby was there for Dad to babysit. I promised Mom, when she stopped her tears, she would get many letters from me and photos of Danny and Linda.

New Year's Day Erwin and Erika came to eat dinner. They had gone out to party with friends and Erwin had a hangover. If Gary had one, he didn't say. Maybe it helped being only a beer drinker. Erwin had beer and mixed drinks, he liked all of it. My drink was one glass of wine and the rest of the time I had Coke. Gary always said I was a cheap date.

Important days were coming up for us. We counted the days to our wedding. The 13th of February 1954, was our set date to become man and wife. It was written in stone, America was our home. The days with family in Berlin were numbered. We didn't have much time from the 1st day of the new year to the 13th of February.

I wanted a small wedding with only family and two of Gary's best friends. Mom would cook the meal and Mom's sister Lene was there to help. Edgar wrote he and family couldn't come. They wished us well and wrote they were there in mind, heart and spirit. He wrote, "Remember when you leave us and go across the ocean, we live far apart but I am there for you and will always be your big brother." Yes, I was not about to forget. I was aware this was also my brother Erwin's mind set. Distance couldn't loosen the strong brother and sister bond we shared.

I knew that I had been the spoiled one by being Edgar and Erwin's little sister and Dad and Mom's baby girl. An ocean or whatever else may turn up between us couldn't change it.

All we planned for this little wedding was always talked over with Gary. He agreed that, he and I being parents, when we married needed to keep it nice but simple. I went shopping for something to wear and Mom stressed the point that being a parent, I should not wear anything in white. I agreed and started to look for something pretty but suitable for this occasion.

West Berlin by this time had some nice stores. Mom and I looked at a few of them. Not having any luck in finding what I wanted. All was too flashy looking, too bridal for me. Till we found the small store hid away from the main street. There I found the dress that suited me. It was satin in a toned-down green, short sleeve with tiny gold buttons. We went to the shoe store Leiser and bought a pretty black shoe with the appropriate heel to make me look more festive. Not bridal but festive was the look I went for. When I looked in the mirror wearing this dress, it was again Mom that shed a few tears.

I had one thought when I looked at me. It is alright that I cannot wear white and look like a bride should look on her wedding day. But I can look nice being a bride and a mother of two. I was happy with what I bought and the preparations we made for this special day. Our day. Gary's and mine.

Gary made the choice to have his friend McQueen to stand up with him. My brother Erwin was the choice I made. I did not go to the hairdresser. My hair was short and had natural curl. My nails and make-up I did it all myself. I dressed our two in the clothing Grandma Monk had sent and thought we looked very nice.

The morning of the 13th was a cold day in Berlin. Mom asked if Gary thought of flowers for me. I told her I am sure he did not, we didn't even talk about this. Mom let me go to a flower shop not far away and I bought my own wedding flowers. Red, long stemmed carnations was what I picked. Not wrapped in fancy paper but tied together with ribbon to make a bridal bouquet.

I thought that the flowers, after the ceremony performed by a Justice of the Peace, could adorn the dinner table. Coming back from the florist, Gary and McQueen stood in the kitchen talking with Mom and McQueen was playing with Danny and Linda. Gary looked very nice in the uniform and was smiling from ear to ear. The smile I saw told me he was just as happy as I was. The day we waited for so long was finally here.

It was early in the morning but I could tell Gary had already had something to drink. The ceremony was not till eleven a.m., but he and his two friends, McQueen and a Sgt. Evans, stopped at Aunt Anna's and drank a few pilsners. The restaurant was the place Gary called his second home. All three told me, when they saw the look on my face, they stopped there for a few minutes to drink a toast to our happiness. Now what could I say to this? Not much, but again I thought much.

I did what I thought was right and bit down on my tongue. I bit down hard and thought Gary and his friends started the happy hour kind of early. I do not remember Gary saying that I looked nice or that our children looked cute in their outfits from Grandma Monk. Nor did he say anything about not giving me flowers. He saw me carry the bouquet of carnations into the kitchen, but it gave him not a clue that he should and could have done this for me.

To tell the truth, all of this did not matter to me. Important was the fact that today we would be proper and legal. We four would share the same last name. What a wonderful feeling this was. Today when someone said you can kiss the bride, we four had the same name. Gary, Dagmar, Danny and Linda Monk.

We waited for Erwin and Erika to come. When Erwin got there, I thought my brother was the most handsome witness a sister could have. Erika stayed with Mom and Aunt Lene, waiting for Dad to get there. Unlike my Gary and his friends, my brother didn't give us an early toast. He smelled of shaving lotion and cologne, not of beer.

Wearing the second coat Gary bought over my pretty dress, the flowers in my arms, down the stairs we went. Holding the pretty flowers, I felt like a bride. Coming down the stairs we met no one in the stairwell. Not any neighbor till later in the day knew it was my wedding day. Gary had two taxis waiting to take us to the Justice of the Peace, or to the Standesamt, like it was called in German.

We got there in good time. Entering the room, we saw we had a waiting period. Many other couples were in front of us. Comfortable chairs and tables to sit at made it nice for us.

This is when the teasing began. I heard from Gary's buddies, "Hey, it is still time to get away from here. You still have time to run for the hills if you want." Or the other I didn't like to hear was, "Hey, Buddy, do you really want this chain around your neck?" We all laughed at this, most of all my brother. He laughed because he was polite but he didn't understand what Gary's friend had said. I understood and was not very comfortable with the chain around the neck statement from Sgt. Evans. I thought if this is true, Gary had three chains around his neck me, Danny and Linda. And he had it around his neck since he was twenty-one years old. I smiled thinking my guy never tried to get away from it. Maybe because I didn't yank on the chain and made him uncomfortable wearing it.

I didn't like the thought, even in fun, that marriage was a chain around the neck. I laughed with them, not because I agreed with the jokes, but like my brother I was polite. This was Gary and my day and I wanted to be happy. This crazy, but meant to be light hearted talk, should not stop me from being happy. And I knew that they really didn't mean anything by it. It was fun talk while waiting for the man to pronounce us husband and wife.

Others were called before us and left as Mr. and Mrs. When our name was called, the ceremony was first in German and second in English. It didn't take long for us to become husband and wife. I came into this room being Dagmar Weiss. I left it being Dagmar B. Monk.

Happy was not the right word for how I felt. It was way more than this. I felt a sense of relief knowing we were now a family unit. I hoped we were solid in our love and commitment we made to each other. Saying the marriage vows tied it all up in a neat bundle. This is what I hoped for when we sat there hearing this noncommittal voice rattling down the words that made us man and wife. The man marrying us spoke fast and loudly, and behind us was a long line of want to be married couples waiting. This is the way it should have been from the very beginning. First the marriage then having the children. We did it the other way around. Many of us did it like we did, we were all children of the times we lived in. We can blame it on the German and the American governments and their rules and regulations. Or we can blame us for not holding hands for almost four years and waiting. Whatever it was, it was behind us.

With a stroke of a pen, with a stamp on a piece of paper, it put everything into the right order. Photos were made inside and outside after the ceremony. It was such a cold day, yet I needed to stand next to my husband outside without the heavy coat to keep me warm. It took a while till the photographer was done. We felt like our smiles were frozen on our faces. But we smiled till the guy with the camera said he was finished.

When we made the taxi ride home, our wedding party again stopped at Aunt Anna's to drink a toast to us. This time I did not say no to a glass of white wine. I had to remind everyone that a nice meal was waiting upstairs or I believe a tab would have been run up at Aunt Anna's.

Coming up the stairs, everyone stood outside the apartment door and was cheering for us. I and Gary were hugged by Aunt Lene, Erika, Mom and Dad. I picked up Danny and Linda and gave them a big hug. The neighbors, Mr. and Mrs. Gnauck, said they would take the children later. If needed, they could spend the night over there. We told them thank you but we thought, since the wedding party was so small, the children could sleep in their own bed.

For Erwin and Erika's wedding we moved the furniture out and stored them for one night across the hallway. There was an empty room with clothes lines all the renters used to hang up their wash on their laundry days. It made it nice for us to use when we needed it. The baby carriages stood there as the apartment was too small to hold these things.

We didn't think we needed to make us all this work for our wedding. We set the dinner table up by the window, put the carnations in a vase on top and this was the way I wanted it.

February 13, 1954 Mr. and Mrs. Gary D. Monk

Chapter Sixty

Everything looked very pretty until my husband couldn't wait to open the bottle of dinner wine. He pulled the cork before Mom got ready to serve the meal. Red wine spilled and decorated the white tablecloth. Mom rushed in looking at me saying, "Don't worry. I have something to put over this. It will hide the stain."

When I saw this, I was disappointed. In the apartment for fifteen minutes, it was more important to drink right away instead of having it with the wonderful meal Mom had prepared. I again bit down on my tongue and did not say a word. But I thought, I hope the rest of this day will go well. I had not any reason to think otherwise.

The surprise came later when Gary told me that he asked another couple to stop by. Mom and Aunt Lene had time to do dishes and I had time to tell them about the wedding ceremony. Telling them about the hurried job the man did because of the many couples waiting. I thought the whole was kind of cold, indifferent was the word for it. While we were in the kitchen laughing and talking, the men sat around doing the same but drinking beer. Aunt Anna would make a fortune today just from us alone.

Our neighbors the Gnaucks came after our two. Since they were the next-door neighbors, we could hear the kids playing and giggling. It echoed right through the wall. Then the couple Gary told me about arrived. I met them a few months ago at the movies. I liked both and knew, like Gary and I, they had a baby boy together.

The men, by late afternoon, had reached the point of feeling good. Mom's pot roast with all the trimmings had settled well and it was prost to the married couple till all went home. I understood a wedding was party time for the invited guests. My husband was the leader of the party. I kept wishing but again not saying it, please Gary, slow down a little. Wishing it and not saying it gives zero result, because slowing down didn't happen.

Then, standing in the kitchen with a glass in his hand, Sgt. Evans took this party one step further down the embarrassing road. He paid the lady that was our guest a very nice compliment. He said in a loud voice that she was the prettiest lady at this party.

She, wanting to be nice, objected by saying he shouldn't say this to her. This kind of compliment today belongs to the bride. By this time, me standing next to them over hearing it all, I was so embarrassed I could have died when I heard him say, no, what is true is true. My face was burning by then. I did not feel well at all. But I knew Sgt. Evans did speak the truth.

Our guest was a slender, blond lady dressed in pale pink. She was dainty and pretty, all that I was not. I walked away and needed to get over the feelings I had. It was my day to be happy and happy I wanted to be. I looked at my family and they enjoyed themselves. Papa and Erwin were the clowns and got everyone to laugh. Telling stories on how they met Gary and some of the fun they had together.

When the big downstairs doors got locked because it was a late hour, it got wild outside. Some of Gary's buddies came uninvited and made noise standing in the street, screaming and whistling up to the apartment window. They screamed things like, "Hey, Monk, all we want to do is wish you and the Mrs. well." They were so loud my family thought the neighbors would call the police. To stop the noise, my sister-in-law Erika went downstairs to let the noise makers in.

It was a group of young men and when they came in to our small place, they turned it upside down and inside out. Drinking, laughing, being a bad bunch to have as wedding guests. Sgt. McQueen and Sgt. Evans and the nice young couple left right after this group took over the apartment. I took them down the stairs to let them out. By the looks they gave me, I could tell what they thought. I knew that my wedding would be talked about for a long time.

Gary and I married on Friday the 13th in 1953. Everyone, when they heard of the date, said to marry on Friday the 13th is asking for bad luck. Other couples married on this day and, as far as it being bad luck, I would prove them wrong.

When I opened the downstairs door for Sergeant McQueen and Sergeant Evans, I thanked them for coming and told them we would see them tomorrow. Tomorrow was Saturday and Valentine's Day. We would meet them at the Outpost Theater to see a movie.

Very slowly I went upstairs wiping a few tears away on the way up. Stopping at the apartment door, hearing all this noise coming at me, I was glad the Gnauck family took care of Danny and his sister Lindi. They slept peaceful in one of the Gnauck's bedrooms. Their apartment was bigger than ours and has sustained less war damage. Standing in the hallway in front of our door, I was thankful to the Gnauck family that they took care of our little ones.

When I entered the apartment, I was ready for all of our unwanted guests to leave. I thought that my new husband needed to help me enforce the law and get his rowdy friends out and on the road, leading away from us. Luck was with me, as my Gary had dropped off to sleep and for his so-called friends, it meant the party was over.

Erwin took them down to let them go on their way. We said good riddance when it was finally over.

My brother helped me roll his new brother in-law into bed. He said that when he woke up, a terrific hangover was his. Dad laughed saying it was not Gary's first one. Over the years in Berlin, Gary had many such hangovers. Gosh, I hated hearing my Dad say this, but it was true. True and not funny. It was me guilty of not speaking up and saying that I didn't like him being hungover so often.

When my brother and I tucked my husband away for a restful night's sleep, I made up my mind to tell him sometime tomorrow that our wedding turned into a mess. I deserved better, because for me it was a forever memory of our wedding. I was a very disappointed bride.

Erwin with Erika left. Mom and I took care of the mess the apartment was in. It looked like a war took place instead of a wedding. I had never seen our small space looking so abused. It was a shame to see it in such a state of upheaval. We cleaned and I kept saying to mom this shouldn't have been like this. She looked at me and agreed, but what is done is done. True and nothing could erase the pictures that were rolling around in my mind.

Early the next day, the Gnauck's brought the children over. They wanted breakfast and hands and face washed. We thanked them for helping the way they did and said sorry for all the noise everyone heard clear into the night. They told us not to worry. It was a wedding. Everyone was expecting to hear noise. I thought yes, but this was more, more than anyone should have to put up with. However, I was grateful that no one was upset over the rowdy bunch of Americans.

Chapter Sixty-One

When Gary got out of bed, little arms and hands were reaching for him. Hangover or not, he had to make time for his children. Mom knew he wasn't feeling well and made him a strong cup of coffee. He refused to eat anything. I thought but didn't say it, with all the intake of fluid from yesterday, there was not room for any food. Maybe by evening there was. Over the years I was with Gary I was a champ in thinking and not saying. Or was I a chump for thinking and not saying. Either way this was something I wanted to change and find the courage to change it.

Since we were going to the movies, we could grab a bite at the snack bar before going to the show. This was my plan for Valentine's Day and to have a little talk about the wedding day. Leaving for the movies, I went to the bedroom to change my clothes. Gary was changing his and I thought it was a good opportunity, with the door closed to the kitchen, to bring up yesterday. Mom and Dad were keeping the children busy and, with the door shut, could not over hear what I wanted to say to my husband.

I started slowly explaining I was unhappy with the outcome of the wedding we had. I really wanted this day to be the foundation to build the future memories on. With friends showing up not invited and rude, I felt very hurt by it all. These were not the memories I wanted to have but since it happened, I could not erase them, nor could we live the day over again. I found all of this sad for me.

Then I made the huge mistake to say, "Gary, you didn't think of how it made me feel with you drinking so much at our wedding. For a long time, I have been concerned about this. And I have been seriously wanting to speak with you about it." Gary just looked at me and when I finished complaining gave me a light slap across my face. I couldn't believe he did this and I was speechless. Besides this he grabbed my blouse and tore the buttons off from the front. I stood there thinking is this for real? Did my telling him how hurt I was deserve me this? I had two feelings going through me at the time. Feeling like a Champ because for the first time I dared to tell him, and feeling like a Chump because I allowed for him to slap me. Without giving me another look or a word Gary left me standing there looking befuddled about what had happened.

He walked to the kitchen and closed the door behind him. What was I to do? I knew I couldn't say anything about this. My parents must never know or find out about it. It would break their hearts. I was a bride all of two days and it broke mine a few minutes ago.

This day was Valentine's Day. A day to give love to people we care about. My gift for this day as a new bride was a slap in my face from my husband of going on two days. What a way to start our life as man and wife.

I looked in the mirror behind the dresser to see if my face was red. The slap was light and it didn't show on the side of my face. Since I looked fine, I put on a new blouse and I opened the door to the kitchen. With a smile on my face, I joined my family. Gary was sitting on a chair smoking a cigarette. Like me, he didn't let it show that something happened between us. Dad was smoking his pipe and said soon he would depart, but first he wanted some of the leftover wedding cake. Mom said for him to eat all he wanted and she would send some home with him

Leaving for the movies, we hugged the kids. Gary promised Mom that we would stop and eat something before going to the show. I am sure that a big hamburger would be his and popcorn at the movie. I was not looking forward to meeting with people from yesterday. Nor their girlfriends.

Sure enough, the word had spread. One girl came up to me and said, "Hey. I heard all about your wedding." I said, "Good. Then I do not have to tell you all about it. It saves me from bragging about it." The look she gave me was priceless and it made me laugh when I walked away.

After the show Gary, wanted to stop at the 48 Club. We went there; it was not far from the Outpost Theater. Other well-wishers stopped by the table. If anyone asked about the wedding, both of us said pointing to our wedding band, we are glad it was taken care of. I got bothered by some that I could tell did not mean it well with the two of us. Gary, however, nothing seemed to bother him as long as he had a beer in his hands. That's my husband, he fell in love with the German beer.

Two weeks Gary was given for us to have a honeymoon. A honeymoon spent in Berlin because the Russians circled Berlin and it became an island. To get out of this island, Gary needed to have a travel pass or use the plane or Allied train. This was the only way to get out of town. We didn't try to get such a travel pass. And for me to travel, maybe even more was requested than from him. We stayed at home playing cards with my parents. We visited Erwin and Erika. She was looking cute with her little tummy. We promised to leave them the bed and the carriages from our kids. They could use them and we didn't want to take them. They knew I would be concerned about my parents because I gave them a little money every month. With us leaving this was over. Erwin said not to worry they would always keep an eye on them for me. And they would pay a little money to Mom for the things like the carriages and so forth we left behind. I thought this was a very good idea. We would tell her it was for her to sell them to Erika and Erwin. Sometimes to help her took some manipulating; she let her pride get in the way. We needed to find a way around all this. And putting our heads together we did.

Gary and I liked taking long walks, we watched Danny make mud cakes playing in an indoor sandbox. And night after night after I put the children to bed, we went for ice cream. I decided to put the slap I got on Valentine's Day behind me. I was sure it would never happen again. The excuse I made for it, my husband still had a dandy of a hangover. He didn't know what he was doing. For me, I really thought this was the end of the story.

We went to order a pass for me to ride on the American shuttle bus and to shop in the commissary if I wanted. Since I was a married woman, the American government paid me a monthly allotment check of one hundred fifty dollars. I felt rich. I never had money to keep in my purse. What I had always went to Mom. This time, after cashing my check at the bank at Truman Hall, after I gave Mom household money, there was some extra for me to do with. For the first time, we didn't have to be concerned how to make it to the end of the month.

When the honeymoon was over, Gary took up residence again in the barracks at Finckensteinallee. He said only because we lived in such a small space. True our apartment was very small, but this has not stopped him before from wanting to stay. We questioned why does it now? The Golden Sun restaurant was still his hangout and he liked going there and shoot the breeze with the guys. Another place he added by the name of Breitzke. So, when he and his buddies got away from one place, they went over to visit the other.

Breitzke was a fancy place while the Golden Sun had the all-time down-home atmosphere. My parents said oh, let him go. All he wants to do is to make the most of the little time he has left in Berlin. We don't think he is doing anything bad. No, I didn't think this of him either, so I let him go and I let him enjoy his last days in Berlin. When he came home to us, there were chocolates for Mom and a bottle of wine for Dad. Erwin and Erika came by and helped by drinking a glass or two.

In this kind of party, I was always the outsider. I did not like to drink and my husband, the tease he was, called me the party pooper. If I was one, so was Mom. We liked a good cup of coffee with a slice of cake or a piece of chocolate.

Chapter Sixty-Two

As Gary's departure date came closer and closer, he and I still sat in offices settling mine and the children's departure from Berlin. When the day came to take Gary to the Allied train for Bremerhaven, Dad stayed behind watching Danny and Linda. He wanted for us to have this time with Gary. But saying goodbye to his son-in-law was hard on him.

Gary said goodbye to Dad and the children the night before. The whole time he was holding his son, Danny was playing with the shiny brass on his uniform. Little Linda didn't know what was going on and just smiled at her daddy when he said, "I'll see you soon." She gave him a love and didn't know he wouldn't be back the next day. She was doing her best to walk and the baby talk she gave us sounded pretty cute.

I went out in the stairwell and waited to hear for the last time how Gary was making it down the stairs till he reached the bottom. I knew I would never hear his steps on the stairs again. This time was over for my family. It would become a memory that in time they would like to recall.

At 6 p.m. the next night we stood at the train station in Lichterfelde West. More hugs and kisses from me. A warm hug from Mom, Erika, Aunt Lene and Uncle Emil. Erwin, my brother, had the hardest time saying goodbye. Gary was his brother-in-law and his friend. Erwin called him his best buddy, it was hard for him to see him leave, not knowing when he would see him again.

Before Gary got on the train, I heard Erwin say, "When you get home, drink a cold one for me. I'll sure miss you." To my mom, it was Gary when he hugged her that said, "I will miss you, Moodie." Moodie being the word for Mutti and it meant Mother.

He got on the train to stand by the window so he could see us for as long as possible when the train pulled out of the station. He was looking at all the people that became his family in the last few years. Besides the family, he also left the town that had become his second home for as long as he was away from home.

At the last minute the rowdy friends showed up. Standing behind us they yelled, "Hey, Monk. The Golden Sun and Breitzke will miss you. They might even close the doors for a day in mourning your departure." Gary waved his hand at them and called back, "Stop it, you clowns. You will see to it that the doors stay open." I thought he was right. The restaurant owners cleaned up and got rich and richer.

The American soldiers claimed the German beer was the best they ever had. All this was going around my head when I looked at my guy on the train and more, much more. The departure song was played and it was "Fraülein" from "The River Rhein". I believe this was it as the train rolled away and taking a part of my heart along.

The departure song did not fit. All the women, all the German ladies standing at this railroad station were from the River Spree flowing through Berlin and not the Rhein. But what did it matter? It was a pretty goodbye song.

I saw tears shed by young girls. Their romance didn't last forever and in time would become a nice memory for them. Even when the couples were in agreement about a short-lived love affair, I would think this was hard to get over. I felt sorry when I saw the sadness in their goodbyes. I cried when the train pulled away, but I knew in a few months, the children and I would say hello to him.

Chapter Sixty-Three

During the day we kept busy. Dad came by to eat lunch. He took the kids out for a walk on nice days. He did a lot of writing and office visits to try to establish West Berlin citizenship. Not any luck so far as we could tell. He did all he could with the talent he had in writing, drawing and fixing other people's radios to put money in his pocket. He wanted so much to stay independent from Mom's help. So far, he was doing very well in taking care of himself. When I came home with tobacco and cartons of cigarettes for both they grinned, but shook their finger at me saying, you are trying to spoil us while you are still here. This reminded me our time with them would soon be over. Yes, I did want to spoil them while I was still there.

Mom was not shy working in housekeeping for others. Erwin and Erika did well. Erika was looking so cute walking around holding her baby tummy. She was tiny for being pregnant. When Mom looked at her, she was sure they were having a boy. Waiting for their baby and getting ready for it was exciting.

Edgar wrote letters and all was well in France. They too had a little baby boy they named Bernard. Now Blandine was not the only child anymore. Edgar wrote she was a proud big sister. And for me, well I missed Gary since he left. When the time rolled around when he used to come home, I listened for his footsteps come rushing up the stairs. Mom did, too. We both missed him.

The mailman brought the first letter saying he was home, we all felt better. He told us of the welcome he got and he was stationed in Fort Leonard Wood, Missouri. He said he was looking for a place to rent in one of the towns in this area. He wrote that he was glad to be back but

331

somehow missed the big city. I always translated the letter for Mom. But I skipped the translations of the loving words that were only meant for me.

When the evenings got too long for Mom and me, Dad offered to babysit. I took Mom to see a movie, but a German movie. The Uffa Studios made some wonderful films. Old film stars like Zarah Leander, Kurt Jürgens, Kristina Söderbaum and Hans Albers made films dealing with the difficult times after WWII. These were the films my mother liked and the Rhein Schloss and the Krone Theater saw the two of us often.

Younger actors like Horst Buchholz, Sonja Ziemann, Hildegard Knef, and Maria Schell came on the screen. Mom and I loved all of their movies. For as long as we had a babysitter in Dad, and he loved spending time with his grandchildren, we went to the movies. Dad did for his grandchildren what he did for me when I was small, he loves, protects and teaches. For me he was and is the best Dad ever. And when we are in America, I need to remember to tell them about him. Not to forget their grandma and aunts and uncles.

Mom took over for Dad when he was not around. Between the two, they gave me amazing, intelligent, little ones. I owed much to both of my parents and the only way to repay this was by never forgetting whose daughter I am. I needed to take with me love, loyalty and strength when I met my new family in America. No matter which way the winds blew when I was away from mine, I must show my new family nothing could blow me away. I was, we were, there to stay.

I let my parents have all the time they wanted with the kids. They took them to the park, weather permitting. Linda was big enough to sit next to her brother in the sandbox. They stood with their grandparents by the window of the Märklin Toy Store and saw the trains buzz by or they stood at the Feuerbach train station to see the real trains come and go.

Double decker bus rides and trolley rides were both kids' favorites. I often went with them on such a joy ride because I was still a kid at twenty. We stopped for ice cream or I went in the store to buy a couple of chocolate bars. The kids got only a little piece of chocolate. It was smart to keep them regular and not hurt with the toilette and potty going.

By the way, itsy bitsy Linda did very well in all of this. I was hoping by the time the travel orders came by mail, my little girl would have learned to be a little, big girl.

After I put the children to bed, Mom made coffee and we ate chocolate and chatted for a while. I told her when I had my own home, I wanted under the Christmas tree every year a big Hershey bar. To remember the two special soldiers that gave me my very first taste of it. She said when you have your own roof over your head you can do all you want to do. Make photos of it and mail them to us. I nodded. I was sure we could do this for them.

In 1945-1946 an unknown soldier played Santa. In 1948 through 1949 it was Lt. Gail S. Halvorsen that surprised me by a parachute he and his crew dropped from the plane. I said to my mother, every time I eat chocolate, I think back to the first sweet taste of it.

My mother smiled and said, "It will be your home. These are your memories you want to keep alive. Go for it. But do me the favor to remember the traditions we have in the Weiss family. The traditions we had when the money was there to have them. Each family member needs to have their own plate with sugar cookies, apple, oranges and nuts. When you do this remember us, all of us, in Berlin, Germany." I promised. There was not any way that I could ever forget any of this. Nor could I forget the hands that worked so hard to give it to us.

When I had time without the children, I walked to the post office. I mailed letters to Gary and his parents and bought a book of airmail stamps to be able to write more letters. I went to Kepa, the store on Rheinstrasse, to buy really thin airmail writing paper in order to write long letters.

On the way home, I picked up a bundle of flowers and at the fruit stand Mom's favorite berries, that she washed right away, sugared and ate till they were all gone. Now having my own money, because of getting an allotment check, I could do a little spoiling that Mom had not had before. It felt nice to be able to do this and it was made possible because Gary married me.

Chapter Sixty-Four

The days went by and then some more. I heard nothing from the American government about us leaving Berlin to join Gary. The doorbell rang on a Saturday morning when we were not yet ready to have company. A General with his German secretary wanted to see me. They had to give us about thirty minutes to make us presentable to have company and then they came back.

Mom looked down to the street from the bedroom window and said a Jeep stood in front of the house. The General and the secretary waited sitting in the Jeep or Aunt Anna had important patrons in her restaurant this Saturday morning. We had to hurry to make up the beds and, get us and two small children ready in a very short amount of time. We did manage it and our place smelled of fresh brewed coffee when the visitors climbed the steps back up to the fourth floor.

Linda made herself at home on the General's lap and he did not seem to mind it at all. Danny brought out his toys from a small cabinet and showed him and his secretary the new fire engine he had.

I was told that my husband wrote a letter saying he was not getting any mail from me and wanted to know what the hold-up was with our coming to the States. I told the General and his lady secretary this is not possible; I write all the time. He has to have mail unless a plane went down that carried the mail. Me saying this brought a smile to their faces.

The book of airmail stamps that I could only use to send such letters proved to the General I was a dedicated letter writer. He then said he would get in touch with my husband or his commanding officer. He wanted this to be straightened out in a hurry. He made the appointment for me to come to see him in a few days. He wanted answers for what he called this unnecessary delay.

When he and his pretty secretary got ready to leave, I thanked him for coming and for his help. On his way out of the apartment, he patted Linda's and Danny's little heads. To me he said, "I will help you to straighten this out, Mrs. Monk." Then they were gone, leaving behind a few dirty coffee cups, and for Mom and me many unanswered questions. I was sure going to his office in a couple of days would clear all this up. When Dad showed up, he added a few of his own thoughts to the many we had. Saying he would like to know why Gary claims not to get mail from me? The letters I mailed never came back. This meant that they reached him.

A few days later, when I went to keep the appointment, the General had the answer. Not about the missing mail for Gary, but about the delay of us getting to the States. He had this to say. "All of this is your husband's fault. If he had seen to it that the rest of the paperwork needed was written and filed correctly, you would be in the States by now."

I didn't know what to say except "I am sorry." I really didn't know there was more we had to do. He understood and told me what offices I had to visit to get a visa for me and the children. I had to have photos taken of Danny and Linda to get the American passports for them. And get the German passport for me.

We went to the American hospital and they got all of their shots. They cried when the needle went in their arms. I and Mom hated to hear and see them cry. It was hard for me not to do the same. My mom, their Oma, shed tears. Maybe for more than the children getting their shots.

The realization hit home, in a short time from now, we would be gone for good. There wouldn't be early morning talks with them, helping me out with feeding them, washing and dressing them. Not anymore laughter or tears shed by two energetic little ones would keep her and me busy. All of this became very real to my mother.

Finances for her and Dad would be less. Us living together under one roof helped a lot. Life for me and mine was changing for the better but not so much for my parents. I was concerned for them. Mom told me she left home to marry Dad. It's natural to leave the father and mother. The difference for them, they didn't leave the country, they stayed in Germany.

When I went to Tempelhof to pick up the visa, it was issued to me getting a lecture from the clerk. He wanted to know if I knew that by leaving Germany, I was a woman without a country. I told him I was not aware of this. I thought for as long as I owned my birth certificate and a German passport, I was still a citizen of Germany. I told him and this shouldn't change till I became an American citizen. When this happened, I gave up my rights. Unless I kept a dual citizenship.

I told him since my children had the American citizenship, I was not waiting too long to apply for it myself. My hope was after study and whatever it took, that America would accept me. Going home, I thought about this man and shook my head.

Before reaching home, I stopped at the flower shop to get something for Mom. I purchased a small bundle of forget me nots. When I handed them to her, she knew what I meant to say. Doing something this small meant much to my mother and I knew this.

In a week or two, the official letter came, giving the departure date to leave family and Berlin on the 6th of October 1954. The Allied train left from the station Lichterfelde West, to Bremerhafen at 6 p.m. From there, by ship across the ocean. 'America, here we come,' is what I thought.

The word that we were leaving spread through the house. Everyone wanted for us to stop to tell them goodbye. I promised the day of our leaving I would ring the doorbell and we would say "Auf Wiedersehen." It means I will see you again. I was sure we would see them again, I just did not know when this would be.

On an impulse, Mom and I with Danny and Linda drove to Lichterfelde West. We thought since Danny liked trains, he would not be scared to climb up into one, if he could see one from up close. It was meant to be for us to be there because I met another young woman doing the same. She was alone and had a three-week-old baby girl to take care of.

Her name was Katie and she and I became instant friends. We promised to help each other, from Berlin all the way to America. And, God willing, to stay in touch after we got there.

From Lichterfelde West, we went by Aunt Berta's for a fast visit. Mom gave her all the news, and a date was set for all in the family to come to our place. Come for coffee, cake, a glass of wine, and have a goodbye party.

The few days we still had in-between, going shopping for a few items, kept me on my feet. My mother-in-law wished for a 400-day clock. It took me a while to find one and make sure it was the right clock. I had never seen or heard of such a clock before. When I found it, it was an item I could not put in my suitcase. It was large and

Dagmar Weiss Snodgrass

had a glass dome. It needed to be packed by the men the military sent to pack the rest of my and the children's belongings.

I shopped to find a Damask tablecloth, a tie for my father-in-law and pen set for my 13-year-old brother-in-law, Eddie. These things I placed in the suitcase. When I looked at what I had to take with me on this trip, I wondered how I would keep us clean. I did not have much for me and the children and hoped, that on the ship there would a place to wash and iron our clothing. I had to trust to find my way in all that was new for me and the children. I wanted for us to look nice when we met Gary's family.

Gary's letter told me we would meet them in St. Louis, Missouri. He didn't go into why our paperwork was not ready for our travel. All this he skipped over and gave not any explanation. But this was the man I loved. I started to believe he was the easy come, easy go kind of guy. I needed to be the woman that kept things straight and organized for the family. I would give it a try and see what happened.

When the man came to pack the big box, my dad kept a few toys. He told me he and his grandson had a favorite spot in the woods and they wanted to bury a time capsule. When Danny came back in his older years, they would dig it up. So, grandpa and grandson went one day to do this and made a whole day of it.

After Danny and Linda went to bed, Dad said Danny was too small to remember what they did today. However, he would remember and would go by there often. They put a time capsule together and it was buried under a tall oak tree next to the railroad tracks in Berlin - Schlachtensee. Dad also asked for Danny's dinner plate and drinking cup. It would from now on belong to him and he would use it every day to eat his meals. All this tugged on my heart seeing and hearing this from my parents.

I realized how hard it was for them to let us go. But go we must and giving us away they had to do. When the day of the going away party came, all the relatives came. The little apartment was filled with people, all had well-meant advice. Most of all, they had love for us. Much, much love for us.

This love and the memory of the day, I would take with me. It was a sentimental time we shared. There was a lot of talk of bygone days. The challenges all of them faced together. I had to be careful not to cry when I heard what they said. Uncle Emil Sauer, my mom's brother, reminded me we would miss being at his birthday party this year.

The 6th of October was the day he came into the world. He was the only son of Emilie and Hermann Sauer. He laughed this nice laugh of his and said, "We will all be at the station to see you off. You can count on it." When they left the apartment, I took them down the stairs and locked the door after them. I stood behind the heavy door listening to their voices when they walked away. It was not easy for them to get home. They used the trolley, bus and subway trains to get to their homes. And getting off at their station, they still had a way to walk till they reached the front door. I must say, I was glad they came to be at my farewell party

The next few days I tried to be calm. I did not find the time to dwell much on the what ifs. I had a few. Like what if Gary was not in New York when we arrived? The General that was kind and helpful was the one to bring this up. His advice was to go to the Red Cross or look for men wearing a red cap at any information booth. He said these people will always help you. I told him I would remember it but I hoped not to have to make use of it.

Chapter Sixty-Five

On the day we left, we started the day as usual. Nothing was done different except the suitcase stood behind the bedroom door waiting. On top laid a harness I wanted to put on my son Danny. With having Linda and she started to walk well but also wanted to be carried; I needed to have control over my fast-moving boy. The harness was to be my help.

My parents and I did not talk much on this day, but all of us had much to think and be grateful for. God kept the Weiss family together. He smoothed the way for each and every one of us to continue the journey. Edgar in France, Erwin and our parents in Berlin, and the children and I in America. The land my family had only read about in books we got from the book store.

Now I and the children would see this land with the wide-open spaces. Cowboys, and Indians that were not wild any more but had much to teach the white man about their culture. It was exciting to think about it. In order to make this change and to be successful, we had to put the old world aside. And with confidence, step into the new world. We must try it on for size and see if it fits us. I wanted to pray that it would be a good fit for us all.

At 4 p.m. I went to see the neighbors to say goodbye. Mrs. Haag handed me three to four apples to put in my large purse in case the kids got hungry. I thanked her but I knew it hanging around my neck would make me hurt. It had important papers, money and beside this it now held green apples. I had a heavy load hanging around my neck. With two small children and a big suitcase I needed to get from Berlin to Bremerhaven.

My boy was wondering about the harness. He had never had to wear one before. When we told him it was to help Mommy, he was fine with it. He was used to being told when they went out, he was Grandpa's helper. He understood tonight he was to be Mommy's helper.

At Lichterfelde West, the train was waiting. Standing on the tracks, dark and long looking. Only on the inside the compartment windows there was light. Katie, my new friend, holding her baby found me. We put my suitcase in the compartment next to hers.

A soldier came by telling us during the night the train traveled through the Red Zone. The Russian Zone. We would hear noises but are not to come out to see what was going on. No matter what we heard, should shots be fired, we needed to know the train for us was like standing on American soil. I had said my goodbye to Mom, Dad, Erwin and Erika, praying I wouldn't turn into a crying mess. I couldn't do this in front of my little ones or they would start to cry. I needed to hold it together till later. I hoped I could do it and not be a crybaby.

I went to the door of the train, while family and relatives played with the kids. I put one foot on the steps of the train but kept the other on the ground and proclaimed, "Look here, everyone. Have you ever seen someone stand in two countries all at the same time? I am having one foot on German soil, my birth place, the land I love! The other foot is on American soil, our home to be and the land I will learn to love."

Everyone gathered around us when we climbed up into the train and stood by the compartment window looking down at the people we would leave behind. Us being on the train now standing 100 % on American soil. Danny was excited to be on a train. Lindi, her doll in her hands, did not care about anything; she only cared about being with her brother and Mommy.

We felt the train jerking back and forth, getting ready to pull out. From all the relatives, Aunt Berta ran up to the window to get a last handshake. Linda, in her small, sweet voice, told her to go away. I couldn't believe my little girl said this, but she did. The goodbye song played over the loudspeaker and slowly, with the children and I standing by the window, looking at now tear stained faces, we left Berlin.

I saw Katie standing at the other window letting the tears roll down. Her baby was in the sleeper compartment sleeping. I did not dare to cry out of fear it would frighten my two. I did want to cry. I left the family that loved us, that supported us, and for the first time had to rely only on me. I couldn't look at Mom or Dad anymore and ask, "Well, what do you think I should do?"

With us leaving Berlin, I was now on my own. I was not anyone's little girl any longer. I was Mrs. Garrett D. Monk. The mom to two cute little kids that depended on their mom to be and act like their mom. I had to be a responsible, grown-up, young lady.

I got busy in order not to have to think. I only removed the children's outer clothing and put them next to each other to sleep. They ate before we left for the train and could not be hungry. Soon, sitting across and watching them, the rattling of the train rolling down the track lulled them to sleep.

I went to check on Katie and found her still in tears. This did not help me much. I was hanging on not to be a crybaby. When I calmed Katie down, I went back to my own compartment to get some sleep. But sleep would not come.

When the train entered the Red Zone we had been warned about, I was still wide awake. I heard voices that gave commands in Russian. I also heard the orders given in English. When the train started up again, it was cleared to continue through the Red Zone in destination Bremerhaven.

In the morning hours we arrived. I had not any trouble with my two. They behaved like little angels. And I was grateful for it. What would I have done if they hadn't? I could not imagine this. The trouble I had was with the heavy suitcase and purse hanging around my neck.

Katie, walking in front of me, turned around and saw me struggling with two children and luggage. She came to my rescue by taking Danny in hand. Her baby was in a small carriage that rolled on two wheels. I had never seen anything like it before. But this little whatever it was made it easy for her with her baby. She had a suitcase about the size of mine. Her purse she hung over the hand bars of this fold away carriage. It was neat to see how much freedom it gave her.

She took over taking care of Danny. She wrapped straps from the harness he wore around her wrist. He was walking with Katie instead of me and gave her not any problem. He was a happy little guy. I had told him a so-called white lie when I said soldiers wore a harness as part of their uniform. It was to protect them and keep them safe. This thing around him would protect him and keep him safe for as long as he was wearing it. Danny believed me and was happy to be a soldier just like his dad.

Chapter Sixty-Six

We were put on waiting busses and taken to a camp. There we were told we would be quarantined for three days and then by ship have a ten-day ocean voyage till we reached America.

Katie and I had rooms across the hall from each other. All of us had our own bed. I was not sure how Danny and Linda felt about it. They shared a bed for such a long time. Having their own bed may be a little strange for them. Looking around and looking everything over, I could not believe how large the room was. My mom's apartment could fit into this one room and there was still left-over space.

The bathroom was as big as Mom's kitchen. We never had a bathtub before but we had one now. I looked around the room and it had three large clean beds and a locker to hang up clothing. The bathroom with a wash basin and a bathtub, I thought I must have died and gone to heaven. This was luxury we never had before. Tomorrow I wanted to write my parents about this.

Katie thought the same. She had no relatives. She was close to the landlady she had. She was like a mother to Katie and grandmother to her tiny baby girl. She wanted to write her a letter or send a pretty postcard. She, like me, wanted for her landlady to know what was going on with her. In the morning we had to find someplace to eat breakfast. We went to the snack bar to buy every meal there. No one told us till later we should have gone to the mess hall. It didn't take money to eat there.

We found the store and purchased postcards to mail home. My two little curtain climbers hung on to me but they did not make it hard on me. Danny could even run around without the harness. When he came to me and asked to play soldier, I put it back on him. I explained that with me hanging onto the harness, I was then his commanding officer. It meant for him to hear and to mind me because this is what all good soldiers had to do. Telling him this really worked well for us. Lindi learned to climb stairs up and down. When she made it up the stairs, she turned her back to the stairs. Coming down with the bottom first, she shimmied back down. Standing at the bottom pleased with herself, she clapped her hands together.

Danny became my helper. Like he used to help his grandpa, he now was helping me. When his little sister wanted to cry, he went to her telling her she needed to be a good soldier like he was. This was cute because Linda listened to her brother. For me having all this time to play with my children was a first. And to be able to do it for hours was really unusual. It was my Dad that got to see how they interacted with one another. He took them walking and to play at the park. Coming home with them, he told me how much fun he had. Now being with them at a much longer time, I saw what I have been missing. They were fun to watch while playing. In Berlin, Grandpa had this pleasure now the pleasure was all mine. I would write him about me having play time with them. He will like this.

Katie and I made everything teamwork. If her baby needed to be changed and Katie had just stepped out of the room, I did the diaper changing. If hands and noses needed wiping and I was not around, Katie did it for me. We were babysitting for each other.

After the children went to bed, we had long talks. We talked about what dreams we had. What did we want out of life? We knew it would not be easy for some of the Americans to like us. The war had left a bad taste in their mouths. Katie and I knew it would take convincing them on our part, and to show them that we are good people and not Nazis.

When we told people that were asking, Katie was going to Jumping Creek, VA, no one knew the place. However, it was different for me. Coffeyville, Kansas was well known because of its history about the Dalton brothers. Gary filled me in on all of this when we had long walks and talks. Going often to the Outpost Movie Theater made me familiar with the Wild West and the outlaws.

Here we were, Katie and I, sharing hopes and dreams we had for us. Would they come true? Only time would tell. Our future, our life, all was in God's hands. Going to bed I prayed about this. I prayed for our family when I was very small and kept it up as a twenty-year-old woman.

No, my family and I did not sit in the church on Sunday mornings. We could have, when the churches opened the doors again after World War Two. But we didn't. For the baptism of Danny and Linda was the only time I was there. In 1945-1946 as an eleven-year-old I was there, but this was it. Yet I always knew who was watching and guiding us. He was with us every time Katie and I sat and had a serious conversation. Next day, we both did what it took. This was not a time for us to be bashful or act like if we were unsure of ourselves. Like my Mom would say, it was time to step up and show what we were made of. For me this too was a first. Having not any parents or brothers to lean on. It was learning time for me. Katie said I needed to pull her along, she wanted to learn. She told me her landlady was the one that held her hand a lot when times were tough. Like me, she wanted to learn. Doctors and nurses checked us to make sure we did not bring a disease to America. Only the healthy people were allowed into the country. After the probing and testing was done, Katie and I got the green light to enter the U.S.A.

In the time at this camp, we have tried to meet other women that had children. But it seemed we two must be the only German speaking women here. We thought we knew better but no one spoke with us unless it was in English. Alright, Katie and I can do this. I gave it a good go around with my two little ones. Now I needed to learn their Daddy's language

At the last check up before boarding the ship, we needed to have X-rays made. It came over the speaker system that German citizen had to go to one room and the American citizen to another. When Katie and I went to the waiting room that was ours, many of the women that did not speak German with us, they were there. I and Katie made it easy for them. Standing with them we spoke only in English, not one word in our home language did we say.

When I looked around the room, I saw a lot of red faces. Later, Katie and I said it was alright that they didn't want to speak German. All of us were on the same journey. The language we all needed to speak is English. We all needed to make an early start and speak it. I started it with my children and they look at me kind of funny. Like what in the world is our mommy saying? For me to keep it up is the key for them to learn.

Chapter Sixty-Seven

The day for us to board the ship, we had to be up and about very early. It was exciting to think about a ten-day ocean voyage. We got ready and stumbling, fumbling with the children and luggage, we made it to the busses. One of the girls looked at me. After I sat down with Linda in my lap and Danny next to Katie with her baby, she turned around and managed to say, "You know, I do feel sorry for you."

I was surprised by this. Then it came to me what she meant. I had Danny in a harness walking up to the bus, Linda in my arms but kind of sitting on my hip. And a heavy purse with all the paperwork hanging around my neck. I knew I was a sight to behold. I did not have time to look pretty like she did. She looked elegant in a poodle skirt and high heeled shoes.

She sat by herself so she was not a mom. To her I must have looked out of breath, hurried and in need of help. I did not ask her why she felt sorry for me. I knew the answer. It was because I was so young and already had two children. She saw my children as a burden. I saw them as my blessing.

The bus started to move away and soon we would board a ship. Linda sitting in my lap started to play with my long hair. She liked doing this, tangling her fingers up in my hair. Sometimes Danny would do it, too. No, I thought, no one needed to feel sorry for me. I was happy to have what I had.

The ride to Bremerhaven Harbor was not long. Looking out the window, I knew this is the last I will see of a city in my country. The next town we will see is New York City. A city not damaged from a war like Berlin.

My little ones will not remember any of this, but I will. When they are big enough to understand, when they have questions, then I will give them answers. I will tell them the story of a handsome American soldier falling in love with a German girl. This German girl happened to be their mommy.

The bus stopped. I heard all the laughing and talking when everyone got off. Katie and I got help from the driver because we had children. The bus stopped not too far away from the ship that would be our home for the next ten days. There it stood waiting for us. The gang planks were down and men wearing white uniforms stood at the doors ready to help us.

The ship was like two, three or four football fields long. It was a huge military ship. I wondered if it had seen battles in the Pacific or the Atlantic Ocean during the war. It was a dark grey color. I could not detect that it showed any battle scars. It looked powerful, majestic and its name was General Patch.

Katie, her baby and I with Danny and Linda walked up the gangplank. It was a steward dressed in a white uniform that took the children from me. He was to show us to the cabin Katie and I would have for this ten-day ocean voyage.

Before I went with him and Katie, I turned around to take one last look. Standing on this ship, I stood on American soil. My last look was a goodbye to my homeland. I was not saying it out loud but saying it with my mind and heart, "Auf Wiedersehen" my heart was whispering. In its translation, "I will see you again." The question I was asking, there was not any answer for. Like my Mom would say, answers are written in the stars above and only found in God's almighty hands.

I and the children wanted to look forward to what was ahead of us. My husband and his family were waiting for us. Our wish was to love them and to have this love returned. Nothing of any value we had to give. We had not money or valued possessions. The war robbed us of it all. What we had to give was respect and love. Much, much love.

With all this going on in my mind, I turned around and followed the steward down the hallway to the cabin door. Katie was already there waiting for me. I walked in to join her and the children thinking, "Is this really happening? Is America ready for us? Because, America, here we come!"

The General Patch – Voyage to Freedom, 1954